Kings of September

THE DAY OFFALY DENIED KERRY FIVE IN A ROW

'Michael Foley has done an extraordinary job in getting inside
the mindsets of the main participants in one of
the most dramatic games the GAA has ever seen.
This book certainly does justice to one of the
greatest occasions in Irish sporting history.'
EUGENE MCGEE

'It was one of the best All-Ireland finals in recent years.
The book gives a great insight into the mindset
and tactics of the different people involved in this great occasion.
For any GAA fan it is a very good read.'
JACK O'SHEA

'An extraordinary book recalling an extraordinary game.
Impossible to come away from Michael Foley's work
without a greater understanding of Irish life. Brilliant sportswriting.'
TOM HUMPHRIES

MICHAEL FOLEY has worked as GAA correspondent for the *Sunday Times* for the past seven years, working principally on Gaelic football. He has also previously written for the *Sunday Tribune* and a variety of national newspapers and publications, and was nominated for an ESB Sports Journalist of the Year Award in 2003 for his writing on Gaelic games. The 1982 All-Ireland football final stands out as his earliest sporting memory, which he watched in front of the television while eating fish fingers for his tea. Now aged thirty, and originally from Killavullen, Co Cork, Michael lives in Dublin. This is his first book.

Kings of September

THE DAY OFFALY DENIED KERRY FIVE IN A ROW

Michael Foley

THE O'BRIEN PRESS
DUBLIN

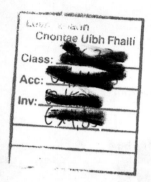
First published 2007 by The O'Brien Press Ltd,
12 Terenure Road East, Dublin 6, Ireland.
Tel: +353 1 4923333; Fax: +353 1 4922777
E-mail: books@obrien.ie
Website: www.obrien.ie

ISBN: 978-1-84717-013-2

British Library Cataloguing-in-Publication Data
Foley, Michael
The kings of September : the day offaly denied Kerry five in a row
1. Gaelic football - History
I. Title
796.3'3

1 2 3 4 5 6 7 8 9
07 08 09 10 11 12 13 14 15

Editing, typesetting, layout and design: The O'Brien Press Ltd
Printed and bound in the UK by J.H. Haynes & Co Ltd, Sparkford

DEDICATED

To Regina for the happiest time of my life.

To Mam and Andrew for endless years of love and support.

To Dad for Thurles, Killarney, Cork
and a love for hurling and football that will last a lifetime.

CONTENTS

PROLOGUE

18 September 1982

Seamus Darby took a deep breath and let the cool night air plunge into his lungs, whooshing through his system like a drug. He felt light-headed. Wired. He floated home, thinking of tomorrow and the All-Ireland final, thinking of Kerry and five-in-a-row. Thinking of history.

The night had passed like a dream. The Offaly players had sat in a small back room in the Tullamore GAA centre for two hours, listening to their manager, Eugene McGee. The silence was immaculate. He told them what they had willed themselves to believe: they were good enough. None of the pressmen who had visited Offaly's training session the previous Tuesday night believed they could win. The bookies had laid odds of 1/5 on Kerry. On the day of the final only one Sunday newspaper would back Offaly. Three days before, the front page of the *Kerryman* was dominated by a picture of 1981 captain Jimmy Deenihan lifting the Sam Maguire cup, with the banner headline: 'A Prelude to History?' The world was treating Offaly like fall guys. But Darby knew. They all knew. Offaly weren't afraid any more.

'If someone threw a ball into the room that night,' says Darby, 'there'd have been someone killed.'

Darby got home and paced the front room. The last few months had been special and promised to live with him forever. When McGee added him to the panel in mid-summer, Darby had waddled in overweight and carrying baggage. When picking championship panels to carry Offaly into the summer, McGee had ignored him for years. Darby had his All-Ireland medal from 1972 and a happy life beyond football. He had kids and a wife. He had a business to run. Did he need all this?

In the end, something tugged at him, and he sacrificed himself for McGee. Now, he was glad. The few months of training had made him the footballer Offaly had always wished him to be. He had lost weight and knocked the edges from all the bad habits that had slowed him up. He already had a place on the team before injury scuttled him. The following day he would sit on the bench, fidgeting and crackling with excitement. If Offaly needed him, he was ready.

He was edgy. Adrenalin was jumping through his veins, making him mad, now. His wife, Veronica, stared at him. 'We're going to win, Veron,' he said. 'We're going to win.'

He needed a drink, something to soften the edges and soak up the tension. He wanted to run into Paddy McCormack's pub next door, but people had a nasty way of twisting those visits into the kind of rumour he'd find hard to shake. Instead, he rang Kevin Farrell, his brother-in-law.

'Have you anything at home?' asked Darby.

Kevin had a bottle of brandy. 'But I've nothing to put in it.'

'Right,' Darby replied. 'I'll be up.'

He found a bottle of 7-Up. The bottle of brandy was demolished. Darby picked up the phone and made some calls. He rang Fr McWee, the parish priest in Edenderry and President of Offaly County Board, and an old friend who always prayed for the team and the players. 'You'll think of us tomorrow morning at Mass?' said Darby.

'Don't worry, Seamus,' the priest replied. 'You'll be on and you'll score a goal or two.'

It was near three in the morning when Darby and Veronica headed for home. That night he slept soundly, the brandy softening his nerves and lulling his senses to sleep. Morning would come soon.

*   *   *

Saturday morning in Ventry had started badly. As Páidí Ó Sé pointed his car towards Killarney for Kerry's last training session before heading to Dublin, he saw something that chilled his blood. A red-haired lady.

It was the worst luck. He knew old fishermen in Dingle who would leave their boats in the harbour all day if they saw a red-haired lady. For the previous few weeks all this five-in-a-row business had been nipping at him. Now this. 'We're fucked,' he mumbled to himself.

That Saturday morning in Killarney, the groundsman, Paddy O'Shea, pulled the gates shut in Fitzgerald Stadium after Kerry's final training session. A faint aroma of olive oil wafted around the dressing room as the players got their final rubdowns and prepared to head for Dublin.

Kerry had trained more than fifty times in Killarney all year, but this was only the visible part of an iceberg that had seen Páidí traverse the hills of west Kerry, the Tralee boys flatten out the bumps on a patch of green behind Banna Strand, and John O'Keeffe and Jimmy Deenihan pump weights in Dinny Mahony's gym in Tralee.

The boys headed to Mickey Doc's at the Park Place hotel for steaks and salmon. Training tonight had been solid. John O'Keeffe sat it out, having taken the previous two weeks off to rest his injuries and prepare himself to mark Matt Connor. Jack O'Shea, Mikey Sheehy and a few lads had taken penalty kicks on Charlie Nelligan. Tim Kennelly had been slamming them into the net. The tables were quiet, save for the occasional squall of laughter from Páidí Ó Sé's corner. His mood had lightened again. Maybe this Kerry team was beyond *piseogs*. There was something of a cause in proving that.

The week in Kerry had passed quietly. The press night in Killarney a few days earlier had gone like all the rest. Jack O'Shea cheerily took questions and joked with reporters. 'Just put me down for whatever I said last year,' he told one. The only player who had seemed jumpy was Páidí. When reporters asked him questions about five in a row and the final, he grimaced, and ducked and dived out of answering. As Ó Sé conducted one interview, a Kerry selector pulled another player aside to arrange a trip to a local school with the Sam Maguire cup the following Friday. No one doubted. No one was worried.

No team had ever given them reason to. No one had beaten Kerry in the championship since 1977. When opponents scrolled through the names and considered their reputations, they were beaten before they even took the field against them. The Kerry team was charismatic, blessed with rogues and genius. In an era when Ireland was racked by unemployment and made dull and grey by emigration, Kerry offered a thrilling splash of colour.

The public revered them. To their coach, Mick O'Dwyer, five-in-a-row felt like destiny. Their mighty rivalry with Dublin that defined the seventies had evaporated and no one in the years since had stood tall enough to stare Kerry in the eye. Five-in-a-row was their reward. Their birthright. Their destiny.

Kerry had already been serenaded through the summer by songs of celebration. Killarney and Tralee had bickered over who should welcome the team home first. T-shirts emblazoned with five-in-a-row slogans were doing hectic business. There were mugs and commemorative plates. A special Kerry jersey was designed for the day. The public were clamouring for history. O'Dwyer had tried to block out the glare, but some shafts of light had already got through to the players. Injuries had hurt his team all summer, and occasionally O'Dwyer's worries had got the better of him. A few nights earlier, he had run a man selling T-shirts from Fitzgerald Stadium, like a godless merchant from the temple. Now he had one day left to get through. Five-in-a-row was theirs to win.

The 1982 final promised to shape lives forever. It would make heroes of some, and shatter others. Some would be jolted from their sleep in the middle of the night, still reliving the moments the game slipped away from them. Others would find themselves destitute and alone. Some marriages and livelihoods would strengthen and prosper after 1982. Others would fall apart. Some friendships would improve. Others would end. Even when their lives would threaten to melt down, the All-Ireland medal would withstand the heat, an indelible image of the remarkable story it represented. It would be the backdrop for triumphs and tragedies, happy times and sad ones.

Like all epic stories, it began simply, with a young man sitting at a typewriter.

PART 1

THE DREAM

1 THE STRANGER

'The uncertainty now is over for Offaly. For the past few years they were being constantly mentioned as threats to the leading teams but that day is finished. The great Offaly team of the first half of this decade is well and truly finished and, barring a miracle, they will not be serious championship contenders for some time.'

Eugene McGee, *Sunday Press*, 14 March 1976

Eugene McGee replaced the receiver on the old wind-up phone, and allowed himself a moment's satisfaction. That piece was good. He rolled the sentences around in his head again. It felt like the best piece he'd ever written. It was sharp and edgy, but was softened by sympathy. It conveyed a sense of drama and loss, but, most importantly, it was bang on the money. He didn't pull a punch, and every blow he threw reached its target. Offaly were buried, and there was no point in dancing around it.

Their last game had felt like a wake. Offaly had travelled to Roscommon for a league game against Mayo, mired at the bottom of Division One. The loser would fall into Division Two. The steepness of the drop promised to wreak damage on either team.

Both counties were burdened by history. Mayo hadn't won an All-Ireland since 1951. Their last Connacht title had come in 1969. Offaly still retained a team dotted with players who had won their first All-Ireland titles in 1971 and 1972, but the team was creaking with age. As McGee took his seat in the ground, the grim awfulness of the day wrapped itself around everything and everybody. A bitter easterly wind whistled through the stand. The scoreboard in Dr Hyde Park wasn't in operation, leaving the few hundred people huddled together for warmth to do their own sums.

McGee looked around the crowd and saw Tony McTague take his seat. When Offaly won in 1971 and 1972, McTague was a warrior hero. He kicked crucial frees and led the attack with verve, but he was retired now, and no amount of cajoling could get him back. McGee thought about McTague's best days and how Offaly had thrived when he was there. Now here he was, sitting in a stand in Roscommon, witnessing Offaly's slow, agonising decline. McGee was transfixed by the depression of it all.

At half-time, Offaly were clinging on, but gradually they faded away. Near the end, they won a penalty. Full-forward Sean Lowry prepared to take it, but minutes passed before the referee could properly clear the players away from the ball. Lowry struck it well, but Mayo goalkeeper Ivan Heffernan beat the ball away. The referee's whistle blew. A reprieve. Something was amiss, and the penalty would have to be retaken.

Lowry placed the ball again. Heffernan saved again and the ball deflected away off the bar. The crowd groaned. When the referee blew the final whistle, Offaly had failed to score for the entire second half and had lost by nine points.

As he thought of Offaly, now withered by age, McGee was moved to recall some poetry.

Even now my limbs tell an answer
To the Croke Park cheer
As borne on the murmurous air above
It fills Ireland from Malin to Clear
And now I raise my head
Not in grief nor in sadness grey
But rather, in pride to whisper,
— I had my day.

For years McGee had scrapped for work as a journalist, but pieces like this one for the *Sunday Press* convinced him he was finally beginning to make progress. He had written articles for the *Gaelic Weekly* magazine, worked on trade magazines and taken subbing shifts and writing jobs with the *Irish Press*. His columns were written under pseudonyms, leaving his mother to wonder whether this Daniel O'Connor truly was her son.

At least he had amassed a few triumphs, even if he was the only person who knew about them. In 1972 he had watched Kilkenny hurler Eddie Keher training alone in Terenure College, preparing for their All-Ireland final against Cork, and built up a friendship with him. Although the bulk of the country was happy to back Cork, McGee was consumed by Keher's dedication and optimism before the game, and backed Kilkenny to win. That Sunday, as Keher delivered a stunning performance and Kilkenny claimed a classic All-Ireland, McGee wallowed in the satisfaction.

For years his colleague in the *Gaelic Weekly*, Brendan MacLua, had written a column for the *Sunday Press*. Now he had a new idea, a newspaper for the sprawling Irish community in London, to be called the *Irish Post*. He asked McGee to join him.

McGee thought about it. He spent a month in 1976 visiting the Irish centres and GAA clubs around London, establishing a network of contacts for the new newspaper, but in the end couldn't leave home. In return for his help, MacLua cut him a break. With his job at the *Sunday Press* vacant, MacLua recommended McGee as his replacement. A public profile – and a byline his mother could believe in – were priceless fringe benefits.

Offaly. Immigrants. Keher. His nature and heritage always drew McGee to the underdog. Donlon's shop in Longford town was the GAA's unofficial headquarters in his home county and from its counter McGee's brother, Fr Phil, held court for years, gleefully chatting to all who would listen and rarely leaving them go without an array of stories and ideas to chew over about football.

Hours could pass with Fr Phil. In years to come, Liam Mulvihill, the

GAA's director general, would remember evenings spent in the Longford Arms hotel after county board meetings listening to Fr Phil's theories on local football – and anything else passing through his mind. As Longford's delegate to the GAA's Central Council, its primary decision-making body, Fr Phil proposed the concept of an inter-county Under-21 championship. In 1965, it came into being.

People always looked to Fr Phil. When their elderly relations took ill, people sent for him. When cows were calving and the local farmers wished to enact the old tradition of blessing the animals to ensure a safe delivery, they called Fr Phil. He worked ceaselessly for the local Latin school in Moyne, a two-hundred-year-old institution that had grown out of an old hedge school. The McGees had grown up in the gentle countryside of Aughnacliffe, near the Cavan border, ringed by lakes and ancient dolmens. While Longford struggled to make any imprint, successive Cavan teams were regarded as gods. Parts of Longford provided willing converts.

Football seasons in Longford came and went untroubled by victories or any ambitions, but Fr Phil never felt comfortable with that. In the late sixties, he turned his full attention to the Longford senior footballers, and the dust began to rise. When it came to seeking a new trainer, Fr Phil sought the best. Mick Higgins was among Cavan's greatest footballers and now coached the Cavan county team, but Fr Phil reckoned he could double-job. He called one evening to talk, and stayed until Higgins caved in. Higgins trained Longford, Fr Phil picked the team, and Longford won their first Leinster title in 1968, along with a National League title in 1966. In a place where the footballers' failure had hardened from an annual occurrence into a state of mind, the county had never known such boundless prosperity. Fr Phil had made it happen.

All the while, his younger brother went to training sessions and learned. In 1969 Eugene headed for University College Dublin (UCD) to begin a BA in English and History, but football provided the greatest outlet for his intellect.

UCD football was in a ragged state. The captain of the football team organised everything. He picked the team. He arranged pitches and starting times for matches, and spent the rest of his time corralling the players to the venue. When McGee took over as secretary of the football club, he assumed some of the workload. He took on the freshers' team alongside the captain and won an All-Ireland freshers' title in his first year.

He followed the team through and as captains changed, McGee emerged as a constant. He never played the game well, but he thought deeply about it. At a time when enlightened thought on training for Gaelic football was confined to a handful of minds scattered around the country, McGee was borrowing ideas from everywhere. He used training concepts from soccer and American sports to devise new drills. McGee wanted to get inside players' minds, figure out how they ticked and see if there was a way to improve them. When GAA coaching courses were organised in Gormanston College in Meath during the mid-seventies and packed by coaches who would apply the lessons learned in the decades to come, McGee shared the same lecture halls as Mick O'Dwyer and Kevin Heffernan. When Gaelic football coaches began exploring new territories, McGee was among the pioneers.

His UCD teams had tactics and schemes like no one else. He had devised a system for taking long frees, withdrawing one player from the full-forward line as a signal to the remaining two that the ball was coming their way. Players took part in workshops to hone their skills. Their kicking style was deconstructed, first learning to kick the ball accurately over six yards before gradually working up to longer distances.

UCD teams were a Babel of accents and origins. There was Colm O'Rourke from Meath. Kevin Kilmurray from Offaly. John O'Keeffe from Kerry, with All-Ireland medals in his pocket and a sense of calm and composure the entire team could feed off. Camaraderie became friendship. McGee shared a flat with O'Keeffe and, after training in Belfield, several players would pile into their flat for breakfast before heading to their lectures. Tom Hunt from Waterford, whose thick accent had them slagging him about getting a translator. Dinny Burke, an Arts student from Tipperary, who ate forwards without salt. Ollie Leddy from Cavan. Mick Fennelly, a meaty Agriculture student from Athy.

'It was a homely atmosphere,' says McGee. 'The big thing about UCD was that they were a disparate group of people and they only came good at periodic intervals when a large group from the same faculty or the one county came together. The vets came good once or twice. Even the medicine people. There was a whole batch of Cavan and Roscommon fellas in the forties and fifties. A clique would form the nucleus for the whole team. I was ever-present when I was there, so there was continuity for the first time. I was able to bridge the gaps between the fellas departing and arriving.'

McGee's personality was abrasive, too. He could be curt. He cut through reputations. No player was greater than the team. Even if they were, he wouldn't let them know it. When he took on UCD's Sigerson Cup team – college football's premier competition – he arranged sessions during deepest winter for seven in the morning. The players assembled in Belfield in the biting cold and darkness, their only consolation the guarantee of warm showers when they were done. He needed to weed the softness out of them. Those who could discipline themselves to show up had the desire he could work with.

'My thinking was, we have to do something exceptional here,' says McGee. 'We have to create a sacrificial situation where the players make a supreme sacrifice. There's nothing more supreme than getting up in November and December and it freezing cold.'

'You'd be shamed if you missed those training sessions,' says John O'Keeffe. 'Nobody missed them. He had terrific control and respect from the players. He had that hold over the team. It absolutely amazed me that he had such an in-depth knowledge of the game for a fella who had never kicked a ball in his life. We used always slag him about that. Though I remember at one tournament game we were short a man – Eugene had to stand in in corner-forward with his wellingtons. He had a terrific way of articulating his ideas. I've never heard anyone in a dressing room as good as him.'

UCD started winning. They owned the Sigerson Cup between 1971 and 1974, missed out in 1975 and gathered another three titles between 1976 and 1978. As the club championships began to take shape, UCD were among those to provide the competition with history and tradition, winning two All-Ireland club titles. (Before Kerry appointed Mick O'Dwyer as trainer in 1974, John O'Keeffe would gently tease McGee about taking the Kerry job.) In the Dublin championship, UCD wrestled furiously with St Vincent's in a rivalry tinged with hatred. Together they created enough waves to raise the tide, and Dublin football prospered.

UCD were young and glamorous. Clubs all over the country invited them to play in weekend tournaments. One weekend in high summer they travelled to Tralee and took on Austin Stack's. They won a seven-a-side tournament in Rochfortbridge, Westmeath, one year and each man left for home with IR£50 in his back pocket. They played a Gold Watch tournament in Bailieboro, beating Castleblayney and Crossmaglen and Cavan.

Then, on a quiet Sunday in January 1976, everything stopped. The day had begun well. UCD had beaten Offaly champions Ferbane in the Leinster club final and celebrated all the way back to Dublin. That night, McGee's phone rang. It was three in the morning. Bad news. Fr Phil had suffered a heart attack, and died. He was forty-six. McGee put the phone down. He knew his life would change forever.

Fr Phil's death left his elderly mother to tend the small family farm alone. Five brothers and sisters were away, unable to return home. Eugene was single and living alone in Dublin, and free to go back. He split himself between Dublin and Longford, continuing to work with UCD while filing his copy to the *Sunday Press* on the old wind-up phone. It was enough to keep him going, but the perfectly manicured pitches in Belfield and the quiet lakelands and hills around Aughnacliffe couldn't contain his ambition. He needed a new challenge.

*   *   *

The summer of 1976 was stiflingly hot, and Fr Sean Heaney was restless. Five years had passed since he had come to Rahan, County Offaly, as parish priest, and his first year as chairman of Offaly County Board had propelled him into the middle of a crisis. Relegation to Division Two was bad, but things were getting worse. That June, Offaly played out a dull Leinster quarter-final against Meath that ended with a scowl. First, Meath's Mattie Kerrigan squared up to Offaly's Mick O'Rourke. Minutes later, Kerrigan was entangled with Mick Wright. Having ignored the first incident, referee Paul Kelly's patience was spent and Kerrigan and Wright were sent off. As Kelly left the field some supporters hurled beer cans at him. Offaly lost by nine points, 3-8 to 0-8, and were sliding. Their manager Paddy McCormack resigned and the usual list of former players were queuing up for their turn, but Fr Heaney wanted something different.

One evening he met Kevin Kilmurray. While the rest of the team's stars had begun to burn out, Kilmurray was a hero, decorated with All-Ireland medals and All Stars, their last remaining source of light. They talked about managers, and Heaney wondered aloud about alternatives. After spending a few years in UCD, Kilmurray knew what McGee could do.

'What's McGee like?' asked Heaney.

'He's the best,' replied Kilmurray. 'Why Longford don't have him, I can't understand.'

Heaney didn't know much about McGee, but he knew enough. McGee was a self-made man. He hadn't won All-Ireland medals but he had twenty-five undergraduates training at seven in the morning a few weeks before Christmas. He could keep them together and bring them all over the country without incident. He could handle people and adversity. He was a journalist with a neck like old shoe leather. To survive in Offaly, managers needed that.

'That's who I want,' he said.

Getting McGee would require work – at home in Offaly, and in Longford. Offaly County Board was filled with delegates from every club in the county – a fifteen-man executive committee, including Heaney and county secretary John Dowling, but the power was isolated to one primary source.

Convince Dowling, and anything could happen.

To most delegates Dowling was a fearsome figure. But Heaney had a bright, sprightly personality, and a good working relationship with Dowling had softened into friendship.

One evening Heaney called to Dowling in Tullamore for a chat. 'The kettle's on, boss,' Dowling shouted from the kitchen. 'Cup of tea?'

Heaney was thinking football. Where Heaney was keen to experiment, Dowling saw no reason to change. Offaly football was just in a rut. These things happen. Look at the size of the place and only half the county playing football.

Even if Dowling didn't, Heaney knew Offaly football needed a jolt. The old story about one former Offaly coach went that, after months of running laps, one player asked if they could shake up training a little to stave off the boredom. 'No problem,' said the coach. 'Ye can run the next five laps in the opposite direction.' Heaney put the idea of Eugene McGee to Dowling. Dowling was suspicious. The man wasn't from Offaly. He had no background as a player, and the idea of a journalist taking over the team worried him.

But there were other issues to consider. Heaney had been Dowling's preferred choice as chairman. Dowling needed him and whatever McGee would do, he couldn't drag Offaly any lower. McGee seemed a harmless indulgence. Dowling gave the nod.

One Thursday evening in July, Heaney called McGee and invited him to a meeting. The conversation was curt.

'What do you want to meet me for?' asked McGee.

'Well, I don't want to talk about it over the phone,' replied Heaney.

'Well, if you don't tell me what you want to talk about, or what you want, I'm not going to talk to you.'

'Okay, well, we'd like you to train the Offaly team.'

'Sure, what would I know about Offaly?'

'Well, I don't know,' said Heaney. 'But we think you'd do a good job.'

McGee was baffled, but intrigued. The following Sunday, as Offaly played Dublin in the Leinster minor football final, McGee lodged himself in the Hogan Stand with his match programme and a pen. Dublin beat Offaly, but McGee saw a spark. Offaly had guts. Spirit. McGee placed a tick beside some names: Gerry Carroll, Vincent Henry, Tomás O'Connor, Johnny Mooney. Maybe he could school them through and build a team around them? It was worth a shot.

Meanwhile, Fr Heaney dropped McGee's name into conversations around the county and created a foothold for McGee among the executive. When the list of candidates was compiled, McGee's name was written at the bottom. He was unknown and untested but, with an absence of any other serious candidates, McGee was proposed. Dowling nodded his approval and the delegates fell into line. Heaney had his man. Word was sent to the newspapers just as the presses cranked into gear.

Westmeath-Offaly Independent
Friday, 13 August 1976

NEW TRAINER FOR OFFALY GAA!
As we go to press, we are told that GAA sportstar Eugene Magee [*sic*] has been appointed trainer of the Offaly senior football team and is to take up the post immediately.

Longford-born Magee attended a meeting of the Co. Executive in Tullamore on Tuesday night, at which his appointment was ratified.

It is further understood he will also serve on the selection committee in company with Messrs Martin Heavey (Rhode), Michael Guinan (Clara), John Buckley (Ballycumber) and John Coghlan (Belmont).

Mr Magee has proved himself an accomplished trainer, if not at inter-county level, then at least as the man who prepared the successful UCD side in recent years.

On a sunny Saturday evening the following weekend, McGee landed into Tullamore with a bag of footballs in the boot of his car and strolled out on to the field in his pale blue UCD jersey. Heaney was in the stand.

Things were already different. Training sessions at Offaly had never been conducted with more than one football.

The players straggled on to the field and McGee brought them into a semicircle around him, twenty yards from one goal. Up in the stand, Fr Heaney held his breath.

'He threw out about a half dozen footballs and said: "Kick them over the bar." Here you had guys with two All-Ireland medals, Leinster medals, club championships. It was the most humiliating thing you could ever do. In other words, he said: You can't do anything. You're not able to kick the ball over the bar from twenty-five yards out.'

A couple of weeks later, Offaly played their first game under McGee to mark the opening of a new club pavilion in Clonbullogue. Kildare came with a shiny new team filled with Under-21s that had reached an All-Ireland final against Kerry. Offaly's team was quickly patched together. A cluster of players was missing, having committed to play for their clubs. Gerry Carroll, one of McGee's cherished minors, had to cry off with injury. Sean Lowry arrived late. But Offaly showed some cut, and won by five points.

'Most of the Offaly side can feel well satisfied with their performance,' said the correspondent from the *Westmeath-Offaly Independent*, 'and with some serious training under team coach Eugene McGee brighter horizons may lie ahead, but patience must be the key as success will not come overnight.'

With the team still plump from the All-Ireland wins of 1971 and 1972, McGee started withdrawing privileges. For years they had trained in Edenderry and gathered in Larkin's restaurant near the pitch afterwards to gorge themselves on steaks. With their guts still churning after a relentless night's training, few plates were ever cleared. From now on, the players would receive a pint of milk. 'When you get to the stage that you earn something better,' he said, 'you'll get it.'

'My image of Offaly was the same as everyone else's,' McGee explained, 'a rough, tough crowd of footballers. I made it clear from the start we wouldn't be trying to copy Dublin or Kerry, and that it would be two or three years at least [before the team made progress]. That eased the pressure straight away.'

In two months' time they would play Limerick in their first National League game, a world away from the planet they thought they lived on. That winter, the shocking poverty of their plight would be revealed to them. Five months before, Offaly had given McGee a canvas to compose his finest piece of work.

Now they needed him to sketch out the next chapter.

2 REVOLUTION

This McGee business appealed to Richie Connor. He was young and McGee had ideas. Big ideas. He talked about the game differently to anyone Richie had ever heard before. Richie respected McGee for what he had done at UCD even if no one else at home took a moment's notice. Anyone who was around Dublin playing football, as Richie was, knew the stuff UCD were up to. McGee was an underground hero.

And he had a nice car.

As Christmas approached, McGee had been in touch with a coaching friend of his at Arsenal, and was taking a trip over to watch them train. He was going to take the boat, drive his Fiat Mirafiori from Liverpool to London, and use his sister's flat in Kilburn as a base. Soccer-training manuals dotted his bookshelves at home, and he knew watching Arsenal would be useful in drumming up a few new drills to run in Offaly, but he'd need a player on the panel to sell his ideas. All winter Connor had been open and receptive. Richie had never been outside Ireland before, and the idea of the trip thrilled him. Plus, McGee had that car.

They met in Dublin and boarded the ferry. McGee pulled out a board game, Scrabble. Connor had never played Scrabble before and muddled through a few rounds. They had a few pints. As they drove off the ferry, McGee looked at the strange city in front of him.

'How the hell are we going to get through this city?' he said. 'Do you want to drive?'

Connor had heard of the motorways in England and his mind's eye had concocted an image for himself. He imagined zooming through the countryside, plunging his foot down on the accelerator, eating up the open road to London. He thought of the other cars on the road and the chance the motorway would give him to see them at full pelt. He wanted to feel that speed, the kind of kick he couldn't get nipping around the narrow bog roads that led home to Walsh Island. Whatever about Arsenal and training methods, the Mirafiori was enough reason to come. They swapped seats, and were off.

After a while, Connor started getting bored. The roads were empty and straight. There were service areas and signposts. True, he could ramp the car up to its maximum speed, but with no chance to slalom in and out of traffic, no chance to propel the car to top speed through wide, sweeping bends, even top speed started to feel slow. After an hour, he settled on making it to London by nightfall.

The following day, they headed for Highbury. After two years with Offaly, Connor had developed a concept of elite training: tog out, take the field and run to the point of throwing up. There was no science, just vomit.

Watching the professionals bemused him. They played weekly games, with the occasional midweek match. Their physical training had been done in the month *before* the beginning of the season. All they were doing now was tipping the ball around. They did a few running exercises. It was harmless, he thought. A child could have done it. For forty-five minutes he watched them, then they headed for the showers. He strolled out to the carpark, trying to pluck up the courage to say hello to David O'Leary or Liam Brady, but instead watched them zoom away in their sportscars. McGee's Mirafiori was getting dowdier by the minute.

Meanwhile, McGee was chatting with his friend, taking notes. He was told that all the players did between games was toning and limbering exercises. Too many games were played for anything more strenuous. Gaelic football didn't have the same span of games as professional soccer, but McGee noted something in the pre-season training plan. The key to summer success, he concluded, was putting the miles in the legs during the winter. He scribbled some notes, and headed home.

The winter of 1976/77 had been packed with experiments. Some worked, others exploded in their faces. One evening McGee arrived at training with a bundle of tickets for the players to sell. The proceeds would go towards buying a video recorder and camera to film matches for the purposes of analysis. The video recorder was a large, unwieldy box, and the camera was bigger. McGee filmed the team playing, but there were problems. A fog fell across the field during the game. When the tape was replayed, the video was unwatchable. McGee took the big box home and it was never seen again.

Otherwise, Offaly had wintered well. McGee had begun the difficult business of cutting loose many of the players who had won All-Ireland medals in 1971 and 1972, but promotion back to Division One had almost been secured and a win against Clare in Lahinch would seal matters.

Nothing would be left to chance. Before Offaly travelled, McGee went to the county board insisting the players be transported to Ennis on Saturday and booked into the best hotel in town. When the Offaly footballers arrived anywhere, they needed to make a statement. Their visit deserved the trappings of an occasion. He wanted people to turn their heads, and the players to notice them looking. Their confidence needed building up. A little attention was a good start.

The following morning, McGee put another idea into motion: a pre-match meal. As the players came down for breakfast, McGee told them they wouldn't be eating until midday. Stomachs grumbled and players followed suit. The pre-match meals finally arrived: twenty plates of steak, nothing else. The players turned militant. Chips were demanded. At the risk of prompting a revolt, McGee agreed. A carefully proportioned dietary plan had now turned into a slap-up feed. With a hefty dinner threatening to burst the buttons on their trousers, the players piled into the team bus and headed for west Clare. As Clare battered Offaly into the mud, the steak sat in their guts like a cannonball. In the end, Offaly survived their stitches and scraped home. McGee had more lessons put away.

His first Leinster championship drew Offaly against Wexford, but McGee was already looking through the draw for Dublin. Wexford, he reckoned, was a game to cruise through. Instead, Offaly were sunk before they even left port. McGee had begun the season without goalkeeper Martin Furlong and would suffer for his absence. He had kept goal for Offaly for three All-Ireland titles – their first minor title in 1964 and their two senior titles in 1971 and 1972 – but he was out of form. Offaly paid a heavy price for his decline. Wexford hit three goals inside the first fifteen minutes and by the time Offaly recovered their bearings the game was gone from them. It finished 4-4 to 1-12. The result prompted uproar. Dropping some All-Ireland medal winners had been difficult politically, and without good results McGee was playing with fire.

PJ Mahon was secretary of Walsh Island, and one evening at the cattle mart in Tullamore told him all he needed to know about McGee's future. The place seethed with talk of a coup. But Mahon knew the players had other ideas. They knew McGee was different. Each club sent two delegates to the monthly county board meeting and Mahon invited Richie Connor to fill one of Walsh Island's berths. At the meeting, Connor looked around a room filled with strange faces. Some he had never seen at a game. When they spoke he could hardly believe what he was hearing. Eugene McGee, they said, hadn't won anything serious in footballing terms. He had no background in football. And, worst of all, he was from Longford.

'Are there not great men in Offaly that could do the job?' asked one delegate.

'I agree with the previous speaker,' said another. 'We're expecting a man from Longford to do the business for us. Sure, Longford have never won anything.'

Connor quietly waited his turn. When it came, he needed to be strong. 'It wasn't Eugene McGee that lost the match,' he said. 'It was the players. As a player I couldn't fault the preparation. It wasn't a case of

Eugene McGee letting us down, as us letting him down. As a team, we'd be anxious to put things right.'

The matter was put to the floor for a vote. McGee survived, but he needed something to happen the following summer. Offaly needed to beat Dublin.

*   *   *

In his years with UCD, McGee had fought battles in the Dublin club championship that left him scarred and battered, but ultimately they never broke him. Few clubs cared for UCD and fewer still chose to disguise their hatred. In the fifties, Kevin Heffernan had led a generation of St Vincent's players to form the core of a great Dublin team and re-energise football in the city. Now Heffernan was busy revolutionising Dublin again as coach, but he always had time for Vincent's. In McGee and UCD, he saw a pernicious influence that must be stopped. McGee was bad for Dublin football.

'Vincent's hated McGee with a vengeance,' says John O'Keeffe, centrefield for UCD. 'It was deep, deep, deep.' For successive county finals, McGee stalked Heffernan along the line and his star-laden team frequently outshone Vincent's. It drove Heffernan crazy. Sometimes his team followed suit.

In 1972, Vincent's met UCD in the county final for the first time. That was the spark. The game was a war. Two players were sent off, but the battle knew no limits. One Dublin official claimed he had to leave Parnell Park after fifteen minutes, so appalling was the violence on show.

'With about five minutes left I looked over and I saw a free-for-all between the two benches,' says O'Keeffe. 'The two sets of subs had a go off each other. But the referee was very sensible, he just let the game run out. It was an effort by Vincent's to get the game abandoned; they were so sore over it.'

The teams met in seven consecutive championships from 1970,

including five finals. In 1974 UCD were forced to give a walkover when the club championship was suspiciously scheduled while the students were sitting exams. Now, with Heffernan and Dublin in their pomp, McGee returned to plague him with Offaly, looking for a way to take them down.

'I knew Dublin inside out,' he says. 'I was the worst person in Ireland, as far as Dublin were concerned, to get the Offaly job. I had walked around Parnell Park behind Heffernan for so many county finals. There was nothing about Dublin football I didn't know.'

Before he could figure a way to take down Dublin, he had to figure out his own team. He needed to find a way into the players' heads like he did with UCD. If McGee wished to talk to the players in UCD, they were easy to find on campus or around town. But the only time McGee saw the Offaly players was at training. McGee would have to go to them.

He hit the road, and visited players at home. He looked around and took the atmosphere in. Did his players have the right kind of background to make it? Did they have a stable home? Were there problems he needed to know about? Was there the required element of steel in their bloodlines to survive championship football? Did they need loving or pushing?

One night he landed in Ferbane looking for Sean Lowry, stayed up chatting all night and slept in Lowry's spare room. The following morning when Lowry got up, McGee was gone. 'You could have a great old chat with McGee,' says Sean Lowry, 'but you'd never feel you'd got inside him. There was a bit of mystery about him that way too.'

The players were all learning about his quirks and his talents. Although he could go months without speaking directly to some of them, they never felt left out. McGee loved meetings. All the analysis and thought he applied to each opposition were distilled into meetings that could stretch deep into the night. The night before a championship game was McGee's greatest stage. The atmosphere was almost always perfectly pitched, balanced between raw passion and the cold steel of logic.

He could talk for two hours and lose no one. He weaved his dry humour through his analysis of the opposition and his own team. Just as with UCD, Offaly were furnished with exhaustive breakdowns of the opposition. And each player received a small slip of paper with a short, typed paragraph detailing their opponent's strengths and weaknesses.

'With the best will in the world,' says McGee, 'players take in about ten percent of what is said to them. This they could look at ten times and concentrate on it. If there was anything they disagreed with, they could check it with me. It meant if their nerves were really at them, they could look at it and it'd bring them back to basics.'

He was drawn to players like Lowry. And Richie. He knew Kevin Kilmurray from UCD and when Martin Furlong returned from his absence, McGee used him, too. He asked them about players in Offaly, and about clubs. Who were the people who ran Offaly GAA? What clubs were strong politically? Offaly was an alien county to him, but he was learning.

McGee's visits and the detail of his training methods confirmed his commitment to the players, but they still found it hard to find a way through to him. Making him laugh was almost impossible. An entire season could go by for some players without a word from McGee, then the phone call might come, or a visit in the night. Some players were harder than others to figure out.

'At the time,' says Richie Connor, 'league matches meant pints. You played your league match, then you went in and drank the evening away. It was nothing to go in and drink eight or ten pints. You'd go in and get your meal, have a few drinks and often a few pints would lead to a few more. McGee would be there drinking his bottle of Carlsberg. He wasn't a drinker, but it was part of the culture.

'Fellas like Gerry Carroll or Johnny Mooney – the only time he'd have talked to them on a serious level was over a few drinks. And they could talk to him. There would've been general respect for him in the team, but that drinking thing in the early years was very important to bond with the players and get their confidence.'

To have any hope of catching Dublin, he needed that, but it wasn't always easy. He had thrown the reins around the team, but some of the players were wild, untameable. Keeping the loosest horses in line would become his greatest challenge.

*   *   *

Everybody loved Johnny Mooney. Johnny was classy. He wore snappy suits. He never got nervous before games and wafted around the dressing room, scenting of calm and confidence. When he played at centrefield, he had the power to reach for any ball he deigned to leap for. He could kick off both feet. He was powerful, yet his footwork was nimble enough to allow him glide past opponents without any apparent increase in speed. At his peak, he was untouchable. But there was a devil in him, too.

Training could be a problem. Winter training was an almost insurmountable barrier. Some evenings when a player would call to his house to collect him for training, his mother would stand at the front door explaining how she hadn't seen him all evening, while Mooney headed out the back. When McGee arrived as trainer, his attention to detail and his innovative thinking appealed to Mooney, but his dry personality sometimes irritated him. Months could pass without a word between them. Then, Mooney could disappear.

'We had a stormy relationship,' says Mooney. 'I was a wild young lad. Not in a bad way, but I would've been a wild one. But I always loved playing with Offaly and I don't believe I ever let Offaly down in a competitive game. But we had our differences. We had a lot of differences.

'I went missing at times. I was having a good life, but we always got it sorted out. We always had a relationship, in that he knew what he wanted and I knew what I wanted, and both included the common good of Offaly.'

The National League was an annual battleground. After a game, most of the players would head out for the night. Sundays could drift into Mondays, sometimes Tuesday. If they missed training that evening, McGee was on their trail. Over the years Mooney's time on the League panels was short and fleetingly sweet.

'I didn't particularly mind because I didn't like playing in the muck and gutter. It suited everybody. You'd be training with the club, you'd play well, then you'd get the recall. It's easy to look back and say it was all planned, but it wasn't. I was only nineteen. Looking back in hindsight you'd say: Jesus look at this fella. But that's not how it was.'

One evening McGee called him over during a training session and asked where he had been the previous night. Mooney protested his innocence, insisted there was a perfectly simple explanation for his absence.

'Oh yeah?' said McGee. 'Well look me in the eye and tell me.'

'How can I?' replied Mooney, 'when you're always looking at the ground?'

Being dropped gave Mooney the anger to force his way back.

'Johnny Mooney,' says McGee, 'was impossible to manage.' But McGee also knew he couldn't be without him. He knew the same about Gerry Carroll.

People in Edenderry had waited for Gerry Carroll to grow into a great footballer since he was a kid, but plenty doubted him too. They remembered his father, Christy, as a beautiful footballer. The older followers always said Christy was ahead of his time. He was small, but in an era of mountainously proportioned men, Christy had survived and prospered.

Christy lived life his way, and applied the same values to football. He liked to shoot pheasants. Offaly might be training on a particular evening, but if the mood took him, Carroll might head into the country with his shotgun instead. He carried Offaly to Leinster finals when they tended to lose them, but when they finally started winning, Christy was losing interest.

He was there when Offaly finally won a Leinster title in 1961, but he let football go soon afterwards. Christy cast a long shadow that Gerry always found hard to escape, but people were missing the precious detail that made Christy's son special. Sometimes he might be standing thirty yards from goal and miss, but he could nail a moving target from forty yards. Full-forwards loved him. His passing was immaculate and clean. Years later, opticians would tell him his eyesight was exceptional for a man in his fifties. The secret, he reckoned, was twenty years spent focusing on the horizon, looking for a spare man.

At the beginning, he and McGee were close. He liked McGee's modernist approach. The meetings and the slips of paper appealed to him, and every note filled him with confidence. 'It made me think: This guy [his opponent] can't play me. If he likes to run upfield all the time, the first ball I'm going to get I'll hit it over the bar and the pressure will be on him.'

Carroll was young and precocious. When the boys went out on a Sunday night after league games, Carroll and Mooney were the ones they watched. From their adventures would pour a fountain of stories to keep the banter crackling along the following week. With Matt Connor in tow, Sunday nights were their break from the constraints imposed by football. They needed those nights, but sometimes it got them in trouble.

Carroll's straight talking often chafed with McGee and they had their scrapes. 'There was good times and bad times,' says Carroll. 'I think I had a good relationship with him. The thing about it was I wouldn't hide my feelings. If I was pissed off, he'd know.'

One spring evening Carroll had his fill of McGee's manner and his training. He took his grievances to McGee, and a row broke out. The following weekend the team was travelling to Tralee to play Kerry, but when the bus arrived Carroll wasn't there. Offaly travelled, and were narrowly beaten.

'At the time I did it because I thought I was right,' Carroll says, 'but I think a lot of players were pissed off with me. I remember Richie Connor saying years later: "If that fucker hadn't decided to go home, we'd probably have won that game." When I thought of it that way, it was probably wrong – then I regret doing it. But I don't regret doing it for the reason I did it.'

He clung to Sean Lowry from the beginning. Where Carroll reckoned McGee was merciless with his criticism and impatient with his demands, Lowry knew when to clap him on the back. When McGee and Carroll began to flirt with all-out war, Lowry was the peace-broker.

'He respected my game and made me feel good about my game. Seanie would take me aside and tell me how vital I was to the team and stuff like that. It was nice to hear those things. That would make me feel good.'

A shared aim kept them all together. Mooney and Carroll wanted to be winners. For Offaly to be successful, McGee needed them around. They learned to endure one another.

*　　*　　*

As 1978 began, McGee continued ripping out the wiring and renovating his team, but it badly needed some load-bearing elements. In 1976 Tomás O'Connor was a scraggly young teenager with a tousled mop of blond hair that had caught McGee's eye with Offaly minors. That year Walsh Island reached the county senior final against Ferbane. These games were no place for quiet men, but Walsh Island were ready to take a chance with O'Connor.

They landed him in at centrefield. It would be his first senior game for Walsh Island, and after years in defence, his first as a centrefielder. Before the game began, O'Connor made a promise: leave nothing behind; empty every drop of effort onto the field. He flung himself into the game against Ferbane's Sean Lowry, survived the fights that raged throughout and dominated the middle. Walsh Island won the county title, and would lose just one championship match over the following seven years.

In the years after 1976, O'Connor became a solid, marking centrefielder, obsessed by the business of stopping his opponent. He had played under-14 football for Offaly with Johnny Mooney and Gerry Carroll, but they were the names that commanded attention even then. Tomás was in the supporting cast, and never felt he could exceed that role.

Football was always a trial for him. He tortured himself when his marker got the ball. All the good things he would do in a game were clouded by his innate pessimism. If his marker escaped with the ball, O'Connor fretted about staying on the field. He terrorised himself into becoming a better footballer, but, in McGee's mind, O'Connor was precisely what he needed.

His bloodlines confirmed McGee's faith in him. In the thirties his father, Tommy, had joined their neighbour Bill Mulhall as the first Offaly players selected for Leinster. They were tough footballers, hardened by their life outside the game. When Tommy O'Connor first married, he settled in Sallins, Co Kildare, twenty-six miles from Walsh Island. Every morning he cycled the distance to the site of his new house back in Walsh Island, and cycled home again every evening after a day's building. He footed turf for Bord na Móna and filled the break times with football matches.

Tommy's brother, Jim, played football for Offaly too and the boys grew up close. When they took wives, they married two Bryan sisters from nearby, and settled their families within a half mile of each other in Walsh Island. They were rooted in football, and Walsh Island. Years later, when Jim died, the locals warmly reckoned that the night Jim spent in Walsh Island church after being waked was the first he had spent away from home.

Tommy and Jim travelled together to watch Offaly play. The Sunday mornings would begin with a seven-mile cycle to Mass in Portarlington. Having returned home for breakfast, they would set out for Croke Park. The same routine was observed religiously for years, and their stories of the epics they had witnessed kept the faith stout at home for generations.

People knew about Tommy, but Tommy was quiet, and allowed his sons find out about their heritage for themselves. At home Tomás occasionally rooted out old newspaper clippings from a cupboard and was swallowed up by his father's past. Football people in Offaly were pleased to fill in any parts he missed. They told stories about his toughness, and how the same traits passed through all the O'Connors. It was nice for his sons sometimes, other times it irritated them. On a football field Tomás couldn't move for the family reputation. Any he time got up to any mischief, he was immediately tagged as one of the O'Connors. His brother Liam was three years older, but he never showed the promise Tomás did. Over the road, Jim had lost the 'O' on his surname along the way, and his sons grew up as Connors. Jim watched Murt grow into a good footballer, then Richie. And in time his son Matt sprinkled his stardust on Walsh Island and made all the Connors immortal. ◈

Other families teeming with footballers surrounded them. The Fitzgeralds had moved from Ballivor in County Meath when their father started a job with Bord na Móna, and settled nearby. Down the road, the Mulhalls were still sending footballers into Walsh Island. During the summer the boys footed turf and played football on Sundays in O'Connors' back field. There were the seven O'Connor brothers. Liam and Tomás O'Connor would call over. Pat and Mick Fitzgerald came and a long supporting cast of Bryans, Mulhalls, O'Sheas and others. The games bristled with intensity, and their own little ecosystem was creating a unique type of football.

'What emerged apart from the toughness,' says Pat Fitzgerald, 'was a lot of good, intelligent play. Eugene McGee encouraged that too – the use of the ball. His idea was to move the ball as quickly as you can to the full-forward line, but don't just kick it on top of them and get them half killed. The Connors were big into that, and that comes from people who appreciate sport generally.

'Take Matt. He could tell you the scoreline between Scunthorpe and Spurs from twenty years ago. He'd talk about rugby, everything. The idea was you were learning from all sports, then you were playing your own as well and honing that intelligence. You needed guts and skill as well, but you can't leave aside intelligence either.'

Their heroes lived close by. Willie Bryan was a cousin of the O'Connors and had brought the Sam Maguire cup to Walsh Island for the first time in 1971. In the final, Murt Connor had smashed a shot to the net that sent rainwater sprinkling into Hill 16 and finished Galway off. Their heritage was deeply ingrained in their past, but still close enough for them to touch.

'I was eleven when Offaly won their first All-Ireland,' says Tomás O'Connor. 'That's a very impressionable age. I suppose I grew up with an unrealistic view of Offaly football. I thought Offaly always won All-Irelands. We expected to win All-Irelands, or at least [went in with] with the expectation that we could.

'I came into a very good set-up in Offaly and Walsh Island. I just knew about winning. Walsh Island won games in Offaly that we shouldn't have won, but we pulled them out of the fire. We never accepted that with five minutes to go we were going to lose a match. Then, as years went on, you could see where teams were used to losing games.'

Offaly were in severe recession, but O'Connor never believed they were truly poor. In 1976 Walsh Island would resume the dominance they last had in Tommy and Jim O'Connor's time, lacing six consecutive county titles together. All the while, the boys from O'Connors' field were massing together with Offaly. Pat Fitzgerald was there, and Richie had already attained the status of McGee's most trusted lieutenant.

One day in 1978, work with CIE landed Liam O'Connor in Longford town. As he strolled along, he heard a car horn beeping. He looked around. It was McGee. 'See you in Tullamore on Tuesday night for training,' McGee shouted, and drove on. O'Connor had never played any football for Offaly before, but standing at six foot three and weighing fourteen stone, he possessed phenomenal size and strength. McGee could teach him the rest.

In training he followed McGee's instructions to the limit. He diligently commuted from work in Dublin and poured everything into training. He dragged himself through the worst training, but stayed cheerful and attentive to the mood around him. If the atmosphere dipped, he could crack a joke or play a trick. One night he reached home in Walsh Island before training in Tullamore without time to eat anything, so he wrapped a steak in tinfoil and balanced it on top of the engine. By the time he reached Tullamore the heat from the engine had cooked the meat to perfection. Nothing would be allowed to impinge on football.

'I never rated myself a skilful footballer. I was more a mullicker. The biggest thing I had was, whatever I was asked to do on the pitch, I did it. If Eugene asked me to do a particular thing, I'd try and do it. I'd know I wouldn't have the same level of skill other lads had, but once you know that, you're fine. I could handle it in my own way.'

He grew up playing football in Connors' field and hanging around the old handball alley with Richie when they were kids. He worked the bogs every Sunday from the age of seven and played football in his spare time. He carried the same size and strength that was bred into the family's bones, but by his late teens he had seen enough. O'Connor had to get out. He went to Dublin, and happily missed out on minor and Under-21 football with Offaly. But, in time, the game began to drag him back. McGee had caught him at the right time.

There was another boy from Connors' field who didn't need teaching. Just a football.

3 THE NATURE OF MAGIC

Life was often hard for the red hen that waddled around Connors' yard. Every day she patrolled the farm, clucking with worry, looking around corners. The daily traffic that busied up the farm was one thing. The mob of children looking to chase her was another. It was Matt and the football she worried about most.

In Matt's mind the farmyard was a shooting gallery. The frame of the stable door was a set of goals. The diesel tank balanced on two supporting walls was another. The second rung on the ladder was a target. And the small window in the turf shed. When the hen saw Matt firing shots, she knew it was time to run.

Everything about Matt was deceptive. He was shy and quiet, but blessed with a sharp, dry wit that could cut to the bone. He grew to six foot two inches when he got older, but, even when he was fully grown, no one really noticed his height. No one could ever fathom how a slender boy could unleash shots fuelled by such awesome power, but those who shared dressing rooms with him were always struck by his thighs, thick as elephant trunks.

Sport obsessed him and he was drawn to beautiful things. Leeds United's sober brand of grit and competence dominated English football when he was a boy, but Matt preferred the irrepressible glamour of Tottenham. When the boys picked teams for those cataclysmic matches in O'Connors' field, Matt was too small to be chanced outfield, so they stuck him in goal. But the goals would never hold him. Soon he moved outfield into the forwards and became the best they had ever seen.

During threshing season, all the Connors would assemble to help, and they passed the evenings talking football. As Matt grew up he watched Offaly players coming to collect Murt for training. When Paddy McCormack, an old Offaly full-back hewn from granite, pulled up, sometimes Matt hid behind a wall for fear McCormack might turn on him.

For years, Tom McTague kicked the frees that kept Offaly alive. To Matt he was a hero and an instruction manual: only three short steps back from the ball, quick run-up, then bang. He liked the theory: the further back from the ball you went, the more you were taking from the emphasis of your kicking style, replacing technique for power. He carried himself like McTague, his head tilted to one side, peering up at the posts, his shoulders hunched like a penitent as though he didn't wish to be noticed. But people couldn't miss him.

He trained as a garda and was stationed in Tullamore. He worked night shifts, and every morning Walsh Island resounded with the thud of footballs being kicked over the bar from all corners of the local field. He would bring home the net of footballs McGee allowed him take, and pass hours soloing the ball, feinting to go right but swivelling to the left, dummying the imaginary defender that stood in front of him. No one was watching, but it felt good. That was enough.

During his first year with Offaly in 1978, Matt's free-taking became the cornerstone of Offaly's scoring tallies, and as time passed he started to express himself more. Matches were adorned with cameos of his brilliance. Some nights he could dominate. Other nights he could lie dormant close to goal for most of the game. One explosion was enough to wipe the opposition out. One night Eugene McGee went to see a titanic club game between Ferbane and Walsh Island, and watched Matt beat five players before smashing the ball to the roof of the net to beat Ferbane. Decades later, he still reckoned it the greatest goal he had ever witnessed.

'If we were ten points up in a match, he could be standing there in the corner with his arms folded,' says Liam O'Connor. 'But if you were two points down, Matt would stick the ball in the net for you. He wasn't a showboater. I don't think there was a vain bone in his body. Reporters would be down in Tullamore and Matt would be out the back door and gone.'

Training sessions were part-masterclass. At the end of every training session, the mandatory shooting practice against Martin Furlong, who had returned that winter, always ended with an epic duel against Matt. In 1978, Matt was eighteen, Furlong was thirty-two. While Matt's career was beginning, Furlong's legend was already enshrined. In 1964, when Offaly won their first All-Ireland title at minor level, Furlong made a stunning save in the final minutes to keep Cork out. When Offaly won their first senior titles in 1971 and 1972, Furlong was there. He terrorised attackers with his manic charges to grab the ball. If a player stood in his way, he risked getting flattened, and instinct told him Furlong was never going to pull out.

'He'd kill you,' says Connor. 'He was fierce brave. If he went for a ball, he went for a ball. At club championship level there would've been people afraid of him, and you could see that. He had that aura about him.

'During one training session, there was a game going on and a big, high ball came in. It was coming to me. I knew if I caught it, Furlong was going to come out and crease me. I thought: he's going to come out, so I'll tap it over his head. So I did, turned around and Furlong was there, waiting for the ball. He bluffed and double-bluffed me.'

Every evening Furlong and Matt faced each other like a pair of gunslingers. The shots Matt took came at Furlong like missiles. He hit penalties and twenty-one-yard frees. He galloped in from distance and shot from different angles. The players and McGee would stay to watch. Every goal Furlong conceded was greeted like a personal insult. Every goal Matt scored was followed by a quiet titter. That drove Furlong even wilder.

'There would be evenings when Matt would take twenty-five shots on Furlong,' says McGee. 'When I look back I can see them hitting all corners of the net and Martin saving some and getting thicker and thicker. He wouldn't give out, but he'd be swearing to himself.'

'He had an almighty powerful shot,' says Furlong. 'You'd have stings in your hand after a night. God, he was special. The best I ever saw.'

One evening Connor buried one shot in the net, and turned away chuckling to himself. Behind him, Furlong was muttering under his breath. 'You can kick those fourteen-yard frees over the bar, because you're not getting another goal!' For the rest of the night, Furlong flung himself furiously around the goals, relentlessly blocking shots, and kept Matt scoreless.

They played for pints. Every goal Furlong conceded, he owed Matt one. Every one he saved went into Matt's debit column. Furlong had grown up playing with Matt's brother Murt and won All-Ireland medals with him; football bridged the years and brought them together. At the bar they could chat for hours. Although Matt was quiet, a few pints always brought the conversation out of him and they passed endless nights in each other's company.

Sometimes Furlong simply couldn't understand Matt. While the public revered him for his skill and teams routinely went out trying to smash him to pieces, Matt would never respond. He took the hits and converted the frees. Matt's icy temperament contrasted with Furlong's fire. At half-time during one game with Offaly, Matt returned to the dressing room with studmarks dotted down the sides of his legs. Furlong finally snapped: 'Would you hit the fuckers back?' But he knew Matt couldn't, and that was why people loved him too.

Furlong had returned in 1978 after his absence the previous year, but the average age of the Offaly team that started the 1978 championship was under twenty-two, filled out by the players who would secure two Leinster Under-21 titles in three years under McGee. Longford and Laois were despatched without any panache, and only Matt's 1-5 against Longford turned any heads. Now, they finally faced Dublin in Portlaoise. Offaly were raw, but they would have a go.

Tomás O'Connor joined Gerry Carroll at centrefield to face Brian Mullins and Bernard Brogan. In the previous year's All-Ireland semi-final, Mullins had delivered a severe lesson to a raw-looking Jack O'Shea. O'Connor was happy to leave Mullins to Carroll, but taking on

Brogan didn't diminish the scale of his afternoon's work. In his own mind, he had everything to prove, but these were his kind of days.

'I just went for everything, and caught it. You just went out in a fury and played out of your skin. You threw everything at it. And that gives you the belief: all of a sudden you start thinking you can beat Dublin.'

O'Connor dominated at centrefield and Offaly flung themselves at Dublin. Midway through the first half, Offaly's Vincent Henry launched a free that found a weak spot on one of the posts – the post split on impact and toppled on to the pitch. The delay didn't interrupt the flow and Offaly strode to half-time in the lead. McGee looked down the line at Kevin Heffernan. He was simmering with rage. Dublin were suffering. As they walked off the field, McGee didn't look for his own players, but the Dubs.

'Some of them were white in the face,' he says. 'They realised, Jesus, we're in trouble here.'

Heffernan had clubs in the bag for this sort of occasion. Kevin Moran was home after his first season with Manchester United, and Heffernan had added him to his bench. He needed him now. With Moran introduced after the break, Dublin were reborn. A long ball towards Bobby Doyle in front of the Offaly goal tempted Martin Furlong, who took the ball in a headlong rush and smashed into Doyle. Referee Seamus Aldridge whistled for a penalty, and Jimmy Keaveney finished the job. Dublin held on by a goal till the end. Offaly were beaten, but now they had hope.

'That was the first sign of life,' says McGee. 'We lost the Leinster Under-21 final after, but there was lots of activity and they could never say get rid of that bollocks because there was always another team coming. Most people were pleasantly surprised we'd got anywhere near Dublin.'

That winter, Tomás O'Connor won an All Star, and Dublin were nursing the wounds inflicted in a heavy defeat by Kerry in the All-Ireland final. Next time, Offaly would meet men with feet of clay.

*   *   *

As 1979 began, Eugene McGee continued pruning his panel and caring for the newest shoots. Liam Currams came from Kilcormac, which straddled the border between the hurling strongholds in south Offaly and the football heartlands of the north. He spent three years with Offaly minor hurlers and footballers, emerging with a reputation as a sweet hurler with enough of an engine to make a fist of football.

In 1979 he left home to start an apprenticeship with the ESB in Lanesborough, just up the road from McGee in Longford town. One evening after a minor football game, McGee visited the dressing room and invited Currams up to a senior match against Galway in Kenagh, Longford. Currams was mobile enough to play anywhere, but the half-back line seemed to suit him best. He was gentle, and he thought deeply about the strange complexities of the game.

'I'd be big into philosophy. I'd read a fair bit on the functions of the human approach. You think of the story of the archer. If he shoots for nothing, he uses all his skills. If he shoots for a brass buckle, he starts to get nervous. If he shoots for a pot of gold, he sees two targets. He still has his skills, but his will to win is overpowering his ability to do his tasks.

'Even when I was in school I couldn't fathom that out: how you could go out and play well on one day and the next day you wouldn't play well. There had to be an explanation. I reckoned if you're not over-worried about the outcome, then you play well. It's the archer thinking of winning. You must stay in the moment and not get ahead of yourself. If you make a mistake don't go back and stay in the history of it. It's an attitude of mind.'

McGee would have to share him with the Offaly hurlers, but he knew he could find a job for him.

As the year began, life had got complicated. One freezing cold afternoon in November 1978, McGee headed to a trial match for Offaly before popping over to a club game in Tullamore; he then repaired to a local pub afterwards. He hadn't paused to eat all day, and as he quelled the cold in his bones with hot whiskies, there was nothing to soak the alcohol up.

He had made it to Edgeworthstown when he was pulled over. McGee's licence was withdrawn for a year. Without a car, McGee was isolated in Aughnacliffe. He couldn't go to games, and training the Offaly team was almost impossible.

At the time, Currams was living in digs and stretching his meagre wage as an apprentice. McGee called him with a proposition. He needed a driver. In return, Currams could move in with McGee and his mother in Aughnacliffe. 'It was the obvious thing to do,' says Currams. 'He had a big house. Piles of room. I was getting free digs and a car. I wasn't going to start complaining.'

They drove to training in Offaly and to matches at the weekends. In the morning McGee would feed the cattle, and leave the evening feed to Currams. Everything about Aughnacliffe's tranquillity appealed to Currams, but his duties as a driver knew no limits. Currams spent nights sitting in the car as McGee visited players and their families. He would read a book, or flick on the radio and sit for hours as McGee made his visitations.

'You'd get a phone call. I used collect him outside the *Longford News* offices in Longford town. Every day you could be heading somewhere different. The days we weren't training we could go anywhere. He used write a column in the *Sunday Press* and he used go up to write his article on a Wednesday evening. You could do it on the telephone, but he preferred to go up and do it. I used go to Dublin every Wednesday afternoon. We'd put over a hundred thousand miles on the car in a year.'

Some nights the journey could pass with hardly a word between them, but Currams grew comfortable with McGee's silence. He learned to understand the nuances of McGee's personality and admired the way he found a route into players' minds. McGee cared. Despite the jagged edges around the margins of his personality, that meant something.

Currams drove him to functions in Dublin. They both mixed in media circles. They travelled to Offaly games. Sometimes McGee would ask Currams about life with the hurlers, or work, but usually the immaculate silence was observed. For those who intruded on their delicate environment, it was a culture shock.

'We were down at an Under-21 match against Carlow,' says Currams. 'Brian Cowen [the current Minister for Finance] was playing for Offaly. Offaly had a good Under-21 team then: Gerry Carroll, Matt Connor, Johnny Mooney were all on it. Cowen was studying in UCD at the time and we were going to Dublin that particular day. We lost the game and McGee was ripping. There wasn't a word spoken the whole way to Dublin. Cowen couldn't get over it. It was as much as if to say, when we got to Dublin: Now, get the fuck out!' Although McGee had his licence back after seven months, Currams stayed in Aughnacliffe for eighteen.

Meanwhile Offaly were progressing. The benefits of McGee's unusual training regimes and practices were rooted in the players and now that results were gradually turning, they were beginning to approach the summers with a different attitude. They made the Leinster final against Dublin, and as the players gathered the night before, McGee was in exquisite form.

'Dublin were a big barrier for everybody,' says Johnny Mooney. 'He broke them down into individuals. People with jobs. People who played football. He talked about their weaknesses and strengths, how they were ordinary human beings like us. He simplified everything.'

'He was fanatical about Dublin,' says Currams. 'He'd smoke cigarettes and everything – even when he didn't smoke – he'd be so uptight. He was passionate against Dublin. Any chance he had, he wanted to beat them.'

The following day Offaly met a team coming to terms with their own crumbling mortality and held them by the throat for sixty-nine minutes. Jimmy Keaveney was sent off, and Dublin struggled with fourteen men. The Leinster title was Offaly's to take. In the middle of the field, Richie Connor took a moment to catch his breath and run some words through his mind for the speech. He had endured four years with Offaly without the solace of a Leinster medal from 1973 or the All-Irelands before that, but his honours were shaped by the respect the players had for him. He was their leader on the field. All the weeks spent training, the hours in the evenings before championship games that he spent walking the bogs at home in Walsh Island with his fists clenched, slowly winding himself up to unleash fury on the opposition, had filtered down to this. The Leinster title was theirs.

Almost.

Only a few moments left. The play has broken down and Brian Mullins bounces the football off the back of an Offaly player's head. Offaly react, and the referee suddenly calls a hop ball.

Mullins's instincts recognise the opportunity. As the ball hangs in the air, Mullins charges and fists the ball deep into Offaly's defence. The ball ends up with Bernard Brogan in front of Martin Furlong. Brogan drills the ball to the net. Dublin have stolen the game. All over the field, Offaly fall asunder.

Richie Connor shook his head. He'd never rehearse a speech again.

The fall-out was poisonous. Although Offaly had gradually worked themselves from losing to Wexford in 1977 to making it to a Leinster semi-final and now a final, and competing seriously with Dublin, the county board delegates hadn't warmed to McGee. He wasn't one of their own. He was too distant. All these meetings and diet sheets and scraps of paper were unsettling. His autonomous regime wasn't working. They didn't move to sack McGee, but instead appointed four new selectors. Democracy, they said, must reign. Eventually they'd nail him.

Fr Heaney was weary from fighting. Much of his time was spent keeping McGee sweet with Dowling, and cajoling the rest of a bucking county board along with him. Offaly hurlers were showing significant signs of life, and the workload was getting heavy. Now, he had to deal with McGee and four new selectors who didn't like him.

'They were anti-me,' says McGee. 'These fellas would've had a slight resentment to me getting that job. They would've expected one of them to get it. If they picked teams I didn't agree with, I had to grin and bear it. There was no point in arguing.'

During one game in Cork, McGee stood on the line while the selectors sat in the stands. When he wished to make a change, McGee had to run up the steps for consultation and a vote. His power had diminished, and something of his dignity, too.

'I was basically a messenger boy. I decided to take drastic action. We had a big tournament match coming up in May in Ferbane against Galway. So I picked the team and didn't tell them [selectors] anything. I told them: "That's the team we're playing." They got thick and stood on one side of the field. I stood on the other. Luckily we won the match.'

That night, all four selectors wrote a letter to Fr Heaney telling him they couldn't work with McGee. The following morning they found a short note in each of their letterboxes thanking them for their services. Heaney quietly appointed himself, John Dowling and assistant county secretary Brother Sylvester as replacement selectors. McGee had regained the freedom he wished for, at a price. 'If Offaly didn't win the Leinster title now,' says Fr Heaney, 'then we were all gone.'

The hurt drove McGee all through 1980. Offaly roared into another Leinster final, and by now Dublin were spent. A cloud seemed to shadow everything about them. Over 150 supporters had been locked out of the Hill. Those inside spent much of the game fighting. That June, Brian Mullins's car had smashed into a lamppost, and he had spent eight months recovering.

The heart was ripped out of the team. Heffernan's greatest creation had expended its last energies in losing to Kerry in the 1979 All-Ireland final, but early on they mustered enough fight to suggest Offaly would be repelled again. Minutes into the game, Martin Furlong raced out from goal to intercept a through ball and dived at Ciaran Duff's feet. Duff powered on, cutting Furlong open over his eye and knocking him senseless. Bobby Doyle finished the loose ball to the net, and, as Furlong resumed with a bandage swaddling his bloodied head, Offaly were lagging behind. They were six points down at half-time, but they weren't beaten.

Johnny Mooney came to centrefield and towered over everyone. Matt Connor was switched to centre-forward, hit two quick points and played the game of his life. With minutes left, he escaped for long enough to win the game. He stood in front of the goal, without an angle to jink away from the cluster of defenders around him or the space to generate some momentum before releasing a shot. 'He hit the ball so hard,' says Fr Heaney, 'John O'Leary didn't even see it. It went past O'Leary about three inches from his side. Eugene McGee didn't even see it.'

Matt finished the game with 1-7, and Offaly had won, 1-10 to 1-8. The team was convulsed with joy. As the stands burst their banks and Offaly supporters streamed on to the field, Richie Connor took a moment. Five years of playing for Offaly had brought ignominy and humiliation. It had brought him to boardrooms defending a manager he barely knew. It had consumed his life.

'I was playing football and getting nowhere,' says Connor. 'I got more relief from that win than any other. I definitely had doubts about us. The final whistle had to be blown and blown and blown. It was such a feeling of achievement. Anything was possible then in my mind.'

The dressing room was the scene of unbridled joy. As the players cradled the cup, Eugene Mulligan reflected on a decade spent labouring to finally beat Dublin again. 'We didn't just beat a team,' he said. 'We beat a legend.'

'That was the end of Dublin,' says Currams, 'and a turning point for Offaly.'

They brought the cup home to Tullamore and toasted it for the bones of a month. With one Goliath slain, they now turned to face another.

Kerry.

4 THE SPECIAL ONES

Spring, 1980

The boys are lined up. Tim Kennelly. John Egan. Ger O'Keeffe. Leaning against the wire and breathing deeply. Facing them is the wide expanse of the pitch in Fitzgerald Stadium. This is wire-to-wire, a training drill invented by Mick O'Dwyer and road-tested in hell.

The drill sends the players sprinting from one side of the field to the other for as long as O'Dwyer sees fit, and serves a variety of purposes. It runs the arrogance out of them. If word filters back through O'Dwyer's network of contacts that a few players have been out the night before, he can run the beer out of them. After their winter's break, some players always come back a little chubby. Even the thought of wire-to-wire leaves the players with sunken cheeks. Wire-to-wire gets them fit, and gets them focused. To some players, it's a creation of such intolerable cruelty that they can already feel their dinners swelling in their guts before they even begin.

O'Dwyer stands a few yards away, whistle in hand. He brings it to his lips. A little smile. He loves this.

The boys are eyeing O'Keeffe. They call him Gadocha. It's a nickname partly rooted in affection, partly rooted in gut-wrenching annoyance. All through the seventies Robert Gadocha had left flaming trails behind him along the flanks when playing football for Poland, incinerating full-backs all over Europe with his speed. O'Keeffe was his incarnation in Killarney, without an ounce of fat on his bones and able to run forever. He was a blessing in the team, but sometimes he was a curse too.

O'Dwyer blows the whistle. Gadocha establishes an early lead, but the boys are holding him. As they pass beneath the goalposts, Gadocha flicks through the gears, and pulls back his shoulders. Gone. The shouts are behind him and starting to get distant.

'Gadocha! Get back here!'

He touches the wire on the other side. And back across. And back again. And back across. And back again. The boys are out on their feet. Gadocha has a sweat broken, no more. This what O'Dwyer loves. The boys never give up. It's springtime now. A few months of this, and Gadocha will drag them all up to his level.

The stand in Killarney is largely empty, save for a few pockets of onlookers and tourists. Out in the centre of the field is Mick O'Dwyer, his whistle hanging around his neck, the central hub around which a great team revolves. Years before his team would ultimately become the embodiment of invincibility, O'Dwyer was an icon for them all. They had grown up with him among their heroes. Now he was their taskmaster. He shaped their ambitions and their expectations. In a career filled with success, his greatest achievement was finding a method into every man's soul, to make them believe in him, and then drive them savagely on like a drayhorse.

Long before he began to gather All-Ireland titles with Kerry like shells on the strand, O'Dwyer's legacy as a player had written a rich legend. He played his first game for Kerry on 11 July 1954 in the Munster minor championship against Waterford and his last against Sligo in Killarney in May 1974. Waterville held on to him for another decade, where he played his last game aged forty-eight.

In between, he smashed records and propelled himself to greatness. He was a fearless player, blessed with unparalleled courage and an unquenchable thirst for success. He won four All-Ireland senior medals and twelve Munster senior medals with Kerry. His eight National League medals remains a record that looks unbreakable.

He played in ten All-Ireland senior finals. He was wrecked by injury, but refused to yield to pain. He almost lost his eye during a football game. He once kicked frees with a broken toe. In a county championship game in 1957 against Kerins O'Rahilly's from Tralee, he took a punch that knocked four of his front teeth out, but he never retaliated. In the mid-sixties two bad ankle injuries forced him to retire, but when Kerry asked him to return in 1968 he won another All-Ireland medal in 1969 and was named Footballer of the Year.

Resilience was bred into his bones. Years later he told the story of the birth of his mother on Scariff Island off the coast of south Kerry. That night his grandmother was alone on the island save for her husband. As the birth progressed, complications began to arise. She needed a doctor, but there was no boat to row ashore. Her husband, Batt, headed for the strand and plunged into the ocean. He swam till he reached the mainland and returned with help. They rowed back to Scariff, where O'Dwyer's mother was born safely.

His father, John, was a quiet, gentle man with little interest in football but a passion for hunting and a life filled with adventure. He volunteered for the IRA when the War of Independence reached Kerry, and remained on the Republican side at the beginning of the Civil War. One evening a convoy of Free State troops came across O'Dwyer and his comrades near Waterville. While O'Dwyer managed to escape to the caves above Waterville, the rest were taken to a mine nearby and blown up. At the end of the war, he jumped on a cattle boat in Cobh, and headed for Canada. Years later, when old wounds had begun to heal at home, he returned to Waterville and started a family.

Football was part of the background hum at home, but always rang clearly in young O'Dwyer's ears. He listened to the radio and worshipped Kerry's Tadhgie Lyne and Joe Keohane. Dublin's Ollie Freaney was an exotic hero from another world. The Galvins from Derrynane were his relations, a tough, hard-living group of brothers who liked their football with a glint of steel. With their cut, and his father's gentle personality, O'Dwyer had an attractive set of genes as a footballer, and a man.

He received his first football aged eight and spent his first evening attempting to kick the ball over the telegraph wires that crossed the road above him. He spent hours in Dr Mellerick's garden in Waterville and the GAA pitch kicking football. When the ball burst he and his friend Jimmy Eric Murphy took it to Eric's father, the local cobbler, to get it restitched.

The boys grew up together. Waterville was its own world, isolated by mountains on one side and the Atlantic Ocean lapping up behind it on the other, but the village still teemed with life. There were fishermen and island people from Valentia. People employed by the local cable station tapping messages out to the world. Old commandants from the British Army often retired to Waterville and promenaded through the town on warm summer evenings, some hobbling on cork legs, all bedecked in their finest pressed suits.

The boys learned to handle every shade and colour of character. The island people were quieter, darker. The tourists came from all over and brought the locals out of themselves. Then some people west of Waterville had never even travelled the ten miles into Cahirsiveen. They were another breed entirely.

O'Dwyer hung out with Jimmy Eric and Brud Sullivan, Brendan O'Sullivan and Joe Griffin. The local orchards were a source of adventure and nourishment. One evening a chap chased them as they escaped with their haul of apples and lost him when he landed waist high in a pool of pig dung. They bought a ferret, put it in league with a greyhound and went hunting rabbits, selling them to those working in the local cable station. O'Dwyer kept lobster pots and went sea fishing with the Galvins.

Cars fascinated him. 'This man would be going to dinner below with a baby Ford,' says Jimmy Eric Murphy. 'Every Saturday morning we'd spot him and be down. The key would be in the ignition. Out the road with it. I'd be looking through the steering wheel and the car hopping all over the road.

'Dwyer'd be saying, you're up to forty now. You're up to fifty-five. Sixty-four was the most we could get out of it with the fall of ground, and you'd have to be thinking of stopping about forty yards before you wanted to. It was a howl altogether.'

Even when surrounded by devilment, every element of his life was shaped to fit around football. His father ran a hackney cab around Waterville and when Mick took it on, Eric picked up his customers from the dances around south Kerry so Mick could sleep if he had been training. One evening in 1956 the lads were caddying at Waterville Golf Club when they saw a man running along the beach, occasionally breaking off to scale the sand dunes but never pausing for a break or a breath.

'Lads,' said Murphy. 'Wouldn't it be great if we could get that man for Waterville.' A few months later they read of Ronnie Delany's gold medal at the Melbourne Olympics, and the stranger had a name.

They could do with footballers back then. Before Mick O'Dwyer ever won All-Ireland medals, played with Kerry or moulded the finest team the game would ever see, he had to deal with prejudice and politics. Between 1926 and 1952, no player from South Kerry had been chosen to play for Kerry. Teams were harvested from the rich soil around Tralee, Killarney and north Kerry and left no reason for selectors to go poking around the barren coves and peninsulas at the edge of the country.

South Kerry football was in mild disarray. Drinking before games was part of the pre-match routine, designed to bolster the local players ahead of the match and scare the life out of the opposition. 'Only a few of us in Valentia trained,' said Paddy Reidy, who played with Valentia before joining O'Dwyer in Waterville in 1952. 'When they'd come into town to play the Mary's [Cahirsiveen] they'd go into Katie's pub across the road from the football field and they'd drink four or five pints before every game. They'd come out then and they'd frighten the life out of the Cahirsiveen crowd. They'd kick and belt and hit. But after the first twenty minutes they were gone. It was left to three or four of us to keep the thing going. They were all conked. But they were tough men.'

O'Dwyer's attitude and ambition bucked against everything around him. He played his first game for Waterville in Croke Park, against St Sylvester's of Malahide, after the club made arrangements to stage the game there with GAA general secretary Paddy O'Keeffe during his holidays in Waterville. The bar was set.

He became the first player from Waterville to play with Kerry. When Waterville won their first South Kerry title in 1956 he was twenty years old and kicking the frees. Around the same time, Mick O'Connell was growing into his greatness on Valentia Island, and in time O'Dwyer coaxed him to play for Waterville when they were reaching county finals in the late sixties.

By then, O'Dwyer was coach too. When Waterville won their first South Kerry title, their captain, Finbarr McAuliffe, had organised training for the team. It was a rare innovation, but this team had come like a comet. If they could help the tail streak across the sky for a little longer, they would. McAuliffe designed a brutal running course on the Lake Road out of town. It tested the players' resilience but it hardened their legs and their minds. When they played the final, Cahirsiveen were run off the pitch. O'Dwyer had taken note.

As the years went on, his store of information began to bulge. He listened to athletes who came to Waterville on holidays. He watched Australian Rules football. In the seventies he travelled to Manchester United's training grounds for a look. He had his own running route around the outskirts of Waterville, out near his mother's homeplace and back into town, that gave him time to work on his fitness and think. In the late sixties he would travel into Con Keating Park in Cahirsiveen to train with Mick O'Connell. They stood a few yards from each other and fired the ball with venom, always catching it in front of their bodies. For two hours their regime was ceaseless, relentless.

By the end of 1974 O'Dwyer had retired and football was changing. But he was slow to follow. The classrooms of Strawberry Hill teacher training college in London were dotted with footballers who came home with their notebooks filled with new ideas. One of them, Kerryman Mickey Ned O'Sullivan, was the most radical evangelist. One day in 1975 O'Sullivan convinced O'Dwyer to accompany him to a GAA coaching course in Gormanston, County Meath. On the way home, O'Sullivan started on to O'Dwyer. O'Sullivan was Kerry captain that year. If he was to fulfil his ambition, Kerry needed a good trainer. Eventually he wore O'Dwyer down, and O'Sullivan sketched out a rough training schedule before O'Dwyer's first session. It was the last time O'Dwyer turned to anyone.

His regime was brutal. Laps accompanied sprints. Players looked after their own stretching requirements. O'Dwyer wanted them to run. To prove themselves. They played 11-a-side games with O'Dwyer as referee. He routinely swallowed the whistle, and the players battered each other, but O'Dwyer maintained control. It kept the players sharp, edgy.

By the beginning of 1975 Ger O'Keeffe was in his early twenties with All-Ireland medals, National league titles and county championship medals already jangling in his pocket. He had played with O'Dwyer like the others. When he became manager, they were devoted to him.

'I remember playing a game against Longford with Mick O'Dwyer and Mick O'Connell,' says O'Keeffe. 'Mick O'Connell was midfield and I was wing-back. The words from O'Connell were: "I'll tell you when to jump." These were our heroes. O'Connell. Dwyer.'

'Dwyer wouldn't bring us in till February,' says Mikey Sheehy. 'Maybe the odd couple of nights every so often. Then you'd meet a couple of fellas and they'd say, "Jesus, I'm dreading going in." Every fella would say the same thing to the other guy: "Fuck it, I'm doing nothing." And every fella would actually be out on Banna Strand. You went training to go training with Dwyer. You'd be tailed off if you didn't. And no fella wanted that.'

No team trained as hard or as often, but O'Dwyer knew when to slow down too. In Sheehy, Kerry possessed the most gifted forward in the country, but he often returned to training needing to shed a few pounds. When he did, O'Dwyer would work on his mind.

'He'd tell you you're going great. You'd be there after doing two hard nights and he'd say on the second night, "Lads, we're getting there. We'll do one hard, good session" and you're dreading it. All of a sudden

Dwyer comes in and says, "Okay, two laps of the field." Then you did your own stretching. Next thing he'd organise a game of football.

'To see the change in fellas! He was a psychologist. Now fellas start jumping. They're on their toes all of a sudden. No fella's stiff. No fella's sore. All mad for ball.'

The wire-to-wires went on. O'Dwyer raced his entire full-back line against each other. Tim Kennelly chased Páidí Ó Sé across the field. None of them wanted to be left behind. None of them wanted to be beaten. In an atmosphere of ferocious competition O'Dwyer moulded his team, kept them sharp, constantly hungry. When Kerry came home with the Sam Maguire cup in 1975, twenty-three fireworks exploded along the railtracks as their train rolled into Killarney, one firework for every All-Ireland title Kerry had won. On the platform in front of the Park Place hotel, Mick O'Dwyer proclaimed his team capable of winning ten All-Irelands. Five years later they had four already won – and years left in them if they could keep going.

As 1980 began, it seemed there was nothing to stop them.

*   *   *

Sometimes, when Offaly were still labouring to pull themselves out of the muck against Clare or finally drive a wooden stake through Dublin in the Leinster championship, Eugene McGee would wonder what life was like beyond the brow of the hill. What would playing Kerry be like? League matches and challenge games against them had always ended with Martin Furlong complaining of an aching back from the amount of times he was forced to bend down and pick the ball from the net, but that was only shadow-boxing. How would they handle Offaly in Croke Park?

The All-Ireland semi-final was McGee's chance. Their brief shared history with Kerry had always been kind to Offaly. In 1972 they drew the All-Ireland final before Offaly inflicted the biggest defeat on Kerry in a final in the replay. They hadn't met since, and they were both in a different place now. They trotted out that Sunday on to Croke Park with the sun beating down on a rock-hard pitch. In their royal blue jerseys, Kerry gleamed a Cadillac. Offaly looked gawky. They knew nothing of days like this. They were in for a world of learning.

The game began at a blinding pace, and Kerry tried to blister Offaly early on, but Offaly held steady. Johnny Mooney had been moved from the middle to corner-forward and won plenty of ball close to goal. Matt Connor was dancing. He began the game having scored 3-22 out of Offaly's total of 3-36 for the championship and although Kerry's defence was mean, he jinked and dodged and twisted his marker, Mick Spillane, into a corkscrew. The ball landed in his hands twelve times during the game, and Matt ended the match with 2-9. Gerry Carroll rushed forward from centrefield to hit 2-1. Carroll and Connor shared all Offaly's scores between them, and even without the assistance of anyone else, Offaly had accumulated 4-10. Problem was, Kerry hit 4-15.

When Offaly hit a goal to pull themselves back into the game, Kerry smashed them with a wave of attacks. At half-time, Kerry led by 1-9 to 1-3. Minutes after half-time, Gerry Carroll hit a goal, but it only roused Kerry again. They hit three points in a few minutes, then Mikey Sheehy slotted home another goal. With fifteen minutes left they had stretched away by 3-14 to 2-6, but Connor and Carroll hit back again, and for a few minutes Kerry wobbled.

Then Offaly ran out of steam. The following month Kerry won their third successive All-Ireland title against Roscommon in a poisonous game, but they never forgot Matt Connor and the sensation of Offaly briefly breathing fire on their necks. Offaly got close, but Kerry had swatted them away like a fly.

'It was a completely ridiculous scoreline,' says McGee. 'They should have won by twelve points. We closed the gap at times, but it was completely false. Six of the goals were handpasses. Only two forwards scored for us. But I was able to manipulate that result. First of all, we had scored more against them than anybody before in an

All-Ireland semi-final. It was a great boost to say we could score 4-10 against Kerry. It was great entertainment, it looked fantastic. We were happy.'

Offaly had their Leinster title, and the defeat to Kerry didn't stain their year, but it still left a mark on McGee. His question had been ruthlessly answered.

5 BELIEVING THE IMPOSSIBLE

The evenings had lengthened and the cuckoo had returned to squat in the nests around Killarney as Mick O'Dwyer brought his players down to a quiet corner of Fitzgerald Stadium in early 1981. They stood in the shade of the stand and caught their breath. O'Dwyer had a question for them. 'Lads. Where are we going this year?'

The trip. While O'Dwyer's torturous training was the stick, the winter trip was always the carrot dangling at the end. All-Star tours and trips to parade the Sam Maguire cup among emigrants had taken them to America. The previous year the cup had got lost on one trip, and Kerry had probably seen enough of the place for now. England had been well conquered over the years. The players needed something different. They were chasing four in a row. Only one Kerry team had ever reached that milestone and almost fifty years had passed since then. This was history. It needed marking with something special.

Spain and other parts of Europe were mentioned. America again. Then Páidí Ó Sé grabbed the discussion by the throat. 'For fuck's sake,' he said, 'the only place to go is Australia!'

The players laughed and shook their heads at Páidí. Always thinking big. Australia was a whole world away at a time when the price of filling a tank of petrol was enough to worry about. O'Dwyer left it with them, and the residue of Páidí's wild notions drifted through their heads as they headed for home.

Later that month, the team gathered in the Imperial hotel in Tralee to discuss their choice. Páidí's idea was still rattling around, and beginning to gain some currency. The team were as famous as they were going to get. People loved them. O'Dwyer's business brain told him their personalities and achievements made them an effortlessly marketable asset. If they needed money, surely people would donate.

Australia was stuck in Páidí's head. This time, he had come prepared.

Tom McCarthy was born in Annascaul and had built his financial empire on hotels. He knew money and he loved football. Now he could mix both.

'How much do ye need for Australia?' he asked.

The players reckoned IR£20,000.

'Chicken feed,' said McCarthy. 'We'll raise a lot more than that.'

The committee set a target of IR£60,000 and sketched out an itinerary – a world tour. The team would travel to New York, San Francisco, all over Australia and back to Hawaii in a month. They started coming up with ideas. Aside from corporate and personal contributions, they would organise a competition to find a Kerry GAA Personality of the Year. An artist would be hired to paint a tribute to the team that had won four in a row.

'In fairness, the lady did it from passport photos,' says Pat Spillane. 'But the trouble with passport photos is you don't know whether the person is 6 foot 9 inches or 2 foot 1 inch! If you look at the picture, Ogie is the biggest in the painting and John O'Keeffe is one of the smallest. I remember my mother looking at it and she didn't recognise Mick, her own son. Dwyer used say to take it in you had to hold it at a distance of a hundred yards.'

Three weekends were organised in Ulster where Kerry played six games against northern opposition and left with the gate receipts. Everywhere they went the locals hailed them as gods. The lads stayed in their houses and lived among them. When Kerry took to the field they smashed the locals to pieces, just as their hosts would have wished. A show was the smallest courtesy Kerry could grant them.

They played Down in the Burren. They travelled to Donegal. One weekend they travelled to Castleblayney to play Monaghan. Mick O'Dwyer knew Declan Loughman from his days booking acts for his dancehall in Waterville, and the entire Kerry team squeezed into Loughman's house before popping across the road to annihilate Monaghan. After the matches, the polite rounds of tea and sandwiches were replaced by some raucous nights that left the locals bewildered.

'The image they had of us was we're fabulous athletes,' says Spillane. 'Suddenly we went up and we were drinking for Ireland. They couldn't get over that, and still go out the following day and beat the living daylights out of whoever.'

One night they played Tyrone in Carrickmore under lights. With no RUC barracks in the town, the pubs stayed open all night and the Kerry contingent made it worth their while. The following morning they headed for Dundalk to play Louth.

'There's no doubt about it,' says Spillane, 'but if there was a breathalyser test on the way into the field seventy or eight percent of the Kerry team would have blown it sky-high. The only thing was, everybody went away happy. Louth went away from the match thinking they weren't too far away.'

The money rolled in. As McCarthy and his fundraising committee threw the nets out for more that summer, Kerry worked their way painlessly through the championship. The evening before the 1981 Munster final, Con Houlihan took his *Evening Press* readers back to another time and place. It was the 1945 Munster final between Kerry and Cork, when Con set off from home on his bicycle to Killarney to witness Kerry perform their annual ritual of removing Cork from the championship. It was a deadening state of affairs. Cork had won only one Munster title from the previous seventeen finals. They travelled to Killarney facing the All-Ireland champions as condemned men, and Con sensed nothing in the wind to change his mind.

As the game began, Cork set about Kerry with abandon and never gave them a moment's peace. By the end, Kerry were beaten 'and Kerry people left Fitzgerald Stadium feeling as though they had seen a river flow uphill,' wrote Houlihan.

Along the way home, a fellow cyclist was grappling with what he had just witnessed. 'Kerry will have to play better than that if they want to win the All-Ireland,' he said. As far back as he could remember, entry into an All-Ireland semi-final for Kerry had always been a matter of course. Their dominance had been so unfettered, so utterly unrivalled, that losing a Munster title was a state of affairs that had never impinged on his wellbeing before.

So it was in 1981. Seven years had passed since Cork's last Munster title. Nothing suggested Cork had any trumps to play this time. The Tuesday night before the Munster final, Eugene McGee arrived in Killarney and witnessed the final nights in the torture chamber. The players sprinted across the field. Jimmy Deenihan led them out in his Adidas tracksuit top. Tom Spillane's Derry jersey was tucked in behind him. John Egan was at his shoulder. Ger Power and Mikey Sheehy led the others home. The team was winding down, but the mood was dark with intensity. Cork in Killarney. That was enough. Along the sideline, McGee sidled up to Mick O'Dwyer.

'I'm a strong believer in the group principle,' O'Dwyer told McGee, 'where a group of players come together and agree to work completely as a unit in all aspects of the game, but particularly training and preparation. Any player who shows himself unable to comply with that is a renegade as far as I'm concerned, and he's finished. Discipline is the number one thing in football today. Without discipline the man in charge loses control and he is left with nothing. As you saw in training tonight, no player ever questions any of my decisions or comments.'

McGee had spent his evening in the stand, listening. 'The winners of this game on Sunday will have the All-Ireland wrapped up,' said one observer. McGee sensed the same from the players. As O'Dwyer left the training field, a child from Armagh sought out his autograph. 'We could be meeting you in the All-Ireland final,' said O'Dwyer.

After years of subjugation, Cork were growing weary of fighting back. In 1977 Kerry's winning margin in the Munster final was 15 points. In 1978 it was 7. In 1979 and 1980 it was 10. A generation of Cork players had grown used to hearing Mick O'Dwyer proclaim them the second-best team in Ireland after each game, and slowly it drained them of morale and hope.

By 1981 Cork had given up on defeating Kerry by conventional means. As the game began, they switched their centrefield pairing, while in attack only their two wing-forwards remained in their original positions. They frantically shuffled their team around, trying to shift Kerrymen into positions of discomfort, but word of their plans had leaked into Kerry during the week, and suitable action had already been effected. With Cork's plans for anarchy foiled, the final became a shambles.

When Cork goalkeeper Billy Morgan was stretchered off seven minutes into the second half after colliding with Eoin 'The Bomber' Liston, Cork lost their spiritual leader. Once they got the scent, Kerry ate Cork alive. The crowd had begun to drift away midway through the second half, and by the end Kerry had skated home by 1-11 to 0-3. It was Cork's lowest score in a Munster final since 1962. 'Cork did not do justice to themselves,' said O'Dwyer. 'They tried to bamboozle us, but instead they bamboozled themselves. In a Munster final, you must go out with a practical plan, which they didn't.'

It was that simple, and that brutal. Even the most complex trickery hadn't even caused Kerry to blink. In Munster and beyond, Kerry were untouchable. As he gathered his notes and left the press box, Micheál O'Hehir fell into conversation with a local journalist. 'Thank God for hurling,' said O'Hehir.

*   *   *

Back in the winter of 1980, Eugene McGee got to thinking about his old trips to Highbury and the notion of pre-season training. In 1980 most teams, including Kerry, shut down for the winter. To catch up with Kerry, McGee knew Offaly couldn't afford to stop moving. When they met Kerry in 1980, no one had truly believed they could win. There was no precedent to sustain them. By the end of the game the players were exhausted. Whatever about their skill levels and their belief in themselves, fitness was something he could improve immediately. But he needed help.

When Tom Donoghue was twenty, he was playing and coaching the Galway Under-21 hurlers to their first All-Ireland title in 1972. A spell in Strawberry Hill teacher-training college had immersed him in different coaching cultures. By 1980, he was teaching in Tullamore and hurling with Offaly. McGee knew what O'Dwyer was doing in Killarney and was also intimately acquainted with Kevin Heffernan's boot-camp regime in Parnell Park. Would Offaly take to the same stuff? They had to try.

McGee needed a hill. He drove around Offaly looking over gates into fields, trying to gauge the right gradient and underfoot conditions. One evening he pulled into the GAA club in Rhode and took in the sight of Clonin Hill. The field stretched uphill for four hundred yards before suddenly steepening halfway up into an almost vertical climb. This would be their Calvary.

A softer approach would be needed to ease the players through the hardship McGee had planned for them. Where his manner was tough, Donoghue was gentle. He had an easy sense of humour, and as an Offaly hurler he was instantly recognisable to them all. After five years under McGee, Donoghue could help freshen the players' bodies, and their minds.

Once summer came, Offaly were playing with a new confidence and finding new players to fill some troubling gaps. The week before the Leinster football final against Laois, Padraic Dunne came home late to Portarlington from training one night, and quietly let himself into the house. All week Offaly had raged with rumour. The last spot at left-half-forward was between Tom Fitzpatrick and Vincent Henry. John Guinan, another new player, was in the mix, but everyone reckoned

Fitzpatrick was a shoo-in. A few weeks before, McGee had arranged a trial game and invited Dunne to play, but Dunne had a problem. He was working in a factory in Portarlington, and they needed him for an inter-firms soccer game. To the boys in the factory, there was no contest. Playing for Offaly wasn't going to happen. This was real. Winning the soccer game meant something. Pointless trials didn't.

But Dunne wanted to try. He agreed to play the first half of the soccer game and then head to the trial. By half-time the match was balanced on the edge. His father sat in the car with the motor running, ready to go. The boys from the factory pleaded with him to stay and not be fooling about. Instead, Dunne went. Now he had a shot at making the Leinster final.

For the previous few weeks he had travelled to training with Fitzpatrick. That evening as they went to Edenderry, Tom was nervous, but Dunne re-assured him. 'Jesus, Tommy,' he said, 'it's your position. Don't worry about it.'

At six foot two inches and fourteen stones, Dunne promised to have the height and strength Offaly needed alongside Tomás O'Connor in the years to come. Dunne was cocky. He liked to hop balls and tug at people's tails. After years of the same voices, Dunne's humour swept through the dressing room like an air freshener. He was also obsessed with football and making it with Offaly. He hung out with the Connors. That was a good sign. At worst, McGee could make some kind of footballer out of him. At best, he could become one of the best Offaly ever had.

That night, Dunne crept into bed and turned the lights out. His father opened the door.

'Well?'

'Ah Jesus,' said Dunne, 'you won't believe it. Terrible decision.'

'Oh no. Who are they after picking now?'

'It's just unbelievable. I don't know what they're doing.'

And his father began dolefully listing players, like the sorrowful mysteries of the Rosary.

'No,' replied his son. 'They're only after picking me.'

'He got a bigger shock than I did,' says Dunne. 'I never minded. Sure, I was nineteen.'

Like Dunne, Offaly feared nothing now. Their squad was easily their strongest under McGee, which gave him room to start expanding their style. Brendan Lowry had been added to the panel at the start of the year having been reluctant to commit to the heavy training and relentless dedication required. He preferred playing soccer with Ferbane Town, but with his brother Sean in his ear and his third brother Michael on the team, he gradually yielded. Now, he helped form a spectacularly potent full-forward line with Matt Connor and Sean Lowry and after a year already stood on the brink of an All Star.

He enjoyed an almost telepathic relationship with Gerry Carroll from the beginning. Off the pitch they lived at opposite ends of the county and rarely met. On the field, their minds moved almost as one. When Lowry ran, Carroll knew where he needed to put the ball. As McGee preached the need for accurate passing, Lowry gave the players something other than Matt Connor to aim at. When delivering a ball into their forwards, Offaly now had a choice of players to aim for.

It was a thrilling combination. Leinster was Offaly's to rule and with an All-Ireland semi-final against the Ulster champions to deal with, they could start seriously thinking about the All-Ireland final. With Dublin in pieces, Laois met Offaly in the Leinster final and were neatly despatched, while Down were smartly dealt with in the All-Ireland semi-final. Offaly were back in the final, but, with Kerry busy making history, their timing didn't seem great.

On the other side of the draw Kerry's dominance was total. In the All-Ireland semi-final, Mayo came to Croke Park with their first Connacht title for twelve years and fell in a heap at Kerry's feet, losing by sixteen points. After the game Mick O'Dwyer stood in the middle of the dressing room and put context on the scale of the challenge Mayo had faced. 'This is the greatest team of all time,' he said, 'and possibly the best we will see in our lifetime.' The money for Australia was rolling in. September was Kerry's to shape.

*   *   *

While Kerry's season was tinged by the quest for four-in-a-row, Offaly was bordering on near delirium. A few weeks before the football final, Offaly hurlers beat Galway to claim the county's first All-Ireland hurling title. The celebrations lasted all week and gently blended into the build-up to the football final.

The Tuesday night after the hurling final, the two hurlers, Liam Currams and Tom Donoghue, arrived late for football training and were greeted by applause. Currams had always felt more comfortable with the footballers. While the hurlers were largely reared in the country, most of the footballers were urban. They liked different music. The footballers were sharp dressers. While the hurlers enjoyed their few pints, a night out with the footballers always seemed more freewheeling to Currams. He could be himself more among them, and the footballers loved him.

Now they could provide him with a refuge from the madness outside. No player had ever won two senior All-Ireland medals in the same year. At twenty years of age, Currams was playing for a place in history.

McGee was worried about him. Currams was shy. He was more sensitive than the older players. He never needed minding on the team, and during McGee's meetings Currams was frequently the butt of his most caustic remarks, but talking to papers and publicity wasn't his natural thing. He simply wanted to play his matches and leave the rest after him. For the next few weeks, he'd need watching and protecting.

'I really couldn't handle it,' he says. 'But McGee screened all that for me. He'd only allow me to take so many phone calls. He'd tell me to watch out for certain individuals. He'd always read the articles I was interviewed for and if he saw something I was saying wrong, he'd always teach me not to do it that way.

'He kept your two feet solid on the ground. Without him I wouldn't have survived it. I wouldn't have been able to concentrate on the games. He allowed you to focus on the game and forget the hype.'

Aside from Currams, McGee had a headful of problems to worry about. In the All-Ireland semi-final against Down, Tomás O'Connor had dominated the skies against Liam Austin. As the days drained down to the final, O'Connor felt a surge of confidence running through him he never knew before. After years of pushing himself and fighting his doubts, he had arrived as a player. The All Star lay between himself and his marker Sean Walsh, but O'Connor was backing himself all the way.

Two weeks before the final, Offaly played a challenge game against Galway. As O'Connor took one ball and prepared to launch a long kick towards goal, his right knee suddenly gave way. In 1980 his knee had suffered some cartilage damage, but an operation had tidied that up. Now, it had returned with horrendous vengeance. It swelled up immediately, and O'Connor was carried off. A few days later, he went to meet Meath footballer Gerry McEntee, a specialist at the Mater Hospital. The x-rays were damning. His ligaments were damaged and a piece of bone was chipped off the top of his leg. The area around the knee was bulging with fluid.

The prognosis was bad. First a bandage would be applied from his foot to his knee. After five weeks, he could begin to use light weights to strengthen his knee. Two weeks later, light jogging. O'Connor looked at McEntee.

'Gerry,' he said. 'That's not what I want to hear.'

He had the fluid drained from the knee, and went home crippled. Then, another pillar of McGee's team came crashing down.

On a hot summer's afternoon, Johnny Mooney was on the bog near the old dormant volcano of Croghan Hill, loading turf on to a trailer. As he climbed on top of the pile to lay the final sods, the drawbar of the trailer that was connected to the tractor broke. Mooney stumbled and fell from the trailer, hitting the ground with a sickening thud. His knees were cut open. Blood was seeping from his head, but the greatest pain came from his shoulder. It was broken.

'I knew when I fell,' he says, 'that I was in big trouble.'

It was later that evening when selector Paddy Fenlon rang McGee in Aughnacliffe with news of Mooney.

'Well, that's fucking that,' replied McGee.

The guts had been ripped from McGee's team. He needed to find a new centrefield pairing, but resources were thin. At best, he reckoned he might squeeze a half each from Mooney and O'Connor.

On the morning of the game, Tomás O'Connor went for a fitness test in Belfield. McGee threw a few balls into the air and O'Connor deliberately leapt off his left foot to camouflage the state of his right knee.

'I convinced myself I was right,' says O'Connor, 'but I couldn't even straighten my leg. Even running around before the game, my knee used lock a bit, then the fluid would clear out and the leg would straighten. I was thinking: once the ball is thrown in here, I'll be fine.'

That morning as Padraic Dunne stepped out from the cheering supporters on the platform and on to the train in Portarlington, he took everything in: the fresh seats, the faint smell of diesel from the engine, the puffs of steam from the vents as the train pulled out for Dublin. He had never ridden a train before.

Pat Fitzgerald pulled up in the station having driven from Newbridge with a hollow grumble in his guts. Having calculated the dietary requirements of the day against the nerves gnawing through the lining of his stomach, he hadn't eaten all morning and didn't think he would all day.

Mooney was on the train with his shoulder strapped up and Tomás O'Connor making himself believe his knee would last the day against Sean Walsh. The team was quivering with nerves. McGee's plans were teetering on the brink of collapse.

He tried to make do. Tomás O'Connor would start against Sean Walsh, with Johnny Mooney replacing him at half-time. Wing-forward

Aidan O'Halloran would revert to defence to try and disrupt Kerry's flowing movement.

'They were such an awesome team you couldn't go in with the blasé notion that we won't worry about the other crowd,' says McGee. 'It'd be absolutely ludicrous.' It was a gameplan based on containment. Offaly weren't set up to take Kerry on, but to stop them.

6 THE KINGS OF SEPTEMBER

Kerry's Saturday night in Malahide appeared to pass off quietly and peacefully, but Mick O'Dwyer's mind was tormented.

It was Spillane.

O'Dwyer never publicly listed his players in order of importance, but the others always sensed he valued Pat Spillane most of all. Football was Spillane's life. He was utterly certain about his own ability and a sense of destiny had already attached itself to him as a child. The night Offaly crushed Kerry in the 1972 All-Ireland final he had cavorted with Páidí Ó Sé around Croke Park when they were two pupils from St Brendan's, Killarney. His bloodlines were impeccable, flowing back to the great Lyne dynasty on his mother's side that provided Ted, Denny Jackie and Michael to Kerry teams over three decades from the thirties to the fifties and won All-Ireland medals as minors, juniors and seniors. By the end of their own careers with Kerry, Pat and his brothers, Mike and Tom, would bring home nineteen All-Ireland senior medals, and Pat would join the small handful with a record eight.

His father, Tom, had won an All-Ireland junior medal with Kerry and died as a young man, leaving his wife with a pub in Templenoe and a young family to rear. Life had hardened them at a young age, but their mother always allowed them time for football. That was their escape.

'One Whit weekend, which is the busiest weekend of the year in Kenmare,' says Tom Spillane, 'we left with people hanging off the rafters to play some challenge against Laois in a place in west Limerick called

Ballyhahill. We drove up a height until we were almost overlooking the Shannon. With the mist on the pitch I didn't think there'd be a game. They sent down a second team. And I thought of it afterwards: we busting our guts to go up there and our poor mother and sister behind at home and the place lifting with people, to go up and play an oul' tournament game against a shadow Laois team. It wasn't important.'

In a team of stars, Pat was among the brightest in a glittering sky. His fitness levels were phenomenally high. His leg muscles were savagely strong, yet he could sprint like a hare. Before every game, Spillane would find a quiet moment, close his eyes, and watch a reel of plays and moments from the game to come. He visualised himself catching, kicking, tackling, scoring. Winning.

Maybe O'Dwyer saw something of himself in Spillane. He couldn't handle him the same way as everyone else, and Spillane's teammates knew that too. He needed to be indulged. He was allowed roam and gather ball. It made space for Egan, Sheehy and Liston in attack, and satisfied Spillane's restless nature. The joke among the boys was there was never such a thing as a one–two with Spillane, but a one–one. Yet, he was an example too. When the Kerry boys arrived in Killarney for training, Spillane was usually there, kicking points, with a patient from nearby St Finan's hospital booting the ball back to him.

He honed his own style constantly. When he received the ball, he often waited for his opponent to come right up against him, before digging his left heel into the ground and pivoting to the right, pushing off his left leg but twisting his knee into an awkward angle while applying immense force to the joint. His ability to twist and turn away from opponents in a tight spot abused his leg joints to a dangerous degree. That August he finally pushed too far.

A week after Kerry had annihilated Mayo in the 1981 All-Ireland semi-final, Spillane lined out for Templenoe in a club game against Waterville. At one point he sprinted for a ball, turned sharply and felt something in his knee snap. The pain shot through his leg. He was carried off the field, but eventually the pain subsided. That night he numbed the remaining pangs with beer and went to the Fleadh Ceoil in Kilgarvan where he danced the Siege of Ennis, unaware that only some tenuous strands of muscle were holding his knee together. The following day, Spillane could barely put his leg under him.

'The pain was worse than anything I'd ever experienced. Savage, savage pain. I'd broken fingers, but it was the first serious injury I'd ever had. No one could really understand it. My muscles were very strong. Any test done by the physio didn't show anything up.'

By the weekend of the All-Ireland final, injuries were worrying Kerry. For a brief few days four-in-a-row seemed in jeopardy. Mikey Sheehy's instep had been aching him for a while and the team for the final was released with two vacancies. The reporters reckoned Spillane was 50-50, but as O'Dwyer gathered his players on the beach in Malahide he was determined they would sleep soundly.

'The team talk that night was as if I was playing,' says Spillane. 'I knew I was codding them. The temptation was certainly great. Sportspeople by their nature are selfish, but the team ethos was very much there. I knew I'd pulled a fast one on Dwyer and the doctor. But I did another little session on my own on the Sunday morning and I knew goddamn well. I was honest enough and said no. I wouldn't play.'

The following day Sheehy's foot was numbed with painkilling injections, and Spillane was withdrawn with Tommy Doyle coming in at left-half-forward. But as Kerry lined out for the team photograph, the players beckoned Spillane from the dug-out to join them. In years to come some of the bridges that linked Spillane to his teammates would be incinerated by the flames of his criticisms as a pundit, and even in 1981 you needed to know how to take him – but every family has one; they still loved him then.

'You'll go through all the little things in life that cling to you from football,' says Spillane. 'That running across the field for that picture was humbling. It really was. Coming on in the last five minutes. It's only really in subsequent years it hit me, because there's only a few of us that played in all eight All-Ireland finals. It was really nice.'

By then, Kerry had the game locked up and secured. McGee's decision to withdraw Aidan O'Halloran to screen in front of the defence only allowed Páidí Ó Sé transplant himself into Kerry's attack and decorate his finest performance in an All-Ireland final with three points. When Offaly did get on the ball, their kicking and passing was imprecise. To beat Kerry, Offaly needed to exceed every level they had reached in the previous three years. They never stood a chance.

Brendan Lowry didn't leave a mark on Jimmy Deenihan. Tim Kennelly dominated Gerry Carroll at centre-back and delivered a towering performance. McGee's plan to start Tomás O'Connor and bring Johnny Mooney in at half-time failed, and Sean Walsh lorded the game at centrefield. At one point during the game O'Connor chased a ball towards the sideline, and sensed Walsh charging towards him. All the worries about his knee, Walsh and the match crossed paths in one jarring moment.

'I remember saying to myself: I can't brace myself on this leg. He hits me and he puts me about ten yards. I can still hear Micheál O'Hehir laughing.'

The All Star was Walsh's, but the day truly belonged to Kennelly. Within the Kerry dressing room, Tim Kennelly could be whatever the players needed him to be. When they needed a ringmaster on a night out, Kennelly would crack the whip and tell a few yarns. They called him The Horse, a carrier of men. When the team needed lifting, Kennelly would drag them up by the collars. Mikey Sheehy could remember talk wafting down from Listowel when he was a kid of a gigantic centre-back in white ankle socks and dreaded the day Austin Stacks Under-14s would be compelled to meet them. When they did, it took a while to find someone who would mark the number six.

O'Dwyer pushed Kennelly hard in training, but Kennelly never surrendered against even the worst onslaughts. He had captained the team to victory in 1979, but the 1981 final was his day. Gerry Carroll struggled to manage him physically, and Kennelly roared into the game, sending raking dropkicks deep into the Offaly half. Whatever Offaly did, they couldn't unsettle Kennelly. He stayed steady, and Kerry were safe.

As a dull game drifted into the final ten minutes, Kerry were heading towards four in a row. Typically, they found a way to embellish the moment. At 0-12 to 0-8, the game was petering harmlessly out as Liam Currams launched a ball into Kerry's defence. Jimmy Deenihan collected the ball near the endline with Jack O'Shea nearby to take the pass. It was an arrangement worked out over the years, but this time Deenihan twisted and turned away, kicking the ball over his shoulder towards the sideline. Tim Kennelly rose, caught the ball. He cleared to centrefield, where Tommy Doyle took possession.

Now, Kerry picked up the pace. Doyle dropped his kick into a space in front of the Hogan Stand for John Egan to collect, sixty yards from the Offaly goal. Egan turned, and as Eoin Liston ran towards him, Egan flicked the ball into his chest. Liston slickly popped him a return pass. Offaly were marking tightly, but as the ball moved further upfield, their team was visibly getting pulled apart.

Meanwhile, Jack O'Shea was jogging along the sideline on the other side of the field, slowly working his way towards the Offaly goal. Of all the attributes that made him great, people marvelled most at Jacko's stamina. When Kerry were attacking, Jacko was there. When Kerry defended, he was in front of the 20-metre line, looking for a pass. His fitness was innate. When he stopped training during the winter, his weight actually dropped instead of increasing. He quit drinking when he made the Kerry team in 1977, while Mick O'Dwyer had stubbed a cigarette out on him years before and finished him smoking. By 1981 he was still a boy in a team of men, but already among their greatest.

With Sean Walsh happy to hold the centre, O'Dwyer never tried to put the reins on Jacko. His style was a perfect mix of athleticism and skill, framed by an unconscious understanding of the game's geometry. When Jacko talked about football he talked about circles, ellipses and triangles. Arcs of running. O'Dwyer had seconded Micheál Ó Muircheartaigh to oversee the Kerry players' training regime in Dublin. At the end of every session with Micheál, O'Shea would kick fifty balls over the bar from inside the 20-metre line. He knew he had the leg strength to kick balls from long distance, it was the mechanics of his kicking style that always needed perfecting.

He watched Dublin in the late seventies and sussed out a simple trend in their gameplan. It seemed that Dublin's style was shaped around gaining possession within a triangle that had its apex thirty yards from goal, and stopping the opposition from gaining possession in the same area in front of their own posts. With the freedom to roam the pitch, he gradually worked out a way to make the best of his role. He watched how Down's Colm McAlarney used the flanks of the field and created a style that merged brilliantly with his natural ability.

'I used play in an oval shape all the time. If the opposition were attacking down one side, I'd jog back down the other. I always reckoned if the ball came to a goalkeeper or a defender, his first reaction is to come out the other way. I'd always try to be available. It wasn't that I was breaking my hole to get from one end of the pitch to the other. When the ball was coming down one side, I was getting back.'

Years of thought and practice were about to come good. As he loped along the far wing and looked across the pitch towards Egan, there wasn't one Offaly player within thirty yards of him. As Egan cut infield and worked the ball to Mikey Sheehy, Jacko went from a canter to a gallop. Sheehy turned round to face goal. Years of matches and nights in Killarney told Jacko what was coming next. Sheehy popped the ball over his marker's head, and into Jacko's hands. He was twenty-five yards from goal. Nothing but glory occupied his mind.

'I just went for it. I wouldn't even contemplate kicking the ball over the bar from there. I never had any doubt I'd go for the goal. Instinct took over.'

The ball flew past Martin Furlong into the top corner of the net. His arms were by his sides. For once, Furlong was powerless.

Jacko turned with his fist clenched, and bounded outfield. In twenty-eight seconds a move involving seven players had embodied every gift and virtue O'Dwyer's team had bestowed on football. It encompassed their speed and their mesmerising passing skills. Six years of relentless work had locked every component of the team together to create a team of near perfection. For a moment, it seemed their years of work had been rising to this moment of crescendo, a great cymbal crash after a thrillingly long drum roll.

Eugene McGee looked at the ground. 1-12 to 0-8. The game was won. Four-in-a-row and greatness had been secured. As Jacko ran past Páidí Ó Sé, he smiled and shouted, 'We're off to Australia!'

*   *   *

That night Offaly gathered for their banquet. McGee was frustrated. Angry. His tactics had failed and the team hadn't performed as he knew they could. The team was afforded a standing ovation when they arrived into the hall, but it rang hollow to him. He knew that criticism would inevitably follow. It had been a poor game, and he knew Offaly wouldn't be spared. All the weeks of thought and preparation were about to be dismissed in the post-mortem. When it came to his speech, he couldn't hold himself any longer.

'We took a so-called super team and reduced their gods to human beings,' he said. 'We're not clowns at a circus. We're a team playing Gaelic football and if the public want to watch, so be it. We are not there to give a show. Every man gave his best and should not be maligned for it.' Gerry Carroll, Tomás and Matt Connor, he said, were great players who hadn't reached the required levels on the day, 'but it's indicative of the relationship I have with the team that I can say that without any embarrassment.'

As Kerry launched themselves into another week of celebrations, Offaly returned to Tullamore that Monday night. Flames from a mighty bonfire licked the air. An open-topped bus edged through the town, where thousands had gathered to greet them. The reception was overwhelming. 'I'm not an emotional man,' said McGee, 'but tonight you made me cry.'

When they looked around at each other, every player had tears in his eyes. That night they promised each other one thing: they would never come home like this again.

'McGee got it wrong,' says Pat Fitzgerald. 'We all got it wrong. When we won our semi-final against Down we thought: right, we're in a final now. This is a whole new ball game. That was a big mistake. We thought: yeah, this is different. The Holy Ghost will come and he'll elevate you a bit. To Kerry, the All-Ireland final was just another game.'

After the final, McGee met with Tomás O'Connor and thanked him for trying to play. Now, it was time to get his knee fixed. Tomás met with his specialist who handed him a letter detailing the difficulties now associated with his knee. The last line was chilling.

'This young man,' it read, 'should never play contact sport again.'

A few days later O'Connor met McGee who asked him how the meeting had gone. 'Fine,' he replied.

*   *   *

The Tuesday night after the final, Kerry captain Jimmy Deenihan brought the Sam Maguire cup to Finuge. Bonfires illuminated the cold night sky and nine of his teammates hopped up on the back of a trailer beside him. Down in the crowd he spotted Offaly's Sean Lowry, Gerry Carroll and Brendan Lowry who had travelled to the Listowel races for the week. As the speeches began, Finuge chairman Martin Whelan plucked Sean Lowry from the crowd, hauled him on to the stage and gave him the microphone.

Lowry touched the cup and smiled. 'It'll be back in Offaly next year!' he shouted and the crowd chuckled. He congratulated the Kerry team and warned their mentors not to keep making promises about five in a row. Offaly had plans.

That week, the cup travelled all over Kerry. From Finuge it went to Ballybunion. Then Kenmare and Dingle. Waterville on Friday for O'Dwyer's annual celebration. Tralee and Killorglin the following week.

The days were submerged in a blizzard of promotional appearances. Players posed for the cameras while picking up cheques from the Irish Permanent and the Imperial hotel, Tralee. Another cheque rolled in from the people at the Concrete Products of Ireland. Jimmy Deenihan modelled a new ensemble designed for the trip: a light blue jacket emblazoned with the Kerry crest, grey slacks, white shirt and white and blue tie. Four days before the team left for the boiling heat of Australia and Hawaii, they were presented with a set of Aran sweaters by Udarás na Gaeltachta.

When the fundraising was over, the final tally reached IR£102,000, dwarfing even the the IR£60,000 Tom McCarthy had aimed at. Every man would receive IR£1800 spending money, with enough held back to top the players up for the final leg of the trip. Seven games were scheduled – in New York, Melbourne, Perth, Adelaide and Sydney, but those would take care of themselves.

Now, it was time to party.

7 THE PARTY BOYS

Páidí Ó Sé craned his neck as high as he could, but he could still feel the water rising against his chest, slowly drawing up close to his neck. Soon it would reach his chin and start to pull him down. He needed to move to higher ground. He stood on his bed and balanced on his toes, but the water kept rising. Thousands of miles from home, New York was being consumed by the sea and taking Páidí with it.

The water had started to rise a day earlier. As the Kerry team's flight to New York was delayed by almost eleven hours, a gang of players repaired to Durty Nellie's near Bunratty Castle and lined up the drinks. Páidí set the pace, and the rest tried to keep up. By the time their flight took off, the boys had almost passed out. When he reached the Statler hotel near Madison Square Garden, Páidí struggled to bed. Now the gin was playing tricks. It was wrecking his mind, sweating out through his pores and making him mad. He was in the horrors so deep, there seemed no way out. He kept his head up, and slowly the waters began to recede. He climbed down and got under the covers, shivering. The trip of all trips had begun.

New York held nothing new for any of them. All-Star trips had made them all intimately acquainted with the sights and unmoved by the sleazy glamour of the city. New York was old hat. They wanted Frisco. Australia. They played Galway in Gaelic Park in front of a huge crowd and lost by three points, but in their minds football had already been left behind till the new year. The party had already begun.

'It was heavy belting,' says Eoin Liston. 'We were fit and in our prime. We just had great crack.'

'People love to get into this thing: "Were ye drinking?" says John Egan. Of course we were drinking. We'd do what you'd do yourself. We weren't professional when we were out on those trips. We were out on holidays. We were doing what any other man would do given the latitude. And maybe more.'

'Some of us,' says Páidí Ó Sé, 'nearly came home in boxes.'

Páidí took the tour by the neck and shook every ounce of crack he could from it. Life was good, and Páidí augmented his spending stash with IR£2000 of his own money. With cash on his hip, every day was merely another story waiting to be shaped.

One night he went for dinner with Sean Walsh, Liston, Ogie Moran and Mick O'Dwyer, with devilment in mind. His plan was dependent on all the players retaining a sober façade regardless of the stress and pressure about to be imposed on their senses. As they sat down to dinner, the players ordered three bottles of wine. Twenty minutes later, they ordered another three. Twenty minutes later, another three. By the end they had demolished fifteen bottles of wine. The following morning, Ó Sé was coming down the stairs to the hotel lobby when he heard O'Dwyer, the teetotaller, explaining the evening's events to a bewildered listener. 'I was there! I saw those fellows doing it!'

A few days later, the same group were invited to dinner at a local Kerryman's house. As his wife prepared dinner, she placed two bottles of wine on the table: one red, one white. As O'Dwyer surveyed the scene and the calibre of guest, he couldn't contain himself. 'I don't know where you're going with that! That won't satisfy these fellows!'

In Melbourne a crew headed to the races on Bomber's birthday where the champagne flowed, smoked salmon was passed around and the day passed like a dream. Páidí Ó Sé and Sean Walsh had a party arranged for that evening, and filled Liston's bath with cans of beer. Then, as the party reached its raucous height, they produced a birthday gift.

'They presented me with a colour television,' says Liston. 'It was a lovely gesture, but of course the television was from the room next door.'

The players' fame exceeded even their own assumptions. One evening, John Egan and a few others set out for an adventure in the bush near Perth. Later they wandered back to a bus station, slightly lost and slightly bemused by the prospect of finding their way home. An old man in a dusty hat stood at the bus stop. Egan sidled up to him.

'Excuse me. Do you know what time the next bus is heading to town?'

The old man looked him and up and down. 'Is that the bus to Killarney you're looking for?'

They partied hard, but they handled themselves with dignity too. As captain, Jimmy Deenihan was interviewed on television stations across the country to explain Kerry's presence in Australia. They attended functions and Irish societies wherever they went, and left memories that were treasured for lifetimes. They played some football, but not much. In Adelaide they played a game of football against the Western Bulldogs. By the end of the first half, Kerry had annihilated them. To even things up, the Bulldogs suggested they play the second half using the oval ball.

'I remember Jacko threw it out to me at one stage,' says Páidí Ó Sé, 'and I soloed up the wing with the oval ball. And Dwyer shouted into me, "Kick the thing! You can't even solo the round one!"'

'We ran at them like a rugby team,' says Liston. 'As soon as they'd come to tackle you, just pass the ball away along the line.'

But mostly they kicked back and crammed as much fun into their days as they could. On their last day in Sydney, Liston and Sean Walsh did a quick tot and realised they hadn't visited a single landmark. They took a trip into the city and ascended a tower. They saw Sydney Opera House, sitting like a sailboat on the waterfront. That's that, they said. Next city.

In Melbourne, Páidí Ó Sé, Paudie Lynch, Tom McCarthy and his wife, Kate, piled into a car and took a drive out of town. Their first stop was Geelong, a dusty outpost on the road to Adelaide. When they went for a walk downtown, they found one off-licence open, and one restaurant.

'It was the biggest ghost town I ever saw in all my life,' says Ó Sé. 'So I rang all the lads back in Melbourne and told them to get into cars straight away – there was massive crack in Geelong. When they arrived in Geelong, we had moved on.'

Jack O'Shea had vague memories of an aunt coming to visit from Perth when he was a boy in Cahirsiveen. Her name was Sr Mary Alban, and she lived in a convent in Subiaco. Her bedroom window looked into the mighty Australian Rules ground across the road. Jacko was the only member of his entire family that had ever been able to travel out to see her. Football had given him this opportunity. Now she wanted to give something back.

Every morning she called to the team hotel and became a familiar face during their stay in Perth. One day, she asked Jacko if the boys might like to come to the convent for a meal.

'But, Mary, there's over a hundred in the party,' he said.

'Well, bring them all,' she replied.

One evening they arrived up to the convent to tables laden down with food. Over a hundred guests feasted on five courses. Irish music provided the soundtrack for the evening and for years afterwards when Kerry footballers thought of Perth, they asked after Jacko's aunt.

Hawaii was their final stop, and their most memorable. They went to Pearl Harbour. Tom Spillane went surfing. Others went snorkelling and windsurfing in the warm Pacific Ocean. In the hotel pool, Jimmy Deenihan and Mickey Ned O'Sullivan tried to teach Jack O'Shea to swim. Others relaxed on Waikiki Beach and absorbed the natural splendour of the scene around them. A few more kept on keeping on.

One day Páidí Ó Sé spotted a cruise that charged $15 a person and gave them access to food and beer for the duration of the cruise. The boat owners didn't see the flaw in their plan, but the Kerrymen did. They piled on board and drank the boat dry. A guitar player hired for the cruise was quickly made unemployed and as the sun went down 'The Rose of Tralee' and 'An Poc Ar Buille' resounded across Waikiki Beach.

On their way home they stopped in San Francisco and stayed in Geary Street where pimps and pushers mingled with Kerry footballers. That Sunday they played a game of football against a local selection and packed their bags to head home. As the plane descended through the murky grey skies into Shannon Airport, Páidí Ó Sé borrowed IR£20 from Paudie Lynch for his taxi back to Dingle and the players handed Australian Rules footballs and boomerangs around the cabin for their friends to sign. The holiday was their reward then. The friendships and the memories that endured since were their ultimate reward.

'There was a great bond between us at that particular time,' says Mikey Sheehy. 'People say we mightn't have been as close as the Dubs, but I don't know. We were all great mates: the Stacks lads and the other lads who would've been around Tralee then: Ogie, Jimmy Deenihan. You wouldn't meet up that often nowadays, but in those days we were very tight.'

They would need everything they could manage for the year to come. The team returned on Friday, 9 November, and headed for their first league game against Dublin in Croke Park three days later, tanned and uninterested. The team photograph captures them looking plump, brown and hopelessly bored beneath a dull, grey sky. Eleven of the All-Ireland final team lined out wearing another new jersey: all green with gold stripes across the shoulders. Dublin were keyed up and Kerry laboured. Their finishing was poor but the afterburn of a long summer was enough fuel to get them home by a goal. 'I got a slap of a fist at some stage,' says Liston, 'but sure you didn't even react. We were still in Hawaii.'

The following Sunday they travelled to Roscommon and concluded a hectic month in Charlestown against Mayo with Jimmy Deenihan in goal and the rest of the team still woozy from a civic reception in Crossmolina the previous night. A last-minute point from Martin Carney gave Mayo victory and as Kerry turned their eyes to the All Stars, they were bottom of the league table and glad of the rest. The following Friday they picked up nine awards. Pat Spillane hobbled up to collect a record sixth award, while Páidí Ó Sé collected his first. At the banquet they toasted Páidí, and worried about Spillane.

'I have absolutely no idea whether I'll be able to play for Kerry in 1982, or at any future date,' he said. 'I'll not be trying out my leg until next June and I'll see what happens then. All I can do at the moment is keep my fingers crossed and hope for the best.'

In another part of the banqueting hall, Mikey Sheehy was hobbling around on the same foot that had been frozen with painkillers the previous September against Offaly. His season wouldn't start till late spring, but at least they knew he would be back. For Spillane, the battle to save his career had begun.

While he recuperated, the team mercilessly pushed on without him.

PART II

THE CLIMB

8 THE HILL

The first meeting of the Offaly County Board after the 1981 All-Ireland final was soundtracked by a familiar, if unexpected, chorus of derision. Delegates were happy to endorse Eugene McGee's appointment for another year, but this time they wanted an advisor appointed to assist him. At the top table Fr Heaney pleaded for calm. An inquest into the 1981 final, he said, 'would not help the cause of Offaly football.' It was too late.

McGee's tactics were torn apart. The non-selection of former centre-back Mick Wright in defence was questioned and became a lightning rod for the delegates' dissatisfaction. One delegate said he was happy with the selectors, but unhappy with the team manager. It was the spark to light a bushfire. Another backed calls for an assistant to be appointed. As the flames started to rise on five years' work, the fire brigade finally arrived, sirens blaring.

A representative from Wright's club conveyed a message from Wright, backing McGee and his selectors. Brother Sylvester, assistant county secretary, added that Wright had been suffering from a knee injury and had completed just three training sessions out of the previous twenty. The recently retired Eugene Mulligan was proposed as assistant to McGee, but Mulligan refused the post. Then Richie Connor spoke, as he had years before when he had saved McGee's hide. The players had met the Monday after the All-Ireland, he said, and they were fully behind the management. The proposal was put to the floor, and after a vote, McGee clung on again. Everyone who had witnessed the ferocity of the attacks sighed with relief, but McGee took no notice.

He was already thinking about 1982.

*   *   *

Offaly's tactical errors in the 1981 final tormented him. Losing Tomás O'Connor and Johnny Mooney had been too much for a small panel to bear. McGee had concentrated too much on Kerry and sent out a team that hadn't been convinced about how good they were. Lads were jumpy on the day. It was all new. He needed the players to see the All-Ireland final as another game, not an occasion. He turned again to the elders on the team for counsel.

'There was a lot of talk between myself and himself,' says Richie Connor. 'The type of ball going in was crazy. Terrible bad ball. Gerry Carroll – what could he do if he was loose for a ball and somebody kicks it to his man? Who's at fault? Gerry Carroll? It's the guy that kicks the ball. He was made look bad by the inadequacy of the backs. There would've been way more emphasis on: right, control the ball and make better use of it.'

That would be the cornerstone on which the coming season would be built. McGee already knew that to beat Kerry his players needed to be precise in everything they did, but he was learning about Kerry all the time too, just as he had about Dublin.

Over the years, when Kerry invited them to play challenge matches, Offaly accepted every opportunity. Some of the beatings they shipped were criminal, but McGee never left without adding a new piece of information to his file. The painstaking work of making his players believe they could match Kerry was taking time, but 1981 had a profound effect on them.

They had limited Kerry to a wonder goal. Remove that, and the gap was down to four points. In 1980 it had been five. They looked around the rest of the championship. Ulster was negligible. Galway looked useful in Connacht. Dublin were in the horrors and the rest of Leinster were a distance behind even them. That left the unknown potential of Cork – and Kerry.

If Offaly got through Leinster, the championship draw placed them against the Connacht champions in the All-Ireland semi-final. That meant Kerry in the final. Of all the teams that started out in 1982, only Offaly were capable of stopping five-in-a-row.

That January, the players returned to the lonely slope of Clonin Hill. The hill is now sanitised by the presence of a neat bungalow at its foot, but in 1982 it reached into the pitch black for an eternity with no sights to lighten the evening until the players reached the summit.

This was where the stamina that would carry them through the summer would be put into the players' legs. The idea was born in McGee's mind, and put into practice by Tom Donoghue. All the boys loved Donoghue. He had a sense of fun, an intuitive ability to know when the players had reached their limits and the skill to push them further without prompting a revolt. Without Donoghue, the horrors of Clonin Hill could have provoked mutiny.

The hill's hidden tricks were the worst thing. About halfway up, the ground imperceptibly steepened and started to extract its toll. When you looked back down at the slope below, it suddenly seemed like running up a wall. Clonin Hill was more than training. It was a cause.

For three months they slogged up and down, making mud of the ground beneath them. It hardened their bodies, but also their minds. Where O'Dwyer had his wire-to-wires in Killarney to reinforce his team's belief that no one trained harder than them, McGee now had Clonin Hill. No team could be fitter than them. Not even Kerry.

They trained there twice during the week and on Sunday mornings. They ran laps around the field and straight sprints up the hill. One exercise was called 'sprinting to exhaustion', where the players dragged themselves up and down until their bodies couldn't withstand any more.

'Those nights were torture,' says Tom Donoghue. 'Of them all, Sean Lowry epitomised that. I saw him on the ground so many nights, moaning in agony. For the sprints to exhaustion he would go as far as he could, flat out up that hill. We might do six in a night. They were absolute crucifixions. Sean suffered more than most, but he'd give every ounce.'

While Sean Lowry wasn't made for the hill, Liam Currams and Pat Fitzgerald glided around the course like two thoroughbreds on the gallops. 'Pat Fitzgerald was like a long-distance race horse,' says John Guinan. 'We'd have to lap the hill and after about two laps, Fitzgerald would be so far ahead he could stop at the top, have a piss, and he'd still be in the lead.'

'I used say to guys like Liam Currams, Matt Connor and Stephen Darby if there wasn't a fence at the top of the hill they'd go further,' says Donoghue. 'You couldn't flatten Liam Currams. No matter how much you'd give him, he'd nearly smile at you and say: give me more.'

One night Donoghue ordered them all into pairs and ordered one man to piggyback the other up the hill. Guinan's partner was Liam O'Connor. Guinan was a light forward, and he conceded several inches and two stone to O'Connor. O'Connor tossed Guinan on his back like a rucksack and trundled steadily up the hill. The test came when they switched round.

'It nearly killed me,' says Guinan, 'but I wouldn't let that beat me. I carried him up. Even if I was Paddy Last, I'd get there. As soon as I dropped him, Liam picked me up and clapped me on the back. He says, "That was fabulous." Everyone appreciated what everybody was doing. No matter what we did on the hill we found ourselves helping each other, praising each other. That happened a lot in Rhode. McGee sensed it.'

'You would literally get sick at lunchtime at the thought of facing it,' says Liam O'Connor. 'It was outrageous, but it did the trick.'

Some nights the players made their own fun. One night, as the players descended the hill for the final time, Richie Connor decided to push harder. 'One more, lads,' he said. The players groaned, but pushed on. As they reached the summit, Liam O'Connor caught up with Richie. By the time the scrum of players had dispersed, they had taken all his clothes with them. The players sprinted down the hill and across the road into the dressing room, leaving Richie to gingerly pick his way down the hill.

Back in the dressing room a slab of milk cartons was left on the ground. Some players managed to drink their carton. With their stomachs still churning from the effort, more left theirs behind. As they drank and regained their bearings, McGee might take the opportunity to open up a forum on a topic he had been chewing on during the week.

'You'd be in a cold dressing room after running up and down a hill all evening and ready to go home,' says Sean Lowry. 'This could be ten o'clock on a winter's night. This man will start talking about some method of playing or training. It used drive me crazy. But he was after reading something about it or finding out something, and he wanted to pass it over.'

Crucially, they had all bought in. One night Gerry Carroll drove from Newport, County Mayo, to Tullamore after a day's work for training and returned to Mayo that night. Liam O'Connor was leaving work in Heuston Station every evening for Portarlington and driving until he met Richie Connor's car along the road. Some nights Richie had called to O'Connor's house in Walsh Island to collect his tea, and carried a plate with a rasher, sausage and slice of bread on the passenger seat. Padraic Dunne was cadging lifts from Dublin with Tomás O'Connor, and thumbing down from Newlands Cross when he missed his ride. At the end of March, they finished their work on the hill. Planning for the next phase had begun months before.

Back in deepest winter, Sean Lowry was looking at the All-Star team and thinking about Offaly. When the All Stars toured America the following May, Offaly would be left without a trainer, a manager and a chunk of their panel. Training would grind to a stop, and making up the ground on Kerry didn't allow for that sort of delay. Offaly would need something to keep the wheels rolling.

It was late November when Offaly travelled to Roscommon for a league game. A meeting had been arranged after the game. Lowry's idea was simple. The team would take a training holiday in Spain while the All Stars were away. They would raise the money themselves, organise the flights and accommodation, and crucially, bring along the wives and girlfriends.

This was revolution on a scale McGee would admire. Teams never thought this way. The only trips abroad ever enjoyed by county players came either with the All Stars or a surreptitious trip to America for a weekend to make some money playing with a local club. To match their ambition as footballers, Offaly needed to think big. If Kerry could tour the world, Offaly could get to Spain.

At the back of the room, Fr Sean Heaney took a breath. John Dowling wouldn't like this. In mid-December 1981 a deputation from the team attended a county board meeting seeking official approval from the board for the team to take a holiday. Eugene Mulligan had been absorbed into the board as PRO following his retirement in 1980 and supported the idea. Fr Heaney said he'd like to see the tour go ahead, but no money would be available to help fund the trip. Some delegates maintained the holiday was tantamount to professionalism and washed their hands of the idea. One evening John Guinan received a brief summary of the likely outcome of the event from his father. 'What are you going to do out there?' he said. 'You're going to live it up and ye'll come back not able to walk.'

The public thought differently. Ordinary people donated what spare cash they could find in their pockets. The big hitters dug deep. A letter was sent to every business in the county and was followed by a visit from Sean Lowry and Richie Connor armed with a persuasive sales pitch. Each player sold raffle tickets. They organised fundraising nights in their local bars. Toyota donated a car for a raffle. In the end, two weeks in Torremolinos worked out cheaper than one, and Sean Lowry and selector Leo Grogan booked the trip through a travel agency in Birr.

When the travel agent checked the vast travelling party assembled, he threw in two free seats. Another raffle with a free trip to Spain for two as a prize topped up their war chest.

They were ready.

As McGee and the rest headed for America with the All Stars, a party of fifty-two Offaly players and partners flew to Torremolinos. Leo Grogan was tour manager, and guardian of the kitty. Stephen Darby and Mick Fitzgerald were chosen to oversee training schedules designed by Tom Donoghue along with Grogan. A few weeks later the 1982 World Cup would kick off and Scotland were booked into the same hotel as Offaly. Until they arrived, the pitch was free. It was immaculately prepared, and was encircled by a running track. Perfect.

For two weeks the players trained every second morning from half ten until midday. The training was short but intense, and while the rest of the day was the players' own, they were obliged to be ready to train. One morning Gerry Carroll and Matt Connor struggled back from a night-long expedition charting the local nightclubs and were late for training. The clock was ticking towards midday when they arrived, but their punishment was merciless. They started lapping the pitch. The sun was sitting high in the sky and the heat was beating down on them. Ten laps later, they were still going.

As the locals watched these strange pale-limbed visitors pound around the running track every other morning, some wondered whether Scotland had arrived early. They challenged the Offaly players to a football game against a local selection, and soon Torremolinos was covered in posters announcing a friendly game between Offaly FC, Ireland and a local team. Matt Connor danced through the game, Offaly won 5-1 and before the end tempers got frayed, the tackles got wild and the locals left the field in protest.

The trip was filled with fun. The players commandeered the swimming pool every day and usually brought a ball with them. As they threw the ball across the pool to each other, they watched for Matt's arrival. The water terrified him, but he occasionally might brave the pool. When he did, the next ball would be lobbed in his direction. As he prepared to catch it, a pile of Offaly men would splash their way towards him across the pool. The ball would go one way, Matt the other.

One afternoon John Guinan and Mick Wright hired a pair of tennis racquets and took to the court. With his shaggy curly hair and pristine white shorts and polo shirt, Wright looked the part. When he topped it off with sweatbands for his head and wrists, he looked a little like John McEnroe. On the court beside them, two women were playing a game.

'See those women, John,' said Wright. 'Watch this. I'm going to carry on the same as McEnroe.'

Wright serves first. It goes long and he races up to the net, pounding the cord and berating Guinan. The women pause to watch. He returns to the baseline, serves again. The women smirk. As far as they knew, John McEnroe was left-handed.

With their wives and girlfriends in tow, the trip bound every element of the panel together: those who trained and sacrificed their weekends to football, and those who were left at home when they did. 'We didn't want people away from home for two weeks, and we didn't want any hassle at home,' says Sean Lowry. 'The one thing I wanted all the time was that people enjoyed going to training. I'd go down some night for a meal and sit beside someone. The next night it could be someone else. You'd go to different pubs and have the crack. When we came back from Spain, the amount of people we had missing from training any night was one. They were all bonded into it.

'They also realised the effort people were making. The women got into it and they wanted us to win as well. It became: You have to go training because we all want to win. It's all in the psyche. You go to a match and the wives know each other. There was no stand-offish stuff. It was just a bigger, happier family.'

After two weeks, they came home tanned and rested. One unlikely dream had been fulfilled. Now, they turned to face another.

*   *   *

After the 1981 All-Ireland final, Johnny Mooney needed to get out of the country. Work at home was scarce, and his money had almost run out. A friend of his promised him work on the sites in San Francisco. All that was left at home was a winter scraping a few pounds together and the muck and hassle of another National League. Mooney didn't need that, but for all the trouble and fights and stress, McGee knew Offaly badly needed him. A few days before Mooney left for America, Offaly played Longford. After the game McGee cornered him.

'So you're going away,' he said.

'Yeah,' replied Mooney. 'I'm thinking about it.'

'Go on,' said McGee. 'We'll win the Leinster next year. But keep training away and I'll bring you home for the All-Ireland semi-final.'

Mooney was thrilled, and confused. The scope of McGee's ambition was stunning. Walking through the Leinster championship was never a privilege allowed to Offaly. Stumping up the cash to bring Mooney home at a time when the country was falling asunder was another day's work again, but Mooney agreed to keep fit. McGee's words stayed with him all winter, filling him with excitement for the summer to come.

The previous year had left a deep imprint on him. Before the 1981 final, his footballing life had flirted with full-blown celebrity status. Drink flowed through the weekends. Ladies were never a problem. He possessed a rare talent as a footballer, and every year had brought a share of glamorous days in Croke Park. At twenty-three, life was an unending carnival.

Then, he fell off the trailer on Croghan Hill, smashed his shoulder and lost the All-Ireland final. The county had bemoaned his absence, and defeat had hurt him deeply. The day after the final, his shoulder screamed with pain. The operation left pins in his shoulder. The time spent recuperating made him think.

'You'd head out on a Saturday night and let fly. Offaly is a small county and word would always get back. But when I got over that part of my life, I realised you couldn't do that and hope to win.

'The realisation about how lucky I was to be playing a sport I loved, playing Leinster and All-Ireland finals – that made me realise: Jesus, a change of attitude could do something. My attitude changed. Whereas before you might've taken things for granted, or taken things a little easier, now you wanted to win. There was a total focus on winning. There was nothing going to stop me. Nothing.'

He settled in San Francisco with his girlfriend and played football with Shannon Rangers. He trained the team twice a week and played a game on Sundays. With hundreds of Irish immigrants in the area, football was strong and training was intense. Every Sunday morning, the radio gave Mooney a link to home. Micheál O'Hehir's voice was his Sunday-morning alarm call, wafting across the bedroom, painting pictures from Croke Park, offering a symbol of what awaited: big days in Croke Park, the sun dappling on his back and Offaly charging at Kerry.

When the All-Star tour came through town McGee called on Mooney, and was impressed with what he saw. The plan was still in place, he said. Mooney would be home in August. One day, the Kerry footballers visited the university where Mooney was on a construction job. When he walked into the cafeteria for lunch, he spotted Pat Spillane, Ogie Moran, Ger O'Keeffe and Tommy Doyle. Soon, the slagging started. Mooney hopped the first ball.

'So, I presume you boys are all set for the five-in-a-row?'

'Well, you can play your part and stay here,' said Ogie.

Mooney laughed. 'It wouldn't be worth your while coming home,' said Pat Spillane. 'You might get an oul' Leinster medal, I suppose.'

They chuckled and munched on their sandwiches. That evening in Balboa Park, Mooney watched Kerry train. For two hours Mick O'Dwyer sent them on lap after lap around the running track that encircled the field. They endured an interminable series of sprints before the footballs were produced. Then, they hit top gear. Mooney never saw as many footballs at a training session, nor had he ever experienced the same intensity of effort.

It was a simple training session miles away from the cynical eyes of the sages that dotted Fitzgerald Stadium every evening, but to every Kerry player every session was a statement of their standing against the man beside them. None of them wanted to be seen as inferior to the other. That was the level Mooney needed to reach. He knew he was getting close. As the All Stars left for home, Eugene McGee reported back to the *Tullamore Tribune* that Johnny Mooney 'has no plans to return to Ireland.'

As the evenings lengthened into the summer back home, Offaly's work went quietly on.

9 CAPTAINS

A week after the 1981 All-Ireland final, Jack O'Shea and John Egan guided South Kerry to the county title. Twenty-three years had passed since South Kerry had last won the championship, and the celebrations fitted the occasion, but all that was quickly overtaken with the business of 1982. In Kerry the county champions were traditionally conferred with the honour of providing the Kerry captain. People wondered. Who would lead the five-in-a-row team?

The coves and inlets around the Iveragh peninsula echoed with rumours. Egan had been on the Kerry team much longer than O'Shea, but Jacko was a special player. Sneem were intent on promoting Egan as their candidate; St Mary's of Cahirsiveen were equally driven to secure the captaincy for Jacko. The winners of the South Kerry divisional championship would normally provide South Kerry's candidate for the Kerry captaincy, but Valentia had already carried the title away to the island. Ger Lynch was Valentia's only representative on the Kerry panel, and his place on the team was uncertain. It was between Jacko and Egan. History was at stake, and everyone wanted their piece.

It wasn't long before the trouble started. St Mary's nominated Jacko. Sneem nominated Egan. While Cahirsiveen had always been richly blessed with footballers, emigration and dwindling numbers had damaged football in Sneem for years. Coming from Sneem often made John Egan's footballing life a battle for recognition.

It had been that way since he was a child. When the Sacred Heart secondary school in Carrignavar in Cork went fishing for new pupils, they often cast their nets deep into south Kerry. In 1965, the Egan twins, John and Gerry, left the tiny townland of Tahilla for Cork, and their footballing education began.

John hurled as well as he could play football. Volleyball and basketball came easily to him during PE. When the boys played table-tennis leagues, he usually won at that too. Fr MacCárthaigh looked after the footballers. He was a man of intellect and ideas. Catch and kick was fine, but he preferred to apply some science to his work.

He studied circuit training, and designed training drills for his teams that the Egan boys brought home to Sneem every summer. In 1969, while St Brendan's College in Killarney was the dominant force in colleges' football, Carrignavar chipped out their own mark at B level. Everything flowed through Egan, and Fr MacCárthaigh reckoned he would benefit from a trip to the Kerry minor trials.

Others weren't so sure. Different people told Egan 1969 was a bad time to be trying out for the Kerry minor team. His first trial game would pit him against John O'Keeffe. O'Keeffe was already considered a star, but Egan kicked a few scores and ensured he wouldn't be ignored. That summer the Kerry minor team was filled out by ten players from Brendan's – and Egan.

In time, Kerry would learn to appreciate him, but years before the incomparable glamour of the seventies and the quest for history in 1982, Egan had seen the darker side. In 1970, he lost an All-Ireland minor medal. In 1971, he lost an All-Ireland Under-21 medal. Finally, in 1973, he collected an All-Ireland Under-21 medal in Ennis against Mayo, but as he began his senior career, Kerry were in a state.

At half-time in the 1973 Munster final, Egan stood on the straw-strewn floor of the Kerry dressing room. With the old Cork Athletics Ground being prepared for reconstruction, the team was shunted into the stables in nearby Cork Showgrounds and the shambling surroundings fitted the mood of the day. Kerry were miles behind Cork and facing ignominy.

Some of the older players had lit cigarettes, and the younger ones worried about the whole barn going up in smoke. Egan looked around. These were his heroes, yet he was on a different wavelength to everyone around him. Kerry lost another Munster final to Cork in 1974 and an ageing team began to fracture, leaving Egan and a handful of others to make something from the wreckage.

'You can imagine growing up idolising these men and now you're in a dressing room where they're all crestfallen. It builds your character. Losing was never a fear to me after that. When you saw they could lose, you'd never be afraid to lose.'

When Mick O'Dwyer retired and took over as coach in 1975, Egan expected little would change. Egan remembered all the good passes he had laid off to O'Dwyer over the previous two years before making a good run, but receiving no return pass. The revolutionary training he experienced at Carrignavar remained the measure of Egan's expectations. O'Dwyer, with his old rituals and ways, couldn't be expected to match that.

Instead, the reverse happened. Egan would become O'Dwyer's template for his new team. Kerry would thrive on swift transfer of the ball and rapid movement. Their fitness would ascend to a level beyond anything any team in the country could match. They would thrive on self-confidence and play with a swagger. When Kerry re-emerged in the mid-seventies reshaped and reborn, Egan was at its core.

Opposing corner-backs dreaded his speed. His movement pulled defences out of shape and made space. Sometimes the detail of his work was lost on the wider public, but Kerry couldn't function properly without him.

In the dressing room he was always quiet and laid back, the epitome of the gentle grin Kerry liked to show the world. There was never a care in the world about Egan, but as the years went on, football made him think about football's place in his world. He thought about his grandmother. She had suffered a stroke when she was seventy-five and was cared for by Egan's mother for twenty years. She lived much of her life in the same room, gazing out the same window, watching the months and seasons drift by. She had never attended a game of football in her life, yet football was still her lifeline to the outside world.

She listened to the matches on radio. When Egan called on her, they talked about football for hours. He described Croke Park to her and the matches he had played. The Dubs. Offaly. The raging clashes with Cork. As he got older, he thought about their chats and realised how the game's importance to him had grown beyond his own ambitions. By 1982, he knew he wasn't just playing for himself any more. The captaincy was more than a simple gesture. It was a deeply cherished badge of honour. Sneem could never have imagined such a privilege as to claim the captain of the greatest team of all time in their greatest hour. Egan could deliver it.

All the politicking that engulfed the captaincy hurt him. Nobody thought about the decade of travelling and training he had given to South Kerry and Sneem. For years he had worked as a Garda in Kildorrery, north Cork, and endured the long, difficult drives to training and matches. People would never know what he had been through to maintain his link to home. Clubs in Cork had come to him over the years and tried to persuade him to transfer to them, but he always refused. When Sneem revamped their playing facilities in 1981, Egan raised pots of money for them. If South Kerry were going to honour him with the captaincy, he shouldn't have to fight for it.

'I never put influence on anybody to nominate me as a captain. I assumed the South Kerry Board would nominate a captain, but it became the biggest disappointment for me in relation to the value they had for players. It became a political football.'

When Jack O'Shea looked around the dressing room in 1982, he still felt like a boy among men. He wasn't going to fight anyone to become captain either.

'It never entered my head,' says O'Shea. 'If I was going to be captain, I'd be captain, but I never expected it. John Egan was older than me. He'd given a lot more service to Kerry. It didn't knock me. All

I was interested in was playing.'

A local spat quickly inflated into a full-blown dispute. The county board were besieged with requests from the South Kerry Board to intervene, but they declined. One evening after a Railway Cup game involving Munster, Egan and O'Shea were invited to a hotel room in the town. Egan thought he was about to get expenses from the Kerry County Board. But when they arrived, a group of officials was waiting for them.

'I was told to sit down,' says Egan, 'and that we're here to discuss the captaincy of the Kerry team. What are ye're views on it?'

In the end Jimmy Deenihan retained the captaincy until the end of the National League, giving South Kerry four months to find a solution. Meanwhile Kerry footballers across the country stirred from their short winter's nap. While collective training could wait until the clocks went forward, the players couldn't. Egan was pounding the roads around Kildorrery. The Tralee crowd could be spotted jogging on Banna Strand and playing soccer on a patch of ground overlooking the beach. Páidí Ó Sé returned to his annual rituals on Slea Head, scaling Mount Eagle, sweating the toxins of Hawaii out of himself and feeling the muscles across his guts tighten up again.

John O'Keeffe and Jimmy Deenihan were in Jimmy Mahony's gym in Tralee pumping iron, trying to top each other with every lift. Jack O'Shea and the other Dublin boys were getting their work done with Micheál Ó Muircheartaigh. Charlie Nelligan was conducting his own goalkeeping exercises in Castleisland. O'Dwyer would call on them soon. Even God couldn't help them if they weren't ready.

Like Egan, the magnitude of the record they were chasing and the careers they were enjoying was beginning to dawn on them all. As their stock grew, opportunities followed them everywhere. In Tralee, Mikey Sheehy was making his way in the insurance business, and five All-Ireland medals never caused hindrance.

'It opened up doors for you,' he says. 'People did business with you because of it. It was always good for your profile to be prominent. If you look at all the prominent players of that era, they did well.'

'We all had agendas,' says Ger O'Keeffe. 'As a consulting engineer, I probably had at the back of my mind that this would be good for business. I'd get an article in the paper and a bit of publicity. We all had something in the back of our minds. We all went a bit individualistic trying to get some recognition, which was to the detriment of the team performance.'

In 1980, Charlie Nelligan had landed in Los Angeles on an All-Star trip with two All-Ireland medals in his pocket. A local Kerry businessman came to him with a proposition. A baker, he told him, could make good money in America. The businessman offered him a location for a bakery and the cash to start the business. Ireland was dying. He had his two All-Ireland medals. Any more, as Pat Spillane sometimes said, was only accumulation.

Nelligan thought of his father. In 1947, when Dan Nelligan had finished his baking apprenticeship in Cahir, he returned home to Castleisland looking to start a business. He found a property in town, but couldn't muster the money to make a bid. He had an offer to go to Australia and it appeared he had no choice. Instead, Charlie's grandfather stepped in. The Nelligans had an old site that matched the value of the property. They swapped the land for the shop, and Dan Nelligan started his bakery.

Now, his son faced the same dilemma. He and his wife were expecting their second child in the winter and home had a hold on him. When he arrived home from America, his father took him for a drive and stopped outside a building near the church in Castleisland. This, his father said, could be Charlie's new bakery. If Charlie wanted, they could buy it. His son smiled, and agreed. Just as well, said Dan. The deposit had already been paid.

For years, Nelligan's battle with Paudie O'Mahoney for the goalkeeper's jersey had kept the public intrigued and gave O'Dwyer an annual platform for devilment. In 1975 when O'Mahoney was in goals for the All-Ireland final, Nelligan was with the minor team and sat on the bench for the senior game. Soon after, he moved to Dublin and began studying at catering college. He played football with Home Farm and began applying soccer training drills to Gaelic football. During an accountancy course in Cork, he hooked up with Billy Morgan and learned many of the revolutionary drills Morgan had brought home from Strawberry Hill. Back in Dublin he trained with Jack O'Shea and a constantly changing cast. The evenings began in UCD with Micheál Ó Muircheartaigh, and ended with meals in Daly's on the quays. 'The biggest job,' says Nelligan, 'was to avoid the second dessert.'

The competition between him and O'Mahoney was intense. One evening, Castleisland played Spa in the county championship that swung on two penalties: one for Castleisland and one for Spa. Both goalkeepers were sent up to take the shots. O'Mahoney scored for Spa, and Nelligan missed. A few nights later in Killarney, O'Dwyer commiserated with Nelligan. Then he started hopping balls.

'But didn't Paudie get a nice penalty?' he said, and walked away, leaving Nelligan's mind turning cartwheels. Suddenly every match report looked different, every comment on the street had a different tenor. Nelligan was driven on. After Kerry's defeat to Dublin in the 1977 All-Ireland semi-final, O'Mahoney was dropped and Nelligan was given his chance. He had won the battle. Like Egan, he was now starting to look beyond himself.

One year, Nelligan took the Sam Maguire cup to a small national school in the village of Lyreacrompane, nestled in the Stacks Mountains a few miles from Castleisland. The school contained just one teacher and, despite its many visits to Kerry, the Sam Maguire cup had never ventured into Lyreacrompane before. As Nelligan waited outside the schoolhouse, he peered in the window.

'Now the All-Ireland final will be repeated on the television tonight,' the headmaster was saying, 'and I'll give you all lessons off if you watch it.' A cheer went up. Nelligan knocked and when the door opened, a little boy was standing in front of him. He was gazing at the cup, his mouth wide open.

'At that,' says Nelligan, 'the hairs stood up on the back of my neck. It just hit me what it all meant.'

Boys were becoming men. Some were married. Others had young families. In Tralee, Mikey was now the most blessed of a canon of great forwards. Castleisland had never seen a footballer like Charlie. In Tahilla and Sneem, Egan was an icon. When he thought about that, he felt humbled.

Now, they all had the opportunity to do something special.

*   *   *

As the spring progressed, a combination of results suddenly put Kerry in with a chance of making the knock-out stages of the National League. To some in Kerry, winning a league was seen as a curse. Of their ten league titles, five had been followed by defeat in the championship, including four of their previous five titles. What made this league campaign more worrying was the presence of Cork.

At the end of February 1982, they sent out a near-championship strength team to meet Cork in Killarney, and staggered out of a bloody ambush. Eoin Liston was carried off while one massive fight drew players from every corner of the ground. 'On the evidence of this meeting,' reported the Kerryman, 'there has to be a lot of bad blood between them as the prospect of yet another Munster final meeting between them looms on the horizon. If they do meet, a strict and authoritative referee will be a priority.'

Kerry's 0-5 to 0-4 win was a mixed blessing, sending them into a three-way play-off with Cork and Offaly for a place in the league quarter-final. The following weekend, they met again. This time Kerry were ready. Ogie Moran traded punches with Christy Ryan, Cork's towering centre-back. Páidí Ó Sé and Jimmy Kerrigan laced into each other early on. Once Kerry had won the fights, they cruised home by seven points.

While Cork got past Offaly, Kerry eased past Derry in the

quarter-finals, and even found time to give a crippled Pat Spillane a run out. His injury remained a mystery. When Kerry travelled to America with the All Stars in May, Spillane visited a knee specialist. Spillane was given two choices. Have an operation, or build up the muscles surrounding the knee to an extreme degree, allowing them to support the damaged muscles inside. The operation couldn't be done in Ireland, and even if he did choose to get it done, it would take him a year to recover. In Spillane's mind, no decision needed to be made.

'It's going to be the sort of injury that if I get a knock on the knee it will go,' he said after the Derry game. 'The more games I play the greater the risk of injury. So it is in my best interests that I play the least number of games possible. The number one aim would be winning five-in-a-row.'

A little makeshift gym was set up in a garage next door to the family pub, and Spillane hit the weights. He spent nights there, flinching as the mice that terrified him scurried about the weights and benches. It was a heroic effort, but even as he forced himself through his regime, he knew it was misguided.

'I was doing everything assways. The weight-training programme was a makey-uppy sort of thing. I was going to a gym in Killarney as well. It was all over the shop. I didn't know where I was. I'd say eighty percent I was doing from 1981 to 1982 was counterproductive.'

When Kerry resumed training in Killarney, he rejoined them, running in straight lines when he couldn't twist and turn, and pushing himself through countless sets of push-ups and sit-ups. After a visit to Manchester United and raising funds in Britain and America, Kerry physio Owen McCrohan had invested in an interferential therapy machine which ran electrical current through Spillane's knee to test its strength.

Even when Spillane could barely walk, his knee could withstand the maximum voltage the machine could muster, the force of the current causing his knee to bounce violently up and down on the table. Sometimes he might try and kick a few balls, but his knee never felt right to him. No one noticed his discomfort, and as the summer began and the doctors and specialists stopped prodding and probing, Spillane said nothing.

'I was very good at camouflaging. I was getting away with it. I could run fast in straight lines. Once I didn't get contact I was all right. When you'd be about to kick the ball, all your weight was down on your bad knee. That's when the pain came. There was nothing to hold it up.

'An operation was the last thing on my mind. The five-in-a-row wasn't a big thing with us – but I suppose it was, in that you wanted to be part of it. And I clung in and clung in.'

The Saturday before Kerry's league semi-final against Armagh, Spillane opted to chance a county league game for Templenoe against St Mary's, Cahirsiveen. On one occasion, he jumped for the ball, and felt his knee buckle beneath him. He lay on the ground in agony. Deep within himself, behind the bulletproof confidence, he knew that no amount of willpower could heal this injury.

O'Dwyer still held on to him like a comfort blanket. Armagh had travelled to Killorglin before Christmas for a league match, bringing with them ten coaches and two special trains along with a convoy of cars to carry their 2,500 supporters. A goal in the last minute by Ciaran McGurk won the game and Armagh celebrated like it was September.

When they met again in Croke Park with the ground hardening and Kerry starting to motor towards the summer, Armagh didn't have the gas to stay with them. Croke Park was stripped of its prestige that day, with no public address announcer, no band and no electronic scoreboard. Barely 11,000 turned up, and even with Spillane missing, John Egan absent, Páidí Ó Sé injured and among the subs and Mikey Sheehy's ankle just out of plaster, Kerry had enough in their locker to win by fifteen points.

At a South Kerry Board meeting the following week, nearly six months of arguing over the captaincy came to an end. With neither Sneem nor St Mary's yielding, the board decided to leave the decision to chance. Fifteen pieces of paper were placed in a hat. Thirteen were blank, the other two bore John Egan's and Jack O'Shea's names. Paddy Reidy was St Mary's delegate at the meeting, but, as the local garda sergeant, he was deemed sufficiently above reproach to pull out the name. When he unfolded the piece of paper, it contained Egan's name.

'It was such a joke in the end,' said Egan. 'I was really disappointed over the captaincy. I know Jack O'Shea was riding high. I don't know why it happened. I'm still disappointed over it.'

When he turned to face the public, Egan put his anger at the process aside. 'It's every player's ambition to be captain of the Kerry team and the honour is very much greater when you're going for the kind of record we're chasing. It would be a marvellous way to finish up if we could pull off the five-in-a-row. If we put in as much effort as in other years, and there is absolutely no reason why we shouldn't, I would be quite confident.'

Meanwhile Jack O'Shea let the moment quietly pass by without a care or a thought. The episode was half-forgotten, but the scars would stay with Egan.

With Cork in the league final, Kerry's run into the championship was getting needlessly hectic. A good winter had renewed Cork's courage. Kerry's injuries were piling up, and they were forced to field a team without Sheehy, Spillane, Páidí Ó Sé, Ogie Moran, Paudie Lynch and with Tim Kennelly hobbling around on a heavily bandaged knee. Suddenly a simple league final had taken on real meaning.

The game was hard and unpleasant. Cork got in Kerry's faces and never backed away, but with fifteen minutes left Kerry still led 0-10 to 0-6. It appeared that Cork had been quelled. Instead, they pushed forward and pinned Kerry back. No one could remember anything like this happening before. Kerry appeared to be sitting on their lead.

Pat Spillane was introduced for his brother Mick late-on, but the tide had turned and no amount of thrashing against the waves by Spillane could change that. In the end, Kerry hung on for a draw, 0-11 each.

A strange silence pervaded at the final whistle. People wondered at the events that had just unfolded. Where Kerry had always made a virtue of burying their opponents, this time they had inexplicably stopped. In the Kerry dressing room players shook their heads and smiled. 'Even when we were four points ahead, they refused to give in,' said Sean Walsh afterwards. 'They were even cocky as the second half wore on.'

The following Friday, Kerry headed on the All-Star trip to America with the lessons of the previous Sunday barely digested. Up in Aughnacliffe, Eugene McGee was thinking. Had Cork just exposed a chink?

10 THE EPIC STORY OF ROCKY BLEIER

Cork seem to have brought the late tackle to a fine art. In boxing parlance, Ger O'Keeffe was put down and only saved by the bell. Jack O'Shea was grounded by solid rights and hooks to the head but refused to take a count. Ger Lynch was put down four times. Ger Power and John Egan had the headlock used on them with effect and John L McElligott was sent to the ground ...

Extract from a May 1982 letter to the *Kerryman*
a week after the National Footbal League final

Kerry returned from America to a county fermenting with concern about Cork. O'Dwyer was used to these occasional outbreaks of panic. He had always told his boys that they weren't playing against 31 counties, but 31½. Always watch for snipers in the ditches. He knew his team, and its engine was starting to make the right noises.

Training in America had been almost flawless. The players were looking lean. A few injuries were still wafting about and Spillane was a loss, but Kerry were showing they could cope. The Sunday before the league final replay against Cork, they travelled to Claremorris for a challenge game against Mayo, fielded a scratch team and slammed in five goals. The following evening, O'Dwyer ran them all into the ground in Killarney for ninety minutes. They were looking lean, sharp. Mikey Sheehy was still troubled by injury, but the rest looked ready.

Five-in-a-row hadn't been mentioned by O'Dwyer, but it was always there. The league final replay was a day to make a statement.

Kerry pounded Cork from the beginning. With the sorry business of the captaincy settled for now, John Egan was buzzing and nailed a sweet goal that finished the game as a contest. Kerry strolled away by seven points, 1-9 to 0-5, and the watching football nation held their heads in their hands. Jimmy Deenihan lifted the trophy in his final act as captain, before handing over to Egan. 'There could hardly have been a worse advertisement for this year's Munster final,' wrote JJ Brosnan in the *Kerryman*, but the worries and fears of a county slowly becoming consumed by five-in-a-row had been assuaged.

The following Saturday, the Kerry team trundled into Sneem GAA club to officially open the club's new facilities. The development was a triumph of local enterprise and generosity. The new grounds encompassed basketball and tennis courts, a playground and saunas and dressing rooms. They had John Egan as Kerry captain and plans already being drawn up for a joyous homecoming in September. This promised to be Sneem's year.

Cork had been booked to play Kerry at the pitch opening, but Kerry had already shown Cork enough over the previous few months. Pat Spillane stood in goals and only three players survived from the League final team. Mick O'Connell refereed the game and Jack O'Shea embroidered the occasion with a fifty-yard solo run that ended with a goal. The crowd gasped. Kerry won by three points. Cork shook their heads again, and headed quietly for home.

Three nights later, Kerry re-gathered in Killarney for training. The first round of the Munster championship against Clare was less than a week away. It was a warm June evening and a summer shower had covered the grass with a light coating of drizzle. O'Dwyer split the panel into two teams. These were the matches that proved the players' collective mettle. For an hour they were dipped into a furnace. The heat either made them, or finished them off.

The individual duels were brutal. John O'Keeffe picked up The

Bomber. Páidí Ó Sé scampered after Pat Spillane. Tim Kennelly tried to snag Ogie Moran. Every summer since they were kids, John Egan and Jimmy Deenihan seemed to end up alongside each other. They had accompanied each other to the peak of their careers. From where they now stood, they could see for miles.

Egan loved marking Deenihan, and Deenihan loved marking Egan. While Deenihan could deal with any physical challenge, Egan was different. He made Deenihan think. When Egan might begin to run in one direction, Deenihan needed to accommodate the possibility that Egan was planning to turn him inside out.

For Egan, Deenihan was a challenge like no other. He never said a word during games, but he stood so close Egan could almost feel his breath on his neck. When the ball dropped between them, the prospect of the sheer physical force Deenihan could tackle with sometimes made forwards duck out of the prospect, but not Egan.

Captaining Kerry had been a proud experience for Deenihan, and the Kerry defence leaned on him like a scrum on a tighthead prop. He was their rock. 'I was really at my peak in 1982,' says Deenihan, 'mentally and physically. You just think about the game. You don't lose any energy through tension or not sleeping, or worrying about a game. I was mature as a footballer.'

North Kerry was good ground for harvesting backs, and Deenihan and Tim Kennelly were the pick of the most recent crop. Growing up in north Kerry, with its fearsome local championship and the locals' appreciation of hard, flinty football, gave Deenihan his grounding, but his football career also passed through an age of enlightenment.

He went to Strawberry Hill College in London in the early seventies to study physical education, played rugby with Mickey Ned O'Sullivan and absorbed modern theories on strength and conditioning. He played for the National College of Physical Education in Limerick under Dave Weldrick, who gave students tuition on modern training methods. While inter-county teams were beating out lap after lap around the country, the students were playing scaled-down football games on small pitches to maintain the intensity and improve their skill levels under pressure. They recalibrated soccer drills for Gaelic football. Weldrick made the boys think about the game and their roles. Every game was planned out. A few years before Eugene McGee was watching his tapes of Offaly get mangled in his video recorder, Weldrick was recording his team's games and showing them to his players, triggering debate and a level of analysis players hadn't been exposed to before.

Deenihan applied the science to what he knew best: marking, hounding, leading. He shaped his teaching career around football: teaching allowed him to devote his summers to football, and when he wasn't teaching PE clases in Tarbert Vocational School, he trained. He roomed with John O'Keeffe before every game in Dublin and lived his entire career alongside him at corner-back. 'I used say I was Johnno's *domestique*,' he says. 'Johnno could always go up for the high one because he always knew there was someone there to clean it up if he missed one.'

They fitted together and the full-back line prospered. In six All-Ireland finals, Deenihan conceded just one point, to Brendan Lowry in 1981. The relationship among the defence was almost telepathic. Deenihan always knew where Páidí Ó Sé was at right-half-back. He could sense when Johnno would come for a ball and where he needed to be. Kennelly was like a brother. These were the foundation stones on which O'Dwyer had built his empire. They would shoulder the greatest burden during the summer to come.

As the evening drew in, the pace of the practice game increased. The entire team was moving sweetly. Even as the light grew dim, it all felt too good to call a halt. 'We'll have one more attack,' shouted O'Dwyer.

The ball was played towards Deenihan and Egan. Deenihan trailed him out. As Egan bent down to gather the ball, Deenihan dashed it from his hands. He stretched out his leg to kick the ball away, but both players' legs got entangled. They skidded on the greasy surface and the sound of Deenihan's right leg snapping echoed around the stadium, as far away as the players at the other end of the pitch and into the stand where pockets of locals gathered nightly to watch the team. Deenihan lay on the ground, writhing in agony. He looked down and saw his foot twisted around, facing in the opposite direction.

An ambulance was called, and the players gathered round Deenihan. 'It's God's will,' he whispered, as he was lifted into the back for the trip to the Regional Hospital in Cork. The impact on the rest of the summer would be seismic. Suddenly, nothing about Kerry's future seemed certain.

'It was a fracture,' says Deenihan. 'My leg was broken in three places. I did a lot of damage to my ligaments as well. It was fairly traumatic. It was there I saw my career with Kerry ending.'

For a moment, he yielded to nature, but his ambition and the environment he had grown up in compelled him to reconsider. 'I was convinced I could get back for the All-Ireland. That's how motivated we were. We all wanted to be part of it. Everybody wanted to be part of winning five in a row. I convinced the surgeon when he was putting the plaster on that I wasn't sore, but it was killing me.'

He persuaded the surgeon to take the cast off early. Deenihan walked Ballybunion strand in the salt water every morning at dawn. A chunk of every day was spent in Jimmy Mahony's gym, pounding weights. He walked as soon as he could, regardless of the pain. He began running long before he should have.

He read books to rehabilitate his mind, and found a soulmate within the pages. People always reckoned that Rocky Bleier of the Pittsburgh Steelers was too small to make a professional player in the NFL. At 5ft 9in and 210lbs, Rocky was small for a running back. He was toast if the opposition got a hand on him, but Rocky played smart and found a way to survive.

The Steelers picked him through the 1969 season but at the end of his first season, the US Army drafted him for service in Vietnam. That August, his platoon was on patrol when they walked into an ambush. Rocky took rifle wounds in his right leg. A grenade exploded nearby, embedding shrapnel in his left leg. They shipped Rocky home with a Purple Heart and a Bronze Star, but he could barely walk. He had lost almost forty pounds and struggled to walk without a limp when he began, but at least, Rocky told himself, he hadn't lost a leg or a foot.

Painstakingly he started to rebuild his career as a football player. By 1980 he had regained his place on the Steelers' starting line-up and collected four Super Bowl rings as part of the greatest team that ever played the game. He also wrote a book charting every excruciating step of an extraordinary journey. Deenihan soaked up the sentiment in every line as if it were written about himself. He could not yield or give in. He could be Rocky Bleier. He could make it back.

Meanwhile, other injuries were mounting around Mick O'Dwyer. After Kerry's challenge game against Cork in Sneem, Jack O'Shea had played with St Mary's against Waterville. O'Dwyer was in the crowd. When O'Shea came down badly on his ankle and lay in a heap, O'Dwyer was over the wire and on to the pitch.

A crowd of people stood around Jacko. Some officials started prodding and rubbing his ankle. He roared with pain. Meanwhile, O'Dwyer was apoplectic. 'Where's the stretcher?' he shouted. No stretcher. They lifted Jacko up and carried him off. Sean Walsh was also injured, leaving O'Dwyer without a centrefield partnership with the championship about to begin. Deenihan might be gone for the summer. Mikey Sheehy was still feeling his way along. Spillane would have to be chanced in attack against Clare. This was no summer for gambling.

*   *   *

Eugene McGee's new column in the *Sunday Tribune* was sparing no one. In his own mind, only Offaly could seriously challenge Kerry and the ferocity of his convictions spilled over on to the pages. By mid-June he had seriously questioned Mayo's ability to regain their Connacht title but assessed Galway as poor challengers. Ulster was negligible. 'Everybody knows that barring earthquake or natural disaster,' he wrote, 'Kerry will dispose of Cork footballers as easily as they did just in the replay of the NFL final.'

Offaly looked good in Leinster, but they began the summer with a simple quandary.

After the sunkissed glamour of Torremolinos, the Offaly footballers came back to find themselves homeless. Finding pitches for training had always been a problem. Some evenings the county team would arrive in Tullamore for training to find a local street league game being played on the pitch, forcing them to wait. Other nights, the pitch could be double-booked, sending them out into the countryside looking for a venue. They wandered the county for weeks looking for a home. Then, by a hump-backed bridge, they finally found a place to stay.

The summer of 1982 was a special time for Ballycommon GAA club. In early June a new clubhouse was opened beside the pitch. Around the same time, Eugene McGee passed the grounds and pulled in. The pitch was firm and sheltered from the wind by the trees that lined three sides of the ground. A telephone mast sat across the road from the pitch, picking up signals from Radio Éireann as well as the telephone company, frequently sending Gay Byrne crackling down the line on a midweek morning!

There was nothing in Ballycommon. A small pub was tucked in behind the bridge, but the blue-and-white-painted gates that marked the entrance to the football pitch was the most vivid splash of colour for miles around. It was quiet and secluded. Ballycommon was three miles from Daingean, perfectly central for the players and nicely tucked away in the countryside to keep too many curious onlookers away. Here McGee could plot and scheme, road-testing new tactics and formations without fear of his plans being leaked. Kerry was on his mind, but first Offaly had the Leinster championship to concern them.

The National League had left them with some familiar issues to confront. With Johnny Mooney gone, they were weakened both at centrefield and in attack. Their scoring tallies were low. An occasional flash of genius from Matt Connor kept them rolling but their forwards weren't clicking properly. Three of their last four regulation league games saw them register just eight points. McGee arranged trial games and ripped the team apart from week to week, trying to find an attacking combination that worked. They made the league semi-finals with their legs weary from Clonin Hill, and took a five-point trimming from a Cork team with the scent of Kerry blood heavy on their nostrils. They began the championship out of public sight, and out of mind.

Louth were Offaly's first opponents in Leinster, but as Offaly people began leaving ten minutes into the second half, a nine-point win did nothing to convince them about the worth of training trips to Spain and cloaked talk of All-Ireland titles. When they met Laois in the semi-finals, the team still churned with uncertainty. Tomás O'Connor's knee was causing him problems and with Johnny Mooney in America, the Offaly attack looked lopsided. McGee continued to audition centre-forwards that might be able for Tim Kennelly, starting with an old defender, Ollie Minnock. The rest of the team looked gauche and unsure of themselves. If Offaly were vulnerable, Laois would be unsympathetic neighbours.

They travelled to Portlaoise for a game that unfolded into an epic. Laois stormed at Offaly. Without Tomás O'Connor, Offaly struggled to hang on at centrefield, but staggered in level at half-time. With twenty-five minutes left, Offaly were a goal down and the noise was rising. The locals sensed victory. Offaly's summer needed to start now.

A few minutes later, a ball broke to Gerry Carroll at centrefield. There was space in front of him. Invitation enough. He pushed on past the 45-metre line unhindered and towards the 20-metre line. Soon, he was closing in on goal and drilled a low shot to the net. Offaly were level.

Laois still hung on. As the game edged towards the last five minutes they were still level. The Ollie Minnock experiment was hitting problems. Sean Lowry was struggling with the pace of the game while Richie Connor was labouring at centre-back. Of Matt Connor's tally of 0-9, only two points had come from play, but by the end of the game Offaly were relying on freakish bounces and naïve defending to survive. When John Guinan raced at the Laois defence as Gerry Carroll had done, the cover melted away again, and his goal eased Offaly clear. Fatigue was starting to weigh Laois down, and as Brendan Lowry hit another goal, Offaly were safe. Just.

A few days later, McGee and his selectors gathered together. They looked at the team. The bulk of the defence was settled, but Richie Connor had a nagging knee injury that was now starting to cause him real problems. The forwards had just scored 3-13, but Matt's frees were forming the bulk of their scores, and goals didn't come easily to them.

The first problem was Richie. He needed an operation that wouldn't wait any longer. If he went into hospital, he would miss the Leinster final. If Offaly survived, he was likely to make the All-Ireland semi-final. It was the first test of McGee's convictions. He had already won the Leinster title against Dublin in his head the previous November. But without Richie Connor? Circumstances dictated Offaly would have to. He had struggled against Laois, and the injury wouldn't heal itself. With Connor gone, Offaly now added a new centre-back to their list of requirements.

They turned to the forwards. Countless trial games and challenge matches had yielded no one. Players flitted in and out of the team and McGee's tactical chicanery in attack had almost been exhausted. They flicked through the files again.

A couple of months before, McGee had seen Seamus Darby nail a goal for Rhode over his left shoulder with seconds left against Daingean in the county championship. The goal drew the game, and relief coursed through Darby's system. It had been a difficult few years, but the goal gave him a break, and from there he tugged the strings for Rhode all summer. A week after Offaly beat Laois, Darby hit four points as Rhode cruised past St Rynagh's in the championship. He was always known as a poacher. Now he was a playmaker.

He looked fresh and eager. His hardware business in Edenderry was thriving despite the recession. He had a young family and a happy life. Football had found its place and didn't bother him too much any more. McGee called him. He wanted him on the panel, but he was guaranteeing him nothing. A few years before, Darby would have hung up the phone. McGee and Darby had history.

When Eugene McGee swept a scythe through the Offaly panel in late 1976, Seamus Darby was among those nicked by the blade. Darby had started in the 1972 All-Ireland final replay against Kerry, and won his All-Ireland medal. He was twenty-one then, but as Offaly declined, some people forgot Darby had ever been around for the good days.

While Darby brimmed with stories and good humour and loved the company of others, he found McGee distant. Odd. Darby was more freewheeling. Most nights before a game he might pop into McCormack's pub and shorten his evening with a few pints. Nothing major, just enough to soften any nerves. As a player he could lie dormant for long spells in a game, then pick his scores like an assassin. In a team of grafters McGee was never sure whether Darby would ever fully pull his weight. They never fully bonded, and Darby struggled to fit into McGee's vision.

'After every county final I seemed to get a run again in the league,' he says, 'and then just drift off again. Then I decided I didn't want the hassle of playing in the league. So when he called me I just didn't bother.'

His last game came in April 1979 against Kildare in Athy, but his name had never fully left conversations about Offaly. After the 1981 All-Ireland final he heard stories about people going to McGee and asking about Darby, but the reply was chilly: 'We've enough Seamus Darbys on the panel.' Gerry Carroll and Johnny Mooney represented all the luxury items McGee could handle in one panel.

The rejection hadn't eaten him up, but Darby never forgot. In 1982 he was thirty-two years old. This could be his final chance. 'I was a bit bitter about being dropped for so long and I was fairly anxious to make a go of it. It was a good thing for me because I was going to make a go of this thing, by hook or by crook.'

Darby's first game came against Westmeath at Durrow the following weekend, but McGee and his selectors had other things to worry about.

The previous week, when Ballycommon had emptied out and Matt Connor had gathered up his footballs and gone home, McGee, Grogan,

Sean Foran, Paddy Fenlon and PJ Mahon settled down to pick a team for the game. They started with finding a replacement for Richie Connor at centre-back. Sean Lowry was the first name into the ring. Lowry had won an All Star at full-forward, but had also won an All-Ireland medal with Offaly at centre-back in 1972. McGee thought his time as a defender was up. 'In the name of God,' said McGee, 'how would you put him there? We had to take him out of there years ago.'

The debate went on. Lowry had struggled against Laois at full-forward. Offaly would need a strong physical presence in the centre against Dublin. Lowry was a cool character. Changing positions wouldn't faze him and he would also fill the deficit in leadership left by Richie's absence in defence. McGee and the selectors danced around the question all night. Darby was picked at corner-forward and Tomás O'Connor was re-introduced at centrefield. The team had a championship feel to it, but centre-back remained uninhabited. They broke up the meeting with nothing set in stone. They would trust their instincts when they got to Daingean.

That night as the players togged off, McGee and the rest repaired to a small room off the dressing room. A few days' thought had mellowed him. The set of selectors he had now were good football men. He never fought with them like he did with others, and this time, he knew they had a point. 'If you want to try Sean Lowry at centre-back,' he said, 'this is the time.'

Seamus Darby was switched to full-forward, and Offaly thrived. Darby scored a point and Sean Lowry comfortably held his opponent in check. Matt hit 1-3 alongside Darby and in the other corner Brendan Lowry took fire, hitting 1-6. The following week they beat Cork in a challenge game in Fermoy, but conceded 4-9. Richie Connor was being missed in the centre, but Lowry was there for the Leinster final now. Dublin might be tighter than McGee expected.

*   *   *

The previous September, a few weeks before the 1981 All-Ireland final and without the pressure of being on the Offaly panel, Darby had spent a week in Kerry on holidays. One evening he had dropped into Killarney to watch Kerry prepare themselves to meet Offaly. They looked sleek. They were moving the ball crisply among themselves. There wasn't an ounce of fat or error between them. He thought about the boys at home. Offaly wouldn't be ready for them.

This time, he knew they were ready for anyone. For three weeks before the Leinster final, Tom Donoghue ran them into the ground. When Seamus Darby weighed himself before joining the panel he was a cuddly thirteen stone. Three weeks in Ballycommon had sweated a stone out of him.

'I thought I was in good shape but the training was savage. I got to the stage where I couldn't eat, not to excess. I realised you just couldn't eat a great, big dinner and go out training, because you'd be looking at it later on.'

The night before the final, Darby went through his usual routine. He felt no nerves, just a simple, uncluttered determination to play well. His ritual had once involved dropping into Paddy McCormack's pub next door for a few pints, then going home to sleep soundly – this time he supped glasses of orange instead.

The sun was high in the sky the following morning, and found Darby bouncing on his toes. With Richie Connor recovering from injury, Martin Furlong captained Offaly in his tenth Leinster final, while Sean Lowry started at centre-back where he faced an imposing challenge. Having recovered from the car crash that should have ended his career, Brian Mullins returned to face Lowry at centre-forward. The legend of Rocky Bleier had a devotee in Dublin, too.

Lowry wasn't bothered. Moving to centre-back was a nice change for him. He had played plenty of good games at centre-back before on worse Offaly teams. He could survive on Mullins.

Dublin won four frees in the first five minutes, but failed to convert any of them. Once Offaly found their feet, Dublin were in trouble. Lowry dominated Mullins. Tomás O'Connor was making a triumphant return at centrefield beside Padraic Dunne. At the other end, Darby had hit Offaly's first three points and was giving Tommy Drumm a desperate time. Kevin Heffernan switched Mick Holden onto Darby, but it only drove Darby on again. As half-time approached, Offaly laid siege to Dublin's goal. Shots by John Guinan and substitute Liam O'Mahony had been blocked out by the Dublin defence, and as the ball bounced around the square, Darby stabbed a shot to the net. Half-time. Offaly led by eight points. Darby had hit 1-3.

Dublin switched Mullins to full-forward for the second half, but Sean Lowry was blocking all avenues to goal. Offaly stretched the margin to nine points at the end, 1-16 to 1-7.

As they took their third successive Leinster title, records tumbled. It was the biggest defeat ever shipped by Dublin in a Leinster final and Offaly's biggest win over Dublin in fifteen championship matches. Matt Connor became the first player to end four successive Leinster finals as top scorer. In Offaly it seemed like the sun would never cease to shine, and the days spent in bondage to Dublin were over for good. The following night Seamus Darby returned to Paddy McCormack's pub to properly toast the weekend and rumours swept through the county that Johnny Mooney was coming home the following weekend. Offaly now bestrode Leinster like kings.

11 CAR CRASH STORIES AND THE RETURN OF THE FRISCO KID

Tom Spillane's desk in St Brendan's College had always been a triumphant expression of family pride. Pictures of Pat and Mike in Kerry jerseys adorned every centimetre. Tom's heroes were his brothers; they were also his best friends. When the Kerry team repaired to the pubs after matches, the Spillanes would always be together. Maybe it came from the knowledge of the sacrifices their mother had made for them so they could excel at football, or the experience of growing up without their father and the support they offered each other that bonded them so tightly together. They mixed happily with the rest of the boys, but they were always supremely close to each other.

As a young boy Tom was routinely smuggled into the Kerry dressing room with Pat and Mick to collect autographs – one evening in Killorglin he was short of paper, so Ger Power scribbled his name on Tom's arm. John O'Keeffe had been his old PE teacher in St Brendan's, and cross-country running had always come easily to him. One day O'Keeffe compared him to John Walker, the great New Zealand long-distance runner, as Spillane breached the finishing tape, his long hair bobbing in the breeze. But O'Dwyer's training pushed him hard. After the first week he learned to confine himself to a sandwich during the day and a slice of brown bread and jam with a cup of tea. He started one championship game in Munster in 1981 as a nineteen-year-old and sat on the bench all the way to the final. Later that year he toured the world with his heroes. He was living the dream.

'If any one of that team asked me: Young lad, that ball is after going down there, go get it. Man, I would be gone so fast for that ball. You're in total awe of these guys. They were my heroes. I'd eat the grass off the ground for them.'

Sometimes his exuberance took him too far. When Kerry played Armagh in the 1982 league semi-final, all the players were instructed to forego the club games scheduled for the night before. Instead, Spillane turned out for Templenoe. The following day he started against Armagh, but after ten minutes O'Dwyer took him off. As Spillane jogged off, O'Dwyer chased him up, slamming his hand into Spillane's fist: 'You weren't meant to play last night!'

O'Dwyer liked to keep Spillane on edge. Spillane shared with Ger Lynch on Kerry trips. Neither of them drank and they prided themselves on their abstention and devotion to training. That pride was where O'Dwyer found his weakness.

'He called myself and Lynch "The Party Boys". You'd meet Dwyer and he'd walk past you nose to nose, so he'd get a sniff of drink. We played a challenge match up in Mayo, and he said it to us this day: "Easy on the drinking now and the parties!" I was incensed. "Micko," I said, "I don't drink!" He was egging us on.

'Even when he ran up alongside you in training, and you might be after forty rounds of the field, and Dwyer might do one and he's flying. But you push on and wouldn't let him pass you out, even for one round. He was like the hare out in front.'

As the 1982 championship began, Spillane was hanging on at the fringes of the panel. Although four players were missing from the team that had beaten Offaly in the All-Ireland final, he didn't make it for the Munster semi-final against Clare. With O'Dwyer's team banged out of shape by injuries, Tommy Doyle and Vincent O'Connor manned centrefield, while Pat Spillane started, even with his knee hanging by a thread. Twenty minutes in, he raced for a ball, took a tumble and stayed on the ground. The crowd was suspended in silence for a few moments. This was the horrible tension that surrounded Spillane's summer. Every twist and turn was analysed. Every slight limp and delay in recovering from a tackle was scrutinised for signs of a flaw in his knee. Spillane knew the danger he was courting, and tried to change his game to survive.

'There was lots of instances where, if I got caught, my knee was gone. You had to be cute in the sense that you had to pull out of certain 50/50 challenges, without being a coward. You had to play it by ear.'

This time, he got to his feet and finished the game with four points.

Kerry did enough to beat Clare by eleven points, but only the sight of John Egan whirling around the attack like a dervish evoked memories of the team at their best. They could save that for Cork.

* * *

Munster finals had become a familiar routine for Jack O'Shea. If the games were on in Killarney he would load the family up and set off from Leixlip on Friday evening to enjoy the weekend at home in Cahirsiveen. If Kerry were playing in Cork, he would travel with Micheál Ó Muircheartaigh on Sunday morning and make his way back later that night. In all his years travelling with Kerry, he had never known the journey to be darkened by defeat. Winning Munster titles had become an annual ritual for the public. For the players, the greatest challenge was surviving O'Dwyer's build-up. None more so than Jacko.

His corralling together of the heavies early in the year reflected Mick O'Dwyer's taste for a challenge. He loved to see bellies and flabby thighs that needed tightening. It gave him something to work on in the spring, something to beat the boys up about. Jacko's return from Dublin was another. Two weeks before any championship game, Jacko would take a week in Kerry for training. Extra sessions were packed into the week to mark his arrival.

First, O'Dwyer would start riling Jacko about the training in Dublin with Ó Muircheartaigh. A spark of slagging would quickly ignite into a flaming bushfire. 'He'd say he was hearing things back: Ye're not working as hard,' says O'Shea. 'Then the boys would be slagging you: Lucky fuckers up in Dublin. He's killing us down here.'

Jacko's first night at home always filled him with dread. It was the night when O'Dwyer would test him. 'One night we did wire-to-wires. I touched the wire and came back. "You go again now, Jacko," he says, and he put another fella with me straight away. I came back. "We'll have one more," he says. Three in a row, and he put Ogie with me for the last one. I hit the wire on the far side and when I was turning round my head started to spin. Coming back across around the middle of the field, I could feel nothing. I had a total lack of oxygen. Dwyer wasn't happy unless he saw you sick or struggling.'

In 1982 O'Dwyer had no worries about Jacko. He never missed league or challenge games, and his form hadn't dipped all year. South Kerry's victory in the county championship seemed to spur him and John Egan on to new levels of excellence. If Kerry were to claim five in a row, South Kerry would be at the centre of the story.

The Friday before Cork were to play Kerry in Killarney, Jacko finished his plumbing work early and collected his wife Mary and their children, Kieran and Linda. The children slept soundly in the back seat and the journey passed quietly as far as Mountrath. He asked Mary if she had the tickets for the game that had been sent up by Kerry County Board. She rustled about in her bag. They weren't in the car. No panic, they had time. They headed back home to Leixlip. Mary got out in Kildare town and Jacko drove on, the children still sleeping soundly in the back seat.

He collected the tickets and set off again, cutting through the bends in the Curragh towards Kildare town. As he left Leixlip, the first rain he had seen for a fortnight began to fall. The road was greasy. Linda had woken up and was getting restless. She was looking for her mother. 'We're nearly there, pet,' said Jacko, 'nearly there.'

He journeyed on through the Curragh. As he rounded a bend, the wheels locked up and the car skidded on. Another car was coming in the opposite direction. Jacko threw his arm across and held Linda in the passenger seat, throwing his other arm through the gaps in the steering wheel to hold it in place. The cars collided and juddered to a halt.

Jacko looked around. Kieran was crying, but he was okay. So was Linda. His own neck was aching, but he was all right. The other driver was fine, but Jacko's car was in pieces. He made contact with Mary in Kildare town, then he rang Ó Muircheartaigh. He was okay, he told him; he could travel Sunday morning.

Minor faultlines caused by injuries traversed the rest of the team as well, but they would manage. Spillane had broken down again in training but Sean Walsh would strap up to play Cork. Even without Jimmy Deenihan, Kerry looked solid in defence. But O'Dwyer was worried. Deenihan's absence had unbalanced the defence. Cork's Dinny Allen could cause Tim Kennelly problems on hard ground, and Deenihan's replacement, Ger O'Keeffe, had played a lot of his best football on the half-back line. After the league final, O'Dwyer had repeated his old mantra that if any team was ready to beat Kerry, it was Cork. Even after routing them in the league final, he feared it might happen this time. O'Dwyer rarely switched his teams round to handle the opposition. For Cork in a Munster final, he would.

Kennelly was back in the corner as the game began. O'Keeffe was at centre-back on Allen. The change worked, but Kerry were labouring everywhere else. Jacko was subdued, leaving Sean Walsh to fight a savage battle against Mick Burns and Dom Creedon.

Kennelly didn't survive the game. Neither did Ogie Moran or Jacko. Mikey Sheehy was brought to centre-forward and Eoin Liston to centrefield in an effort to trigger something, but only two Kerry forwards managed to score all afternoon.

Cork were revelling in the scrap and with seven minutes left they led by a point, 0-9 to 0-8. On the line, Kerry mentors and officials were braced for the worst. Having edged a mighty hour against Dinny Allen, Ger O'Keeffe wrung the last drops of stamina from himself and set off upfield. He was brought down within shooting distance, close enough for Sheehy to tap the ball over the bar.

For the final minutes, Kerry pinned Cork back, but shot three bad wides. Finally, John Egan took control. He won a ball close to goal, and spotted Ger Power. A quick one–two prised open some space as Cork frantically funnelled players back. Mikey Sheehy popped up to take a pass and found Power in front of goal. He kicked for the winning point, but the ball screwed badly off his foot and drifted left of the posts.

The final whistle blew. Draw. Kerry were shattered. Cork were inconsolable. A county board official hopped a ball with Power about his miss as he left the field. 'Ye'll make a few bob here yet,' replied Power.

While the players cooled their tempers and their legs, the battle for supremacy spilled over into the committee rooms. There was a replay date to fight for.

The following Friday the Munster Council convened for a meeting that left blood on the floor. The Council had four Sundays to choose from before an All-Ireland semi-final against the Ulster champions on 15 August, but each of them was loaded with problems. Cork wanted to draw Kerry into battle quickly again, and proposed the following Sunday in Killarney, 18 July, but Kerry dodged their advance, insisting it was too close to the drawn game. It wouldn't allow sufficient time to print tickets, trim the grass on the banks around Fitzgerald Stadium, and allow the media to promote the game. With the Siamsa Cois Laoi Festival scheduled for 25 July in Páirc Uí Chaoimh, Waterford delegate Tom Cunningham suggested Saturday, 24 July, but that was quickly dismissed.

When Kerry suggested 1 August, Cork resisted. Cork's Christy Ryan would be in Canada that weekend. The reason prompted a furious response from Kerry delegate Dave Geaney. Ryan, said Geaney, would be on the pitch if the game was fixed for 1 August. Cork secretary Frank Murphy responded that Mick O'Dwyer himself had said that a month's break would be ideal for Kerry. The atmosphere had turned sour. A proposal to play the game the following Sunday was rejected, leaving Murphy to suddenly suggest a Friday night fixture on 16 July.

The meeting dragged on past midnight. There were calls for Croke Park to intervene but the meeting broke up with neither side in the mood to flinch. Then, Cork capitulated. The following Wednesday night, the Munster Council issued a statement announcing that the game would take place on 1 August in Killarney if both counties agreed. Cork conceded. Having lost the boardroom battle, Cork were now in danger of losing the war.

With Pairc Uí Chaoimh occupied by the stage built for the Siamsa Cois Laoi festival, the team hit the road, training at five different venues. In comparison, Kerry's camp in Killarney was buzzing with the usual business of the summer. Interest in the game was growing. Calls came from Northern Ireland to Kerry County Board looking for tickets. For a few short days, the Munster championship was brimming with life again.

Kerry were ready to dampen that dust down. The Thursday night before the replay, O'Dwyer convened a trial game. It was murderous stuff, but players were blooming with good form. Pat Spillane played ten minutes and managed to kick two stunning points from the right wing. After a summer with the Under-21s, Tom Spillane dominated Jack O'Shea. It was enough to get him into the team at centre-forward, with Ogie Moran moving to the wing and Tommy Doyle switching to wing-back. Ger O'Keeffe had excelled at centre-back, but Tim Kennelly needed to start there. Either way, O'Keeffe's form was so good now he could do a job wherever he was put. Confidence was high. 'If we can beat Cork,' said selector Joe Keohane, 'we will win the All-Ireland. This is my fifth year saying that, and so far I've been right four times.'

It was another boiling day as they took the field in Killarney in front of over 34,000, and as the game began, Cork were worrying Kerry again. Charlie Nelligan was forced to make two superb saves from Ephie Fitzgerald and Declan Barron. Dinny Allen missed a penalty and Tadhg Reilly fluffed another goal chance. John O'Keeffe was gone with an injury after twenty-three minutes and Kerry were rattled.

Then, as the heat increased, Cork started to burn up. Sean Walsh was continuing a storming summer and Ogie Moran was looking comfortable on the wing. Ger O'Keeffe continued his run of form while Tim Kennelly was reborn at centre-back. By half-time, Kerry led 1-10 to 0-4 and steam was billowing from beneath Cork's bonnet. Midway through the second half they had blown up. By then, Tom Spillane had properly announced himself in the grand way Spillanes liked to. He embellished his day with four points, and with minutes left, intercepted a pass to begin a move that ended with Mikey Sheehy deftly chipping the ball over goalkeeper Michael Creedon into the net. By then the crowd were drifting away. Kerry won by 2-18 to 0-12 and all the good Cork had done over the year was lost in the wreckage of a 12-point defeat.

'It was a Kerry team that simply was not prepared to lose,' said the *Kerryman*, 'a Kerry team with the killer instinct as strong as ever.' After the game Ogie, Eoin Liston and Sean Walsh supped their pints in Killarney among the Kerry supporters, warmed by the evening sun and the satisfaction of sending Cork home beaten. All around them the talk wasn't of five-in-a-row any more, but six-in-a-row.

With Cork out of their hair, there seemed to be nothing for Kerry to fear. They trained six days out of thirteen before the All-Ireland semi-final against Armagh and headed for Dublin that Saturday morning. The small crowd that travelled from Kerry confirmed the quiet belief that the Ulster teams were incapable of competing with them, but in comparison to other summers, the year had already borne its share of frights and scrapes.

Only 17,523 turned up at Croke Park but the opening minutes brought them to the edge of their seats. Inside twelve seconds Kerry's full-back line had been torn apart and Charlie Nelligan was forced into a save from John Corvan. Fran McMahon rattled a shot off the crossbar before half-time. Brian McAlinden saved a penalty from Mikey Sheehy. Joe Kernan was bustling away against Tim Kennelly, and the noise from the disparate pockets of Armagh supporters echoed around the ground.

A goal from Mikey Sheehy appeared to restore order after fifteen minutes, but instead Kernan punched a cross past Nelligan minutes later. Armagh were only trailing by a point, 1-5 to 1-4. With their defence in ribbons and Armagh making progress at centrefield, Kerry suddenly straightened up and kicked for home. Five unanswered points put Armagh away, and in the stand Eugene McGee was reminded of Offaly's experience in the 1980 semi-final. For all their endeavour, Armagh still had much to learn.

The second half descended into a rout. Ger Power and Ogie Moran burned the flanks up with their pace, while Egan maintained his glorious form. His goal finished Armagh, and as the game wound down, Pat Spillane jogged on for Ogie. They won 3-15 to 1-11, but O'Dwyer and his selectors could see problems. The full-back line had been stretched, and this talk of five-in-a-row was about to start blaring in their ears wherever they went. As Mikey Sheehy left Croke Park that evening, a group of Armagh supporters approached him for autographs. One little girl held out a scrap of paper. 'Can I get your jersey from you after the final?' she asked. Sheehy thought for a second. If Kerry won, he knew the jersey would be worth something, not financially but emotionally. In itself, the sweat-soaked jersey would represent his lifetime of football, but he had never placed too much stock in mementoes, and he wasn't going to start now.

'Of course you can,' he replied.

They had a date and a meeting point. Two weeks later, the Rose of Tralee competition took the county's attention and Kerry disappeared behind the gates to their sanctuary in Fitzgerald Stadium. There, as the evenings grew colder and September weather started creeping in, they could start thinking about history.

*　　*　　*

That August, Johnny Mooney returned from San Francisco with a face as red as a beetroot and looking sleek, but as Offaly prepared to play Galway in the All-Ireland semi-final a few days later, there was nowhere to put him. Richie Connor had returned from injury and Seamus Darby was flying in training. The Sean Lowry experiment had been an unqualified success and with Connor available, McGee had options.

He had thought about Richie Connor as a centre-forward from the beginning of the year, but had rarely used him there. Such a fundamental alteration threatened the entire structure of the team without a proper replacement. Richie had the size and the brains to match Kennelly. For now, McGee slotted him in at centrefield, with Padraic Dunne at wing-forward and Gerry Carroll in the centre. Even if it didn't work, Galway, McGee reckoned, wouldn't get near them.

Then his plans started to fray at the edges. Seamus Darby tore a hamstring before the game and spent the weeks before the semi-final in physio Amy Johnson's waiting room in Dublin alongside Jimmy Deenihan. Darby's injury was Mooney's chance at starting. He hadn't done much training with Offaly, but, after a year away, he could see a difference in the team. Their passing was quicker, sharper and much more accurate. Their training games were now played at a lightning pace. There was an edge to their attitude, too. After a year psyching himself up to perform when he came home, Mooney fell effortlessly into the groove.

'I came in with a very clear head. I knew I was going to play well in that semi-final. There was nothing dragging out of me at all, I only had to play football. I was carrying no baggage.'

By now McGee's attitude almost unconsciously dictated the mood of the players, and his belief that Galway would be dismissed had seeped across. The night before the game, he spoke to them with less fervour than usual. The training had been scaled back to slow Offaly just enough to get past Galway and give them a chance to peak again for the final, but it was a gamble that almost cleaned them out. With ten minutes left, Galway were ahead by a point. McGee started Johnny Mooney at corner-forward and only a consummate performance was keeping Offaly alive.

It was vintage Mooney. He won everything in the air and his kicking was razor sharp. The pace of the game didn't trouble him. As Offaly leaned on his shoulders all afternoon, he had no trouble bearing the weight. At one point Offaly had trailed by five, but a glorious crossfield pass from Mooney put Brendan Lowry through for a goal.

Elsewhere, Offaly were threatening to buckle under the pressure. McGee had moved Richie Connor to centre-forward, but on the sideline, John Dowling had the piece of paperwork completed to withdraw him. With eight minutes left, Connor launched a shot from near the sideline over the bar. Offaly were ahead for the first time. Connor had saved himself.

'All we had to do was keep playing,' says Padraic Dunne. 'I never even thought once that Galway were going to beat us. I went over to the dugout with about ten minutes to go to get a drink of water and someone says: "Would you ever get back out there!" And I says: "We have them beat." It was extraordinary. We had Galway beaten and that was it. I never dreamed they could beat us.'

The game ended with Galway missing frees and Offaly hanging on by their fingernails. They won by a point. The final whistle brought no reaction. No emotion. 'It just felt like destiny,' says Mooney.

He finished the week as the *Irish Independent*'s Sportstar of the Week, and being home and playing for Offaly felt good. That night Jimmy Deenihan's old coach, Dave Weldrick, analysed both All-Ireland semi-finals for 'The Sunday Game' and produced a series of clips to highlight the gap between Kerry and Offaly. It helped pitch the public mood, and maddened the players in Offaly. The following Tuesday, McGee took them back to Clonin Hill and ran them into the ground. Sprint after sprint to exhaustion. More crushing piggyback rides. Laps piled up on laps.

McGee watched the players for a reaction, but they never flinched. He watched Martin Furlong as the old man bounded to the top of the hill. Their Calvary had almost killed them in the spring, but now they had conquered even that. One mountain left to climb.

12 SIREN SONGS

The Scór club in Our Lady's Psychiatric Hospital in Cork city was a feisty, cheery collection of singers, storytellers and dancers. Three girls made a fine-sounding ballad group, and people liked to hang out on the fringes with them. On the evenings they weren't in competition, they would sing songs in the pubs around the city. They had won All-Irelands and drawn recognition everywhere they went. They were the Scór club's shining jewel, but one evening in 1979 they hit a problem.

With a local competition in Coachford a day away, two of the girls fell ill. They needed to find replacements. The secretary of the Scór group knew where to go. He went looking for Declan Lynch.

Lynch was a psychiatric nurse in the hospital, but he was known as a singer too. When the group's set list dried up on their nights out, Lynch was always there to pick up the slack. He was blessed with a rousing voice and a personality that demanded – and commanded – the stage. In the hospital he had befriended people who loved folk music, could play instruments and belt out songs when the night called for it. Could he pull a group together for the weekend? He agreed to try. He got three friends to join him. By Sunday, the roof on the hall in Coachford had been lifted off, and Galleon had taken to the skies.

Lynch was the front man. He was gregarious and boisterous on stage. He wore costumes and filled his songs with jokes and catchy hooks. In time, Galleon filled pubs and venues all across the south. Noel Magnier was their manager and he sensed big things. There was a wild streak in their songs and their image, and the crowds loved them. All they needed, reckoned Magnier, was a break.

Aside from music, their weekends were built around football. The group was filled out by two Corkmen, Mick Mangan and Ger Walsh, and Kerryman Tim O'Sullivan, from Killarney. The boys followed Kerry everywhere, but nothing beat the adventure involved in heading to Dublin.

They had arranged a string of pubs into their weekend routine over the years, and filled them all with their own songs. There was one tune that never seemed complete, but always stuck in their minds. Lynch had liked the melody from the first evening he composed it. It swung gently along, almost like a languid version of 'Auld Lang Syne'. In the pubs, lads would ask them for a song, and as long as Kerry kept accumulating All-Irelands they had a verse to fit the tune and the occasion.

In 1979 it started as 'Two in a Row'. In 1980 it expanded to 'Three'. By 1981 it had reached 'Four' – and the free pints were more than paying its way. By September 1982 the song was due another alteration, but Magnier and Lynch sensed it had the capacity to achieve even more than a few laughs. The right song this September could change their lives for good.

*   *   *

One evening in early September, Lynch started to work with some lyrics. He dredged up a few lines that had been rolled out on previous September Sundays, and laced them together with some new ones. Praising the Kerry players came easily, and prodding the Offaly team with good humour came quickly to him, too. Matt Connor was the only player any right-thinking Kerry person was concerned about – but Lynch could puncture that notion. By the end of the night, he had a song. It felt good. It felt right. He called it 'Five in a Row'.

Five in a Row

You've read in the papers
Of teams from the past,
Of Galway and Cavan
And Dublin so fast,
But none can compare
With the green and the gold,
Who are first to be champions
Five times in a row.

It started in a downpour in '78,
Against the Super Dubs who thought
We just didn't rate.
Paddy Cullen's hindquarters
We'll never forget,
'cos he picked it five times
from the back of the net!

CHORUS
And it's five in a row,
Five in a row,
It's hard to believe
We've got five in a row.
They came from the north,
South, east and the west,
But to Micko's machine
They're all second best.

'Twas the Dubs once again in '79,
Jimmy Keaveney was trained
On gin and slimline.
But the blackguards with placards

Were up on 16
When the Dubs were mowed down
By O'Dwyer's machine.

Next came a soldier,
Dermot Earley by name,
His regiment had plans
To win the big game.
They couldn't win Sam
At the match in Croke Park
But we wonder who stole it
In far off New York!

CHORUS

In Offaly Matt Connor
Is a footballing star,
He scores goals and points
From both near and far.
In Kerry we call him
A meteorite,
Because his star, it had fallen
By All-Ireland night!

Offaly will win in '82
We'll hammer John Egan's
Famed green and gold crew'.
But The Bomber and Jacko and Sheehy said, No!
'Cos we're keeping Sam
For our five-in-a-row!

CHORUS TWICE

They talked about getting Micheál Ó Muircheartaigh to add a commentary to the track, but the music and the chorus were enough of a hook. Galleon were in business. To relieve their consciences of any concerns about loading pressure on to the players before they even played the game, Lynch ran the idea past a few players. 'To be quite honest we didn't lose much sleep over it,' says Lynch. 'We couldn't see Kerry being beaten.'

No one objected. One player even sold copies of the single. 'Five in a Row' was ready to released to the world.

For the month of September it dominated Galleon's set list. Before they played the song, Lynch would put a Kerry jersey on and pull out a green and gold hat and scarf. The crowd loved it. Later that month, Galleon headed to a recording studio in Ballyvourney and recorded the track. They ploughed IR£5000 into launching the single, and the song was stitched into every playlist across the country. It was a hit.

The players were happy, the public were delirious. If sales kept rising, Galleon could become the boys' fulltime occupation. One more All-Ireland title for Kerry, and a new life could begin on Monday.

Back in Kerry other people were working the angles. With five-in-a-row as part of every conversation in the county, there was money hiding behind the phenomenon. Down in Lacca Cross near Ardfert, a man had an idea about some T-shirts. Although Dublin had generated support draped in colour during the seventies, and Cork crowds were always splashed with red, Kerry hats and flags were a rarity in the crowd when they played. The era of the replica jersey was still twenty years away. The market was wide open. Printing a five-in-a-row logo wouldn't cost a fortune, and there was a population certain of victory and ready to buy them.

He sold them outside Fitzgerald Stadium. They were available before matches. A newspaper advertisement appeared one weekend in the *Kerryman*. Tom's T-Shirts were available by mail order, emblazoned with the logo 'Kerry 1982 5 In a Row Year'. T-shirts were IR£5. Sweatshirts IR£7.50. Commemorative plates and mugs followed. At a county board meeting, the concept behind the T-shirts was embraced as a proud show of local pride. Football had seen nothing like this before.

'It was seen that the five-in-a-row T-shirt was a great thing,' says then Kerry County Board vice-chairman Sean Kelly. 'People said, okay, it's a bit presumptuous, but it was a fitting memento for something that was going to happen.'

There was something in five-in-a-row for everyone. Down in Tralee, the GAA clubs were getting restless. Football has always been at Tralee's heart, helping pump the blood that makes the town live and breathe. In time, the streets were named after great football men – John Joe Sheehy Road, Dan Spring Road. Strand Road was where Kerin's O'Rahilly's were based. Rock Street was home to Austin Stack's. Boherbee housed the John Mitchel's club. Great players tumbled from their histories and stitched the rich fabric of Kerry football together. Now, on the cusp of Kerry's greatest footballing achievement, Tralee wanted a piece of the action.

The talk had already begun a month after the world tour in 1981. At the December county board meeting, the Tralee delegates were keen to discuss the plans for the next All-Ireland homecoming. The routine had been set in stone for years. On Monday night the train from Dublin arrived in Killarney first. The following evening the cavalcade always moved on to Tralee and a welcoming procession through the town, but now Tralee were feeling left out. The clubs wondered why Killarney should always get Monday night with the team. With five-in-a-row on their minds, it was a good time to buck the trend.

That evening's meeting sparked with annoyance. 'We feel they should come to Tralee on the Monday night,' said Ted Fitzgerald of the John Mitchel's club in Tralee. 'Once every two years at any rate.'

'Monday night is *the* night,' said another Tralee delegate. 'Let it alternate between Tralee and Killarney.'

The mood at the top table was unsettled. As vice-chairman of the Kerry County Board, Sean Kelly was quietly climbing his way through the administrative structure. He was interested in hurling, but when the footballers were training in Killarney he often joined in. Other nights he might be asked to referee a practice game. He knew that the players' attitude contained nothing of the hubris he could sense among the delegates before him. It made him uneasy.

'It was seen as a bad omen,' says Kelly. 'Even discussing it wasn't a good idea. That was part of the over-confidence there. We were going to win, so we've to make sure we're in for the glory.'

The argument quietly rumbled on into the summer and gradually seeped through to the players. One afternoon, Tom Spillane was driving when a radio discussion turned to the homecoming. 'Some woman rang in and says: "I think the cup should stay in Tralee because it's much better fun." We hadn't even won the cup yet, and to be talking like this! I hoped no one else heard that comment.'

If the players didn't hear on the radio or read about the impending feud in the newspapers, there were plenty in the streets to let them know.

'That annoyed me,' says Charlie Nelligan. 'That brought me back down to earth fairly fast. I was thinking: what the hell are they doing? We've nothing won yet.'

The hype was starting to swirl around them. Hawkers were selling T-shirts and mugs and commemorative plates around Fitzgerald Stadium and across the county. 'Five in a Row' was steadily climbing the charts.

'Any time you were out in the street, people had you as roaring hot favourites,' says Ger O'Keeffe. '"Ah, you'll make the five-in-a-row now. You'll make history." Nobody in the county could see defeat. I was on a wave of complete belief. Eventually some of that is bound to stick.'

The Saturday morning before the All-Ireland final, the members of Galleon gathered in a record-pressing factory in Dublin as their single was pressed and sleeved. A huge raft of employees had been brought in to work the weekend, as demand was expected to soar following a Kerry victory. The Dubs slagged the Kerry boys about ruining their weekend even when Dublin weren't in the final, and all seemed right with the world.

Behind the gates down in Fitzgerald Stadium, the players remained unperturbed. Galleon's old songs had always been wafting around in the background. After every All-Ireland a portion of the local newspapers' letters pages had to be devoted to a collection of poems proclaiming the team as the greatest. O'Dwyer sheltered the players as best he could, but the wave of hype and colour was becoming too much. The gravity of the day was starting to weigh on them all.

'You try and hide yourself away from it,' says Tom Spillane, 'but it's always there.'

The final couldn't come soon enough.

13 COUNTING DOWN

A few weeks before the All-Ireland final, Eugene McGee took a phone call from David Walsh of the *Irish Press*. He was looking for a new angle on the jaded old topic of a team on All-Ireland week, and he had an idea he wanted to run by him. Walsh wondered if he could train with the Offaly team for a night. McGee respected Walsh and liked his suggestion. They settled on Monday night, six days before the final.

Walsh arrived in Ballycommon early, jittery with nerves. All week he had fretted over the smallest details. He worried about the dress code. He didn't want to look too formal in a pristine new jersey, or too scruffy in a battered old training top. He called Liam Lyons, an old friend who had won an All-Ireland minor medal with Mayo. He had kept his jersey as a memento, but agreed to lend it to Walsh for the night. An old county jersey would look worn enough, and carried some street cred. As Walsh jogged out on to the pitch, McGee looked at the jersey and frowned.

'What the hell are you wearing?' he asked. 'Get that off.'

He rummaged in a bag and pulled out an old Offaly jersey. With that he turned to the players. 'This man is from the *Irish Press*,' said McGee. 'He has come to train with us. He won't interfere with you and I'm sure you won't interfere with him.'

Then, without warning, McGee named the team for the All-Ireland final: Martin Furlong, Michael Lowry, Liam O'Connor, Mick Fitzgerald, Pat Fitzgerald, Sean Lowry, Liam Currams, Tomás O'Connor, Padraic

Dunne, John Guinan, Richie Connor, Gerry Carroll, Brendan Lowry, Matt Connor, Johnny Mooney.

There was silence. Between the lines was contained the story of Offaly's summer and the breadth of McGee's thinking. Mick Fitzgerald and Michael Lowry had been swapped to allow Fitzgerald follow Mikey Sheehy. Matt Connor was switched from wing-forward to full-forward to give John O'Keeffe something to chew on. Richie Connor stayed at centre-forward, and Sean Lowry at centre-back. Having used John Guinan's heft at full-forward against Galway, he was now released to the wing where he could physically match Tommy Doyle.

Gerry Carroll had moved to wing-forward during the Galway game and was retained there. From the team that had lined out against Louth in their first game in the Leinster championship, three players had been dropped and only five held the same positions all summer. It was a team that had transformed itself throughout the championship, though the hand of its creator was constantly evident.

The players arranged themselves in a circle and Tom Donoghue eased them through their stretching exercises. 'You know, lads, we've been very lucky with injuries this year,' he said. 'It'd be a pity if things went wrong now. So stretch those hamstrings.'

Offaly were on a high. Two days earlier, on Saturday night, they had crushed Down in a challenge game that left the Down officials certain Offaly could win. Now they played a match that concentrated on the handpass at blinding pace. In the middle of the field, marked by Tom Donoghue, Walsh tried to keep track. 'The game was one with a purpose,' he wrote. 'All passes had to be fisted, and preferably of the short and safe variety. McGee argued that long and loose punched passes wouldn't do against Kerry and they wouldn't do now. The Offaly team coach also insisted on the absolute need to have the man in possession supported. The Kerry style has won friends and influenced people.'

There were a few hits, but nothing severe. A few balls were even popped in Walsh's direction. He was their guest, and the players were gracious hosts. Then, the last ten minutes were played in utter silence. On All-Ireland day, said McGee, the noise means you won't be able to hear even the person beside you. They needed to learn how to get a pass when they couldn't call for it.

The following night the rest of the assembled press travelled to Ballycommon and filled their notebooks with tales of the quaint little pitch by the humpback bridge and the gutsy little team it was hosting. All the work had been done, but the mood was tense among the players. A shipment of football boots had arrived from Adidas with instructions that all players were to be seen wearing them. Gerry Carroll never cared for Adidas boots. His feet were wide, and these sponsored boots pinched his feet. He'd stick with his own.

When he told McGee, McGee's face turned to thunder. 'Why aren't you wearing them?'

'Because they don't have my size,' replied Carroll.

McGee walked over to a pile of shoeboxes filled with boots and found some in his size.

'There.' He threw a box of boots at Carroll. 'Now fucking wear them,' said McGee and headed for the dressing-room door.

Carroll snapped. He caught the boots, flung them at McGee and watched them fly past his ear before landing at the feet of RTÉ reporter Mick Dunne. McGee kept walking.

Sean Lowry sensed mutiny. He stood up, slammed the dressing-room door closed, and turned to Carroll.

'Gerry, you have to apologise to him. Otherwise we're at nothing. You can wear what you like the day of the All-Ireland, I don't give a shite. But let on you're wearing them anyway, and apologise to him.'

Deep down, Carroll knew he must. The team wasn't playing just for McGee. They had bonded together like family. Endangering that bond was the most treacherous thing he could do.

The players assembled in a circle before training. McGee was almost purple with rage. Some reckoned Carroll was about to be sent home. Just as McGee was about to speak, Sean Lowry made an announcement.

'I think Gerry Carroll has something he'd like to say.'

Carroll apologised to McGee and his teammates. The tension evaporated, and the players trained. Afterwards, the press descended. As Pat Fitzgerald chatted to one journalist, he sensed a tone behind his questions. Finally, the journalist got round to the point: 'Pat, ye can't be serious about beating these fellas. Sure, they're going to hammer ye!' Fitzgerald bristled, and left the conversation at that. If that was the feeling in the outside world, he thought, they're in for some fright.

That night McGee flicked on the radio as he drove home. The late-night sports news carried Kerry's starting line-up. Although his own team were looking good, he had one concern. Ogie Moran.

He knew Ogie from UCD. His mobility was one of Kerry's greatest weapons. His passing was exceptional and his relationship with the forwards around him, particularly Eoin Liston, was intuitive. In reshaping his team to beat Cork, O'Dwyer had nudged Ogie out to the wing. It was never something that bothered Ogie, but Ogie preferred the centre and Kerry always moved more fluidly with him there. He had played at wing-forward in the 1976 All-Ireland when Dublin defeated them. When Dublin beat them again in 1977, Ogie had again been shunted out to the wing to handle David Hickey. Ogie at centre-forward had always been a good omen for Kerry, and it seemed to make sense against Offaly. Pitting Ogie's pace and cleverness against Sean Lowry could severely stretch the Offaly defence, while Tom Spillane's strength against Pat Fitzgerald might be too much to handle. In contrast, Fitzgerald had the pace for Ogie, while Lowry had the cuteness and the power to handle Spillane.

McGee listened to the announcer work his way through the team: 'Charlie Nelligan, Ger O'Keeffe, John O'Keeffe, Paudie Lynch, Páidí Ó Sé, Tim Kennelly, Tommy Doyle, Jack O'Shea, Sean Walsh, Ger Power …'

McGee braced himself.

'Tom Spillane, Ogie Moran …'

Yeeeesssss!!!!

McGee's emotions came tumbling out. He roared and cheered. He banged the steering wheel. He stopped his car and leapt out. He punched the air with delight and relief. Ogie was on the wing. He could feel the Sam Maguire cup tickling the edges of his fingers. Everything he could control was in control. Everything beyond his reach was falling into place, too.

Training ran like clockwork for the rest of the week. Sometimes McGee simply stopped the session when the intensity of the action got too much. No point in burning them out now. One evening he stopped a practice game and gathered the players in the middle of the field. He had one question for them. Could any of them see their fellow team player being bested on Sunday? Could Brendan Lowry see Mick Fitzgerald being destroyed by Mikey Sheehy? Could Michael Lowry imagine Paudie Lynch holding Johnny Mooney all day? Could Tomás O'Connor seriously see Sean Walsh coping with Padraic Dunne? Would Richie Connor allow Tim Kennelly the run of the field? Players shook their heads. As McGee sent them to the dressing rooms, they could feel the confidence starting to race through their veins.

In the three weeks before the All-Ireland final, Offaly trained nineteen nights out of twenty-one. Some nights they concentrated on running drills and passing. Others were devoted to marking. To disrupt Kerry's systems, they would need to mark their opponents with rigour and supreme discipline. Kerry's flowing style was based on one-twos – laying a pass off to a colleague before receiving it again, leaving the marker caught out. Stop that, and Kerry wouldn't be able to tear their defence apart.

McGee and his selectors had built little tripwires and traps into their line-up. With Mooney, Connor and Lowry as his full-forward line, McGee had stumbled on a stunning combination of skill, speed, strength and unfathomable genius. The options at his disposal were now endless. From training games, Matt Connor sensed that McGee had decided to use him as a decoy. McGee encouraged him to drift away from goal, leaving room for Lowry and Mooney inside. It was something McGee used to do with his Under-21s back in the seventies and with UCD before that, but it carried a steep element of risk now. Offaly had fêted and relied on Matt Connor for years. Now, they would mask their best punch and hope Matt would tug the strings from deep. When Kerry dropped their guard, Lowry and Mooney would provide their winning combination.

Aside from the need for Richie Connor to keep Tim Kennelly occupied all day, the management also thought about Jack O'Shea. Given his mobility and endless thirst for hard work, Padraic Dunne usually seemed more suited to following Jacko about the field. This time, Offaly would try something different. If the rest of the team disrupted Kerry in the manner McGee had planned, much of Jacko's running would be in vain. Dunne's movement might be something that could bother Sean Walsh. Walsh would probably expect a physical challenge like Tomás O'Connor, but O'Connor was vulnerable. His knee was still troubling him. He worked on the fourth floor with Bord na Móna, but had to take the elevator to work every day. Sometimes people joked with him about a super-fit footballer taking the lift. He smiled back, and wondered what they'd think if they realised he couldn't even manage one flight of stairs.

One evening Paddy Fenlon had taken O'Connor aside to talk to him about his fielding. 'He had noticed I was dropping quite a few balls,' says O'Connor. 'He said it to me, and I thought, he's right. "You're doing everything right," he says to me. "You're jumping, you're catching. But when you catch the ball, you're looking down to the ground to see where you're going to land." The minute he said it, I knew he was right. It was because of the knee.'

How they used O'Connor would be crucial. They needed him to mark Jacko. Don't chase him, they said, just hold the centre. 'Wherever he goes,' McGee told him, 'stay calm and stay where you are.' The plan went against everything O'Connor believed in. It hurt O'Connor any time his marker ever got the ball. It made him question himself. He knew that every time Jack O'Shea would get the ball praise would be showered upon him and questions asked about O'Connor. He had seen the abuse heaped on Aidan O'Halloran after the 1981 final when McGee had sacrificed him from the forwards to sweep around as a defender, allowing Páidí Ó Sé to rip Offaly apart as an extra attacker. Would *he* be made the scapegoat this year?

Otherwise, the team was flying. Every night they finished up with sprints and their jerseys stuck to their backs from sweat. Every night Sean Lowry came home with news for his wife, Nuala. 'It's getting better,' he would tell her. A week before the game, he started talking about winning.

McGee worked relentlessly on their minds. The Thursday night before the game, the players were gathered in Edenderry to collect gear for Sunday from Fr Heaney. McGee had organised a video for them to watch. When he pressed play, the 1981 All-Ireland final illuminated their screens. There was no commentary, and no interruptions from McGee.

For seventy minutes, the players watched the screen. They sighed and shook their heads at the wayward passes and the missed chances. The room bristled with annoyance. When the tape was over, McGee turned the television off, and wished them good night. He sensed the fury in his players. They knew they were better than that. If they were better than that, then they were ready to beat Kerry.

*   *   *

In Kerry the hype had got louder and louder until it started to give Mick O'Dwyer a pain in the ear. Another problem loomed. The jerseys.

No team, apart from Dublin, had ever caught the public's imagination like Kerry, yet the rewards for their hard work and dedication were modest. When he was a child, O'Dwyer's mother worked as head chef in the Butler Arms hotel in Waterville, and after dinner her son would collect leftover tomatoes from the plates to sell on. The money would pay for footballs and other luxuries, and his ability to spot opportunities hadn't diminished through the years. Kerry were a marketable asset. O'Dwyer knew how to work the angles.

The Kerry jersey provided fertile ground to generate money, but also formed the backdrop for years of battles. The GAA's rules said only Irish-made sportswear could be used by its teams, but as the markets opened up, foreign manufacturers took an interest. Kerry had first taken tracksuits and boots from Adidas in 1972, and by 1977 a formal arrangement was in place. Although Adidas was a foreign manufacturer, McCarter's of Buncrana, Co Donegal, carried the contracts for making Adidas jerseys and sweatshirts in Ireland, while Three Stripe International in Cork distributed the products. Although Kerry couldn't line out with an Adidas label, or take any payment for using their gear, they used their boots and jerseys while supplying posters of the team bearing the Adidas logo for sports shops around the country. When the press descended on Killarney, the players were regularly kitted out in Adidas shirts. O'Dwyer was rarely seen without an Adidas tracksuit.

The entire business had always made sections of the county board uneasy. Before the 1980 All-Ireland final, a mild spat arose between O'Dwyer, the players and the board about wearing Adidas boots for the game. In 1981 a contribution of IR£5,000 towards Kerry's world tour appeared on the accounts. No firm officially claimed the money, but Adidas were considered the likely donors. The 1982 All-Ireland final and another clash of colours with Offaly provided an opportunity for Adidas to provide a new design. They had big plans.

The new jersey was mint green with pencil-thin gold pinstripes. The Kerry players were happy, but the county board were edgy. 'It began to surface about a week or two before the final,' says Sean Kelly. 'People weren't too happy about it. It [the Adidas deal] used be mentioned on and off, but things like that were never really tackled.'

The first tremor had been felt around the Munster final. Before the drawn game, county chairman Frank King had threatened to resign over a dispute between the players and Croke Park over the origins of their shorts and shirts. Now, Croke Park was objecting again. The Friday before the final, word was sent to Kerry that the GAA was preventing the team from wearing the newly-designed jerseys. O'Dwyer was stunned. With two days to go, Kerry had no jerseys.

That night, McCarters in Buncrana received a call from Three Stripe International looking for a set of replacements. Taste or design concepts went out the window. Kerry needed something green with a hint of gold. Mild panic gripped the factory. They needed to find material for the jerseys, and staff to sew them together. The jerseys needed to be in Dublin by Saturday night. They pooled together what resources they could, and set to work.

That Saturday afternoon the Kerry team caught the train to Dublin, rolling north through the footballing heartlands they had conquered over the years. After weeks of talk and hype, the only place they could escape was here, among each other and those who understood the pressure they carried, but the frenzy around the team that had capsized the entire county's faculties was never far away.

As Mikey Sheehy and Sean Walsh stepped on to the platform in Heuston Station, the mania had come to meet them. 'Make sure ye're down on Monday night with the cup,' said one official, conscious that the players might make their own arrangements for the celebrations. Sheehy and Walsh bristled with annoyance. 'Will you give us a break,' replied Sheehy. 'There's a game to be won first.' No one was listening.

They reached Malahide and disappeared to perform their own rituals. That night, they regathered in the pitch dark on the beach, with aeroplanes droning overhead and nothing to illuminate the space in front of them but a cloud-covered moon. The players stumbled along before O'Dwyer brought them to a stop. His speech was an annual staple, never altered but consistently spellbinding. The instructions were simple: Sean Walsh was to stay in the middle when Jacko roamed, and while Jacko could roam wherever he wished, he was still required to win his share of ball around the centre. Bomber was to drift out from goal, allowing Sheehy and Egan to switch corners. The rest were to play their own game. O'Dwyer had them fit and believing in themselves. Quietly he worried to himself that his defence was beginning to creak badly without Deenihan, but there was no more he could do.

On these nights before he headed to bed, Jack O'Shea usually shared a pot of tea and a plate of sandwiches with O'Dwyer. They exchanged local gossip from home in south Kerry and lulled each other into a relaxed state of mind. O'Dwyer had watched Jacko grow from a ball-boy into one of the greatest players the game had ever seen. They had travelled together to Jacko's first training sessions, when Jacko would sit by his front window peering out, waiting for O'Dwyer to arrive. Some nights he came in a racy Ford Granada. Other nights he could pull up in a hearse borrowed from his undertaking business in Waterville. Some evenings on the way back to Cahirsiveen, they might be forced to make a stop to collect a corpse.

Now, Jacko was miles away in Dublin, grown up, with a wife and children, and for all the slagging and prodding Dwyer gave him, he knew he could trust him to the marrow.

They would talk on as the clock ticked past midnight. The hotel was silent. Mikey Sheehy was tossing and turning. Eoin Liston had switched off the greyhound racing on television and drifted off to sleep. John Egan slept the sleep of a contented man, one day away from delivering Sneem the greatest gift he could ever bestow on them. Their nerves were quelled. That night, as the players headed to bed, the new jerseys had arrived from Donegal and the intrusion on the players' evening was minimised. The jerseys and the songs and the squabbles over homecoming had drifted away into the background noise of All-Ireland weekend. Now the team were together, and alone. They would leave their mark on the day to come for all eternity.

*   *   *

Above: Kerry team before the 1982 All-Ireland football final. *Back row (l to r)*: Jack O'Shea, Paudie Lynch, Eoin Liston, John O'Keeffe, Charlie Nelligan, Tim Kennelly, Tom Spillane, Sean Walsh. *Front Row (l to r)*: Mikey Sheehy, Páidí Ó Sé, Tommy Doyle, John Egan (capt), Ger O'Keeffe, Ger Power, Denis 'Ogie' Moran. (*Photo: Don MacMonagle*)

Below: Offaly team before the 1982 All-Ireland football final. *Back row (l to r)*: Sean Lowry, Gerry Carroll, Padraic Dunne, Liam O'Connor, Liam Currams, Matt Connor, Tomás O'Connor. *Front Row (l to r)*: Michael Fitzgerald, Pat Fitzgerald, Martin Furlong, Richie Connor (capt), John Guinan, Johnny Mooney, Brendan Lowry, Michael Lowry. (*Photo: Joe O'Sullivan*)

Above: Martin Furlong, Seamus Darby and Richie Connor get ready for training at Ballycommon. (*Photo: Offaly Archaeological and Historical Society*)

Below: Offaly captain Richie Connor shakes hands with Kerry captain John Egan with referee PJ McGrath. (*Photo: Sportsfile*)

Above: Kerry's Jimmy Deenihan clears his lines during the 1982 National Football League semi-final against Armagh. A few months later, Deenihan's season and his career would be ended by a terrible leg injury.

(*Both photos: Don MacMonagle*)

Below: Kerry's John Egan prepares to shoot as the rain pelts down during the second half of the All-Ireland final as Offaly's Stephen Darby closes in.

Above: Contrary to every instruction he had received in the previous few weeks, Offaly's Liam Currams hares downfield to score the first point of the final, leaving Sean Walsh, Ger Power and Páidí Ó Sé in his wake. (*Photo: Sportsfile*)

Right: Kerry's Tommy Doyle bursts out ahead of Offaly's John Guinan. (*Photo: Sportsfile*)

Above: John O'Keeffe, Kerry's imperious full-back, during the 1982 Munster football final against Cork. 1982 would prove to be O'Keeffe's last All-Ireland final with Kerry. (*Photo: Sportsfile*)

Below: Offaly goalkeeper Martin Furlong evades the attentions of Kerry's Tom Spillane (11) and Eoin Liston during the last frantic minutes of the All-Ireland final. (*Photo: Sportsfile*)

The goal. (*Photos: Sportsfile*)

The goal. (*Photos – above: Sportsfile; below: Don MacMonagle*)

Above: Kerry officials Sean Kelly and Gerald Whyte console devastated Kerry manager Mick O'Dwyer at the final whistle. (*Photo: Don MacMonagle*)

Below: Offaly captain Richie Connor raises the Sam Maguire Cup behind a scrum of delirious Offaly players in the Hogan Stand. (*Photo: Sportsfile*)

Friday, 17 September 1982

The cars were pulled up on the ditches and kerbs outside Paddy Edwards's house as the evening drew in around Moate and the last of his relations, neighbours and old friends filed their way through his house to pay their respects. His mother, Rose, had died, and even the furthest branches of the family tree had travelled to mark the evening.

Paddy saw his first cousin arrive with his wife, and shook Sean and Nuala Lowry's hands. They sat together for a while. He was pleased to see Sean, especially this week. They talked about Paddy's mother and the family. It was hard. Sean had lost his own father four years before and still missed him, but you get over things. You move on.

As Paddy greeted more visitors, Lowry found a quiet corner and cradled a cup of tea in his hands. He could have done with his father this week. When Ned Lowry came home to Ferbane from Manchester in the fifties he brought a small platoon of children with him. Years later, people would say Offaly football's gain was Manchester United's loss.

For ten years Lowry had played for Offaly and seen every stage of the team's mortality: peak, decline and now regeneration. Lowry had earned this Sunday. At thirty years of age, time was starting to catch him, but he trained harder and smarter. He had cajoled his gifted younger brother, Brendan, away from soccer and into the team. Another brother, Michael, was there too. When Michael started getting his game with Offaly, people used to slag Seanie that it was great to see his son getting a run on the team with him. He was like an old oak tree in a team of saplings, sturdy and unshakeable. He understood Offaly and grasped the meaning behind Sunday's final. There would never be a final like this again. Of all the people he knew, his father would have understood that feeling best.

People recognised Lowry and shook his hand. He could read their smiles. They wished him well, but their faith was shallow. When Offaly met Kerry on Sunday, a vision of the team's mortality would surely pass before their eyes. Offaly would visualise their last hours: the avalanche of scores that would bury them, the crushing sense of powerlessness in the face of a vastly superior opposition. Lowry thanked each person for their interest, and wished the time away, waiting to leave.

A man came and sat by him. He introduced himself as Declan Carolan, an old friend of Paddy's. He talked softly about nothing in particular at first, but he knew Lowry and he knew something about sport. This weekend, of all weekends, Declan had a story he needed to tell him.

As a young boy, hurling had been Declan's game. Tipperary were his team and Pat Stakelum was his hero. When Tipperary won All-Ireland hurling titles in the forties and fifties, Stakelum was a vision of heroism. The radio at home sat on the window sill and as Micheál O'Hehir described the games, Declan imagined Stakelum at the centre of the whirl of action, dominating like a god, infallible and untouchable.

In time, Declan grew up and Stakelum retired and the memories were despatched to a corner of his memory, but sometimes he wondered where Pat Stakelum was. One afternoon in Athlone Golf Club, Declan was eating lunch and idly talking hurling with the man at the next table. His companion nodded towards the bar. 'Do you know who that fella at the counter is?'

Declan looked up at the stooped, grey man.

'That's Pat Stakelum.'

Declan froze. The longer he looked, the more the years fell away and the same features he had memorised from the pictures in the newspapers regained their vitality in front of his eyes. It was Stakelum all right. He had to meet him. He made his way to the counter, and tapped Stakelum on the back. 'Are you Pat Stakelum?'

Stakelum turned around. 'I am,' he said.

'You played for Tipp?'

'I did.'

They talked a while. They remembered games and players, and for a few minutes they were both young again. Now that he was older, everything about what hurling and Pat Stakelum meant to him was clarified. Players could never know their impact on the people who watched them, but Declan did. He leaned in towards Lowry.

'Remember that. When you go out on Sunday, you're going to be playing for people that you'll never see. People you'll never meet. You'll have people in Australia and New Zealand who'll have their chest out Monday morning if Offaly beat Kerry, but you'll never see them or have the feeling they're feeling.

'There's two days people take off in the year: the Grand National and the All-Ireland final. They're the two events people watch all the time. There's old women living down lonely roads in Tyrone and Fermanagh and these places, and they're rooting for you on Sunday, but you'll never meet them. You'll never realise the lift you'll give them if you beat Kerry on Sunday.'

Paddy Edwards looked across, thinking his cousin was cornered, but Sean sat with the man and talked with him for an hour. He had heard speeches of every tone and tenor in dressing rooms all over the country. He had heard them before Offaly won All-Irelands and when they were in decline, but he had never thought about his footballing life like this before. That night he thought about the All-Ireland final. This was a game for the ages. This game could change lives. He would remember that story on Sunday.

On the same evening, Eugene McGee had called into Peter Clarke's pub on Dublin Street in Longford for a drink and sat down with his evening paper. At the other end of the bar, a customer had struck up a conversation with the barman about Sunday's game. They didn't take long to get to the point. 'Offaly haven't a chance,' said the man. 'They'll be beaten out the gate.'

McGee gripped his paper and quietly raged to himself. For six years he had built Offaly up from nothing. He had made mistakes and learned. Kerry were great, but Offaly were good enough. He would tell them so the following night at their meeting in Tullamore. For two hours, McGee would hold the room spellbound. He would work his way through the Kerry team again as he had done all week. There was nothing there for them to fear. They had run Kerry close in the 1981 final and made mistakes. He would hand a slip of paper to each player, detailing their opponent's strengths and weaknesses, distilling years of information and tactical discussion down to a simple set of instructions. They could see it for themselves in games and training sessions. He would tell them. They were good enough.

He supped his pint and stored the anger for another time. Sunday would settle everything.

PART III

THE PEAK

14 THE MORNING

Athletic interests dominate your activity during the week. Perhaps you participate in some real competitive sport. If your particular interest is football you should get a lot of satisfaction as a result of being on the right side just now. A particular feature of this week's events is the way success comes in the most unlikely situations. Start off this week on a really positive note, and you can't go wrong

Sunday World horoscope for Scorpios, Sunday, 19 September 1982,

Eugene McGee's star sign

Sunday morning came hurtling at Seamus Darby like a freight train. He reached out from under the covers and looked at his watch. The time was heading towards ten. The train to Dublin was pulling out at 10.40. Veronica was asleep beside him. Furry feeling in his head. Stale taste of brandy on his lips.

They were late.

He scrambled his gear together, pulled on his green team jumper and got into the car. As he pulled out of Edenderry for Tullamore, he noticed the fuel gauge on the dashboard dipping into the red. They had to stop for petrol. Tommy Cullen's was the last stop out of town. Tommy had played football for Offaly and lost an All-Ireland final to Down in 1961, but this morning he was manning the pumps. When he saw his latest customer, he paused for breath.

'Are you not meant to be in Tullamore?'

'I was,' said Darby. 'I'm on the fucking way.'

Tommy filled the tank, and dug deep for a piece of wisdom for Darby to carry through the day. 'Well, you're late. You better move.'

As he swung his car into the train station, the last of the team was boarding. Tom Donoghue had returned from a quick trip home to gather up the net of footballs he had forgotten. Darby leapt on the train and the team were off.

With a carriage to themselves, the players settled down for the short trip. With the footballs safely stored away, Tom Donoghue regaled the boys with a dream that had visited him the night before. Offaly were playing Kerry in a schoolyard, scuffing the ball across the tarmacadam. In the end, he said, Offaly won by a point. 'I tell ye, lads,' he chuckled, 'it was one dream I didn't want to wake up from.'

That morning, all the Connors had been to Mass in Walsh Island. As he concluded his sermon, the local priest wished them the best of luck – and a hundred eyes drifted towards them. At that moment, something inside Richie Connor tightened up. It was strange. Walsh Island wasn't a place for heroes. Usually, people simply saw neighbours who were footballers, though cabinets all over the parish groaned with county medals. Willie Bryan and their brother Murt had brought Offaly's first All-Ireland back to Walsh Island, to the bonfires and the pouring rain. Today was different. There was history in this final, and the four Connors were bringing that to their neighbours' doorsteps that Sunday morning.

In Newbridge, Pat Fitzgerald was up and about early, breakfast eaten, bags packed. He was driving to Dublin, and leaving his car with his brother-in-law. There was nothing about the day that could creep up on him. There was no fasting, no worrying. Everything was ready. The butterflies were zipping around his guts as normal, but this time they were flying in formation.

When the train arrived in Heuston Station, the team bus outside whisked them away to the anonymity of the team hotel. McGee was waiting for them.

*   *   *

That morning, the trains pulling out of Kerry teemed with people. When the first train reached Killarney, Weeshie Fogarty and his son Ciarán stepped aboard and found some seats, the inheritors of an undying ritual. Fogarty had grown up in the town watching great teams roll out of the railway station for matches in Croke Park before returning with All-Ireland titles. In 1953 he listened on the radio as Kerry met Armagh in the final. Just before half-time, Bill McCorry of Armagh missed a penalty, Kerry cut loose in the second-half and poor Bill carried one unfortunate moment to his grave. Down in Killarney, it made heroes of local men.

'When that final was over and the full-time whistle went on the radio, we had arranged to go to the seminary field at St Brendan's College and we had a fifteen-a-side game. The match was gone into your blood and into your mind. The week previously we'd been collecting jam jars in the Killarney dump pit. We'd collect the jars, wash them and sell them. We were after buying a football for ten shillings and sixpence. When we were collecting the jars we found an old oil lamp and I brought the lamp home to my mother. It was shaped like a cup and she got out the Brasso and polished it up. And we played our All-Ireland final that Sunday for that cup with the ball we bought from the jam jars we had collected.'

Two years after the 1953 final, Fogarty travelled to Croke Park as Kerry beat Dublin, and never missed another final. He grew up among All-Ireland winners and learned to aspire to the same things. Fogarty would eventually play for Kerry at every level, and for years had lodged himself at the back of Fitzgerald Stadium to watch Kerry train. He had been there on Mick O'Dwyer's first night. He had witnessed Dr Eamonn O'Sullivan prepare teams at the end of a career that saw him win All-Ireland titles in five different decades stretching back to the twenties. He had worked under O'Sullivan in St Finan's, the psychiatric hospital tthat overlooked Fitzgerald Stadium.

O'Sullivan had been a revolutionary. A bell hung in one corner of his office, tinkling to notify the doctor of impending company. He carried himself with a certain air of detachment, as though more profound thoughts and ideas were always arresting his attention. He committed his thoughts on occupational therapy to print and allowed some of his patients work on the building of Fitzgerald Stadium. He also produced a training manual: *The Art and Science of Gaelic Football*. It quickly became a bible.

In time, Fogarty had become a referee and had officiated at Offaly's All-Ireland semi-final against Galway. Sometimes he wondered how many finals he might have refereed if only for O'Dwyer's team. Kerry's prosperity always doomed their referees to a career in the wings.

The mood around him on the train was cheery. The supporters weren't worried, and from what Fogarty had seen at close quarters, Offaly had nothing for Kerry to be overly concerned about. The journey passed merrily. They would be in Dublin soon.

The Kerry players' morning began with all the familiar trappings of September. For Mikey Sheehy, a day's fretting always began when he drew back the curtains and looked to the skies. This morning was grey, but no wind. Good enough, he thought. Too much wind was a free-taker's nightmare. The rain he could handle.

Downstairs, the hotel was emptied of supporters. The usual gaggle of players congregated in different groups, waiting for the day to begin. Jack O'Shea headed for the local pitch-and-putt course with the younger players and played a few holes. The same cackles of laughter that had followed Páidí Ó Sé the previous day in Killarney were there in Malahide. All the talking had been done on the beach and over the previous six years. There was nothing left to say. Time to head for Croke Park.

Some travelled by bus. A few travelled by car. Some players felt a tension that had never been there before. Mikey Sheehy had never known anything like it. Ger O'Keeffe had been worried for a while now, and the feeling in his guts didn't improve his mood.

'I was unbelievably nervous. The butterflies were extraordinary. A lot of us were mentally drained, and subsequently physically drained. Even Dwyer was tense. There was no cooling impact. But how could there be? We were there to make history. You had other teams who had won four in a row. It had been said to us: "You'll never be as good as the John Dowlings, the Paudie Sheehys, the Joe Keohanes." There would've been that little thing there in fellas' minds as well: if we win five in a row, we'll be known as the greatest Kerry team of all time. If you add all the little psychological bits and pieces knocking on your brain, you'll have enough of a collective amount of bullshit that you'll believe in the end.'

Back in the city centre, McGee had sent his players for a walk in Merrion Square. Now they were back for one final chat. The same simple message floated around the meeting. 'If each man doesn't believe he can outplay his opponent,' said McGee, 'there's no point in being there. We've worked for fifty-two weeks in the muck and dirt for this day. When the time comes, don't go out and waste it.' He turned to corner-back Mick Fitzgerald, and prodded him to speak. Fitzgerald had been added to the Offaly panel in 1973, the season after they won their last All-Ireland. He had been known as a centrefielder and in time would end his career having played in every position for Offaly aside from goalkeeper, but McGee had transformed him into a corner-back designed to hold Mikey Sheehy.

Fitzgerald burned with intensity. He had no patience for those who didn't put the work in, and over the years he reckoned some of those sorts had made the team before he did. When he questioned McGee's decisions, they butted heads. Both were stubborn, and in the end Fitzgerald had left the panel for a few years.

Since his return, the defence had solidified. Along with Sean Lowry, Richie Connor and Martin Furlong, he had become part of the team's conscience. Some players feared him. On match days he sought peace and quiet for his nerves to settle, and growled when people came near him. Training matches spent in his company were as brutal as competitive games. He demanded everything from those around him, but gave everything in return. Now, with a few hours left before the greatest challenge of their lives as footballers, after years of scrapes with McGee and tetchy training sessions, Fitzgerald was the one McGee sought.

'The only thing on my mind was that white thing. The ball. McGee had already mentioned it at an earlier meeting, about the importance of making sure Kerry didn't get it too easily. If we had our hands on it, we had to use it or put it out over the sideline. That was what was up here, in our heads. We had to put all the other stuff aside. Concentrate on this white thing.'

To Mick Fitzgerald every layer of hype and tactical thinking melted away. It was that simple.

*   *   *

Inside the Kerry dressing room, players were settling down, but county secretary Gerald Whyte was getting twitchy. Having conjured tickets from nowhere for the general public all week, now he couldn't secure one for himself. A limited number of sideline passes were issued to the senior and minor teams and, having squeezed as many people as he could into the dugout, Whyte realised he had nothing left for himself. As he argued with a Croke Park official for more space, he stormed out the door, cracked his head off the doorframe, and passed out. When he awoke, they had got him a ticket and others he was looking for, but a difficult afternoon was only beginning.

The new jerseys were missing. Whyte swept the dressing rooms. Nothing. He remembered bringing them out to the bus. Now, they were gone. He struggled back out to the bus and searched the baggage hold. He looked in the overhead racks and around the seats. Nothing. Then, at the very back, piled up in a tatty cardboard box, he found them. He sighed, lifted them up and headed back inside.

As the jerseys were given out, the players looked at them but didn't pause to consider their sartorial merit. It was just as well. They were green. Lime green. The yellow collars and cuffs didn't distract from the horror of the jersey that was being foisted on them for the biggest day of their lives.

'They were hideous,' says Tom Spillane. 'They weren't even a proper green. There were issues with that jersey. It didn't affect us, but our preparations were blighted.'

But in the end Tom didn't care. None of them did. Kerry had been chopping and changing jerseys for a few years against Offaly. 'The jerseys could be purple with pink spots,' said Mikey Sheehy. 'Whatever the people might say at home, Kerry jerseys wouldn't win a game against this crowd.'

They all went through their rituals. Charlie Nelligan sat silently, his back against the cold wall, eyes closed. His mind was in a state of near-delirium. When he opened his eyes, he felt dizzy, but it was familiar and made him feel better.

Ger Power was cool. John Egan sat beside Ogie Moran with a gentle grin playing around his lips. After all the political pulling and dragging of the summer, he had made it. Pat Spillane sat in his tracksuit top, willing his knee to be right. On the other side of the dressing room, Jimmy Deenihan sat, feeling a strange kind of satisfaction. He had never worn a tracksuit on All-Ireland final day, but at least he had made it. Páidí Ó Sé was starting to stoke the fires, while down the line John O'Keeffe was thinking of Matt. Only Matt.

Offaly were arriving. As the bus trundled over the Canal Bridge, 'Five in a Row' came blaring from the back of a van and wafted through the open windows. They got off the bus and waded through the crowd. Outside the ground, stand tickets costing IR£6.50 were being sold for IR£60. All down Jones's Road the flag and hat sellers were making a killing on five-in-a-row gear. As Richie Connor forced his way towards the players' entrance, a woman weighed down with five-in-a-row scarves stood in front of him.

'Hey mister! Buy a scarf! They're lovely!'

Connor pulled his kit bag from behind him and showed her the Offaly crest on the side.

'Ah go on,' she said. 'You'll take one anyway!'

As the minor final between Kerry and Dublin continued, Pat Spillane wandered out to the corner of the tunnel. A few minutes later he was joined by Liam O'Connor and Padraic Dunne. A few minutes passed before Dunne hopped the first ball.

'Who's winning?'

Spillane looked up. 'Kerry.'

'Right,' said Dunne. 'Who are you, now? Are you with one of the Kerry teams?'

O'Connor stifled a chuckle, and before Spillane had a chance to compose a reply, the kid was gone.

Down the hall, Eugene McGee was pacing. The old masseur, Ossie Bennett, was at his table, going through his list of patients. As McGee walked by, he grabbed his arm and pulled him in. 'They're as finely toned as you're going to get,' he whispered. 'They're perfect.'

Sean Lowry was talking out loud for anyone who would listen: 'Remember to change the studs on your boots just before you go out, so the loose grass won't stick to rough edges on the old ones,' he said. Other players and selectors moved through the players, calming some, rousing up others. All the pressure that had followed Liam Currams into the 1981 final had fallen away. Now it was just him and his friends. He was living in the moment, just as he knew he had to. As he slipped on his boots, he never felt the medal of the Holy Spirit his mother had quietly placed in it the night before.

Tomás O'Connor was winding himself up. Today he would quieten some people. A knot of nerves sat in the bottom of John Guinan's stomach and no amount of trips to the toilet could shift it. Mick Fitzgerald had entered his own world of silence. Only Mikey Sheehy could intrude on his thoughts.

It was almost time. Fr Heaney was flitting around the edges of the scene when McGee approached him and asked if he could say a prayer. 'I was totally flummoxed,' says Fr Heaney. 'But I said okay. There I was, stuck, wondering what was I going to say? So Eugene said: "Before we do anything else I'll ask Fr Heaney to say a prayer. We usually go to Mass together but we left it to yourselves." I just said one or two sentences. The main thing was to give us the conviction and the relaxation to perform. To show our talents. To thank God for the gifts we have and to take this opportunity. To have no fear.'

Then, McGee spoke. The message was simple. Remember what they had spoken about the night before and that morning. He told Gerry Carroll to avoid solo runs on his left foot, and Liam Currams not to hare upfield. Finding himself up there would be considered a crime. Shooting for goal was tantamount to murder. Then there was that song.

'They're talking about Matt Connor being a fallen star,' he said. 'Let the stars fall in that dressing room. You could go down as the team that gave the Kerry team the five-in-a-row, or as the team that stopped them. You've nothing to lose.'

Then, at the last moment, Sean Lowry told his story. He asked them to remember the people at home. Their people. They were carrying a small, noble tradition with them. Generations of players from Walsh Island and Ferbane, Rhode and Edenderry could never have imagined that an Offaly team could position itself so close to history. The mood lifted again. They walked out the door, leaving the lives they knew behind them.

*　　*　　*

Offaly trotted out on to the field and ran into a wall of noise. Michael Lowry jogged alongside the Hogan Stand and heard a shout: 'Come on, Ferbane!' Kay and Sean Flynn were neighbours from home and he waved back. For a second he thought about the hype and the noise, and the Artane Boys' Band and the thousands of others in the stands and terraces, and amid all the madness, he had heard a familiar voice. There was comfort in that.

The Kerry boys knew the track better and the noise and ceremony melted into a background hum. Charlie Nelligan brought Jacko in to take a few shots on him. Mikey Sheehy practised some frees. Grey clouds squatted overhead. The oncoming rain heavied the air with foreboding and mingled with the growing tension around the ground. The moment was upon them all.

The teams dispersed around the field and picked up their positions. Tim Kennelly jogged back towards the 65-metre line looking for Richie Connor, but first he met a fist that hit him plum in the chest. It stopped him dead. The wind whooshed out of his lungs, and as the pain spread through his chest, he went down on one knee. The Horse had fallen. He got up and looked for Richie Connor, disguising the pain as best he could. Ten minutes would pass before he could properly catch his breath again.

Meanwhile, the game had begun.

15 THE FIRST HALF

Everyone was ready. Weeshie Fogarty and his son Ciarán were in the upper deck of the Hogan Stand on the 20-metre line. Sean Grennan and his mother had travelled from Ferbane with their family and stayed with relations in Balbriggan, but tickets were hard to find. In the end they got enough for his mother and his aunt – and they lifted Sean over the turnstiles and took their seats behind the Offaly dugout, waiting and hoping.

Football needed Offaly to perform. The previous year's All-Ireland final had attracted an attendance of just 61,489. It was the lowest attendance for an All-Ireland final since 1947, and back then Cavan had played Kerry in New York. Kerry had taken their training and preparation to a new level, but few teams possessed the ambition or the application to follow them. When the Kerry boys in Dublin trained with other inter-county players in Dublin under Micheál Ó Muircheartaigh, many of the other players from different parts of the country would opt out as the Kerry boys piled lap upon lap. They were broken before they even played on a football field. Some commentators and football people blamed Kerry for draining the game of its excitement and variety, but it wasn't Kerry's fault. It was everyone else's.

Jimmy Eric Murphy, Mick O'Dwyer's oldest friend from Waterville, held O'Dwyer's son, Karl, by the hand as they ascended the steps of the Hogan Stand. Down on the sideline, Karl's father sat in the dugout with his selectors, wondering what Offaly might do to buck the trend. In 1980 they had sparred Kerry without ever laying a punch that hurt. In 1981 they had tried to tie them up, but Kerry got free long enough to win on points. What now? Trying to slug it out with Kerry seemed pointless. But Roscommon had tried to rough them up two years before and still lost. Cork had already plotted all manner of ruses and schemes in 1982 and only managed to knock a few feathers off them. What, wondered O'Dwyer and the world, could McGee conjure?

McGee had already told him. In *The Irish Times* the previous day, McGee suggested that O'Dwyer couldn't see his team losing the game unless the weather turned '… wild and wet. It is that belief which dictates the preparations of Offaly for this final. The conviction that to beat Kerry they must, to put it quite simply, play better and more skilful football than their rivals.'

His plan was simply rooted in faith. Every move had been choreographed and shaped to meet the demands of this day. One step out of place and the entire routine would fall asunder. All week McGee had believed his team were ready, but he worried too that Kerry could lift themselves to even more stupendous levels. They had already shown there was no limit to what they could achieve. As far as McGee knew, there was no limit to what they could produce in a game like this either. There was nothing he could do now. All he could do was believe in his players, and hope they truly believed in him.

They did. As the game began he watched his players moving around like pieces on a chessboard, seamlessly putting his plan into operation. He looked at his full-forward line. Matt Connor was wandering away from goal and John O'Keeffe was following him. Brendan Lowry was already feeling liberated without Jimmy Deenihan snapping at him. Ger O'Keeffe was different. O'Keeffe trusted his pace against anyone, and the confidence gained from a summer spent playing the best football of his life was coursing through him. He was a brilliant ball player, but Lowry was happy to stand toe-to-toe with him. In an even start, there would be little left between them, and the day was still playing on O'Keeffe's mind. Now it was seeping into his legs.

'I'd normally be on the tips of my toes fighting for the ball,' he says.

'But I was missing that burst off the mark that would get you to the ball. Possibly doing those extra sessions as the hare when the heavier fellas were coming in hurt me. If they were doing those scientific tests on me then, they'd have said I needed a rest rather than more training. By the time it came to the final, and all the pressure, I didn't perform.'

While Ger O'Keeffe worried, John O'Keeffe's heart was lifting. The further Matt drifted from goal, he reckoned, the less damage he could do. Even now he could match Matt's speed. He just had to watch his turn. But so far from goal? And McGee knew all this. What, thought O'Keeffe, was McGee at?

When he turned around towards his own goal, the pieces started to come together. Lowry and Johnny Mooney stayed close to goal. Lowry was a good match for O'Keeffe. Mooney was physically equal in stature to Paudie Lynch and moving irresistibly well. When the players around centrefield looked up, Brendan Lowry was darting from his corner across goal, looking for a pass. Everything else was lofted towards Mooney. By half-time, Lowry had gathered three points and Mooney had played a role in five scores, including one of his own.

Meanwhile, the hounding of Tim Kennelly continued. As Sean Lowry emerged from defence with the ball, Eoin Liston bumped him aside, sending the ball out over the sideline. Offaly worked the ball upfield before launching it towards Kennelly and Connor. A roar greeted Kennelly's catch, but out of his eyeline John Guinan had him fixed in his crosswires. First Richie Connor caught Kennelly with a shoulder, then Guinan clattered him. The hits sent Kennelly one way, then the other, snapping him in two like a twig. He hit the ground with a deadening thud. A moan whooshed through the crowd. Brendan Lowry tapped the loose ball over the bar, but referee PJ McGrath had already whistled for the free. The hit was worth even more.

'It wasn't intentional,' says Guinan, 'but I was going to run into Tim Kennelly no matter what. Kennelly was going to say: Well, Richie Connor didn't hit me, who did? Who's going to hit me next? Is this get Tim Kennelly day?'

Charlie Nelligan trotted out and boomed a huge kick beyond centrefield, where Padraic Dunne cleaned up the break. Out of the corner of his eye he saw Liam Currams warming his engine up for a burn. The first breach of McGee's regulations came after four minutes. If Currams got a point in training, he got a round of applause. Now he was haring forward towards the Kerry goal. On the sideline McGee was close to a seizure. He knew Currams better than any other player on the team, yet he was also the first player to go against McGee's instincts and trust his own. Out on the field Gerry Carroll was behind him, screaming at Currams to keep running. The space in front of him kept opening up. Ger Power raced back, attempting to catch him, but couldn't keep pace. Tim Kennelly joined the chase, but Currams left him behind too.

As he reached the 45-metre line, he braced himself, half-shut his eyes and kicked the ball in the direction of the goal. The ball sailed into the clouds, hanging in mid-air, before dropping incredulously over the bar. The crowd rose. His teammates rose. McGee shook his head. They would clap that one for decades to come. Offaly were one up. The archer had hit the target.

All over the pitch, Offaly were conceding nothing. The quicker Kerry tried to play, the harder Offaly ran and covered. When Offaly had the ball, their passing was short and quick. Their kick-passing was immaculate. Few passes were being risked without being fully assessed for their percentage worth. When Kerry attempted to set up plays, Offaly didn't allow them an inch, but Kerry were a team capable of unleashing forces beyond anyone's control.

When Tom Spillane got his first touch, he turned and beat Sean Lowry. He had Egan nearby and calling for a pass, but instead he kicked a soaring point from 40 metres. After nine minutes, Paudie Lynch set Ger Power racing at the Offaly defence. Currams shadowed him as Power laid the ball off to Liston. Conventional tradition usually saw Liston give the ball back to Power within milliseconds, allowing Power in on goal, but when Liston looked, Currams was at Power's shoulder, blocking his eyeline and preventing the pass.

For a second, the attack was floundering until Liston saw Egan. He took the ball 20 metres from goal near the Cusack Stand and jinked. With Michael Lowry on top of him, a point seemed unlikely. Egan only needed room to swing. His kick dropped over the bar. All Offaly's hard work was rendered useless by one touch of genius. People in the stands applauded and Offaly shook their heads. What hope had they?

The game continued to sort itself out. Padraic Dunne was doing well at centrefield. John Egan was leaping out of his skin. Eoin Liston was grappling with Liam O'Connor and bouncing off Sean Lowry, but making his lay-offs and setting up the plays. Páidí Ó Sé had taken some hard hits from Gerry Carroll, but he was starting to get forward and grabbed himself a point. Tom Spillane was also starting to run at Lowry. Offaly had stifled them, but Kerry still had room to manoeuvre. Offaly needed something else to get Kerry thinking. They needed another spark.

Out on the right wing, everything Pat Fitzgerald had thought about the final was coming to pass. It already felt like his day. Ogie Moran was nippy and skilful, but Fitzgerald had the pace to match him and his form was good enough to keep Ogie in check. Years later, when people talked about consistency, Fitzgerald would sometimes lay out a selection of dusty old programmes dating back to 1979, and ask them to check the owner of the number five shirt. Always Fitzgerald.

He was as reliable as the changing seasons, but McGee always wanted him to be more. For years he pushed him to broaden his game, to get forward. Fitzgerald tried. Sometimes it worked. Sometimes it didn't. Some evenings he would head to the pitch in Newbridge and practise attacking on his own. He would start his run deep in defence, see the pass coming in his mind's eye and pretend to grab it. Then he would push on for goal and take a shot, repeating the procedure all evening. Getting forward and taking risks was never in his personality, but Offaly needed something now. If he got the chance, he had to take it.

Padraic Dunne won another break, and fed the wandering Johnny Mooney. Fitzgerald saw space. He left Ogie behind and started to race towards Mooney. The pass lobbed into Mooney's chest, and he set off.

He was back in Newbridge. The crowd had melted away. All that was left was him and the black spot on the crossbar. Ogie was floundering. He cut in from the right and hit a shot with the outside of his right boot. The outside! Swerving and dipping, the ball dropped over the bar. Offaly were level again.

With nerves shaken out of them, Offaly were playing with abandon. Brendan Lowry darted from his corner to collect a couple of points. Richie Connor was dominating Kennelly, who had yet to gather a stray pass or begin to spread the ball about as he liked. The Fitzgerald brothers had Mikey Sheehy and Ogie Moran tied up in knots. Eoin Liston was winning some ball, but Liam O'Connor was a powerful stopper and Offaly were surrounding Liston at the breaks like an army of Lilliputians. Early in the game Liston stepped across Sean Lowry to stop him coming out with a ball and hit Lowry on the side of the cheek with his head. The second time, he stopped Lowry again.

'I was going for a pass and the next thing he walked out in front of me like an oul' cow. The next time I got the ball, I gave it to Pat Fitzgerald and he got in the way again. I pulled and hit him with my dead-level best [on the cheekbone]. He dropped down in front of me. I jumped across him and never looked back.'

Liston called to referee PJ McGrath and pointed Lowry out, but the referee waved away his complaints. Meanwhile, Lowry had another matter to settle. Tom Spillane had kept Kerry's score ticking over, and Lowry needed something to take into half-time for himself. Spillane's second point levelled the game after twenty minutes. As Tomás O'Connor jogged back out to contest Martin Furlong's kick-out, Lowry called to him. 'Next time you get the ball,' he said. 'Give it to me. I'll be gone.'

A few minutes later, Lowry's chance came. Having won another break, Pat Fitzgerald gave him the ball, and Lowry set off. More space yawned in front of Kerry's goal. Behind him Ogie Moran was frantically making ground. With every two steps Lowry took, Moran's speed was making up the gap in one stride. With 30 metres to go, Lowry had to shoot. Moran dived through the air and fell on Lowry's boot, but the ball was gone. The ball sailed over the bar, and Lowry punched the air.

'I turned round and there was a Kerry footballer giving out to Tom Spillane. Why wasn't he up after me? And Tom Spillane only nineteen and after scoring two points. I was delighted to see him doing it, but it shouldn't have been happening.'

All of Offaly's half-back line had scored. In the stands, the crowd hailed McGee's tactical chicanery. On the sideline, McGee took these freak occurrences in his stride. He had changes to make.

Offaly were on top, but Kerry were troubling them in parts. Michael Lowry had stuck like a limpet to John Egan and poked a few balls away, but Egan was like a ball of fire and leaving scorch marks on his man. McGee turned to the bench. Having seen all three half-backs score, Stephen Darby had quietly pulled a veil over his season and settled back to watch the final. Beside him, Seamus Darby's knees were jiggling. The forwards were going well, but things were tight. Of both Darbys, he was more likely to get the call.

When it came, they were both surprised. McGee swung around, calling for Darby. Stephen looked at Seamus, who was already getting his tracksuit top off. McGee looked behind again.

'No! Stephen Darby!'

Darby had never played corner-back at championship level before. His place was as an attacking wing-back. On the way home from training the previous Thursday night, Darby, Johnny Mooney and a few others talked about who they'd hate to mark on Sunday. Without hesitation, Stephen picked John Egan. Egan had strength, Darby was light and quick. On current form Egan was almost unmanageable. Now Darby was forced to confront his greatest fear.

With half-time closing in, Offaly had taken control. Brendan Lowry's third point put them three up, 0-10 to 0-7. Seconds after Lowry's last point, Egan had the ball out from goal and popped a pass towards Tom Spillane, who had wandered in near the endline. As Spillane miscontrolled the pass and the ball rolled towards Hill 16, Martin Furlong smelled blood. He thundered out of his goals and tapped the ball to Padraic Dunne. Dunne's foot-pass travelled 15 metres to Mick Fitzgerald who found Gerry Carroll. Carroll's chipped kick landed in Liam Currams's arms. He found Tomás O'Connor. Kerrymen were rooted to the ground like lime-green traffic cones as Offaly neatly slalomed through them. Kerry were being poked in the chest and pushed back towards a wall. They needed to respond.

With two minutes left to half-time, a long ball from Jack O'Shea finds Mikey Sheehy drifting across an empty corridor of space 30 metres from goal. He hits it to The Bomber, but Liam O'Connor beats him to it. Under pressure, O'Connor holds on to the ball too long, and Mikey taps his first free of the game: 10-8.

From Furlong's kick-out, Tim Kennelly gathers his first ball of the game, escapes Richie Connor and pushes forward. He kicks another long ball towards Liston. This time he beats O'Connor and turns to face Furlong. As he opens up to shoot, Pat Fitzgerald flings his arms around him, one hand attempting to block his shot, the other wrapped around his back. Liston loses his balance and falls out over the endline, and for a moment Kerry think about claiming a penalty.

Instead, the game has left them all behind. At the other end of the pitch the ball has found its way to John O'Keeffe, who is fouled by Matt Connor in a scrum of players. Richie Connor gives Jack O'Shea a nudge. Johnny Mooney steams into Jacko's back. Tim Kennelly and Paudie Lynch are hovering as Jacko squares up to Mooney. Kerry are at breaking point.

The free is worked downfield. John Egan races outfield and gathers the ball. Jack O'Shea is back in Kerry's attack to take Egan's pass. Two men converge on O'Shea, but he dodges them both and lands his shot over the bar. Suddenly Kerry are only a point behind: 10-9. PJ McGrath blows his whistle. A classic is taking shape.

No half in the history of All-Ireland football finals has ever witnessed 19 points, but that is only the beginning. Offaly have peaked at the very moment McGee wished, but Kerry have matched them. The crowd take a breath and the first heavy droplet of rain begins to fall. Officials are borrowing jackets and umbrellas from stewards to make it across the field without getting soaked. As PJ McGrath jogs to the tunnel, an old friend calls out to him from the stand. 'That's great stuff,' he says. 'Keep it going!'

As he runs across the field to the dressing room, Mick O'Dwyer's mind is racing. Ogie will be substituted. This is no time for weakness or misplaced loyalty. Time for change.

16 THE SECOND HALF

The Kerry dressing room was a worried place. Ogie Moran slumped down beside Egan and pulled his tracksuit pants on. The tension that had heavied the atmosphere before the game began hadn't lifted. Meanwhile, Pat Spillane started to warm up. O'Dwyer was gambling with high stakes, and the players knew it.

He had plenty of options. John L McElligott's form had been excellent all summer. Vincent O'Connor had been a reliable panellist for years; he could operate at centrefield or along the half-forward line. Tommy Doyle could switch into attack, allowing Ger Lynch to come on in defence. But in the All-Ireland semi-final against Armagh, Spillane had replaced Ogie. The players reckoned O'Dwyer had made a mistake, but O'Dwyer trusted Spillane. Maybe too much.

Spillane knew he wasn't ready. His knee was heavily strapped, but the joint still felt unstable. At times he thought of the 1981 final and how he had codded the doctors and O'Dwyer about the strength of his knee. He had done it again, but now O'Dwyer had unwittingly called his bluff. Spillane had to deliver.

Down the hall, Offaly players were bouncing off the walls. 'Where are the falling stars now, lads?' asked McGee, remembering Galleon's lyrics. 'Where are they now?' Lowry and Furlong, Richie Connor and Seamus Darby moved among the players again as they had before the game. Believe, they said. Believe. This time they had thirty-five minutes of perfection to back up their argument.

Only Matt didn't feel too good. The first half had passed him by.

Little of the play was running through him, and he reckoned John O'Keeffe had him in his pocket. He had gathered the first ball that landed between him and O'Keeffe. He tried to sell a dummy, but O'Keeffe wasn't buying. Connor bounced the ball but O'Keeffe slapped it away in mid-air and collected the ball as it hit the ground. In frustration Connor fouled him, and the crowd cheered. O'Keeffe had drawn first blood. By half-time, the wound still hadn't been staunched. Connor was being hard on himself. He had gathered three points, including one from play where he sold two dummies, left O'Keeffe on the ground and rifled a shot from 25 metres that skimmed the top of the crossbar.

Outside the rain was falling in sheets. Where the first half had been an epic game of perpetual motion and fluidity, the second promised a war.

When he hit the field, Spillane flexed his knee and shook hands with Pat Fitzgerald. Offaly returned unchanged. For six years, Kerry had learned to absorb pressure early on and blitz teams in the second half. Inside five minutes, Offaly were sent sprawling.

Mikey Sheehy pointed a free. Minutes later, Liam O'Connor spilled the greasy ball and Eoin Liston fed Pat Spillane. Spillane took a quick look and kicked with his right foot. Point. He punched the air and gritted his teeth. Kerry led by one. Spillane looked fit and ready. The pitch was getting heavier. Kerry were beginning to rumble.

Another Kerry attack. Eoin Liston stands alone at the front of the square as Tom Spillane bursts through the centre. His pass finds Liston, who lets the ball drop to the ground and shoots on the half-volley. It seems bound for the net, but bounces off Jack O'Shea. Offaly survive, but a loose pass allows Tim Kennelly pin Offaly back again. Offaly break out, but Matt Connor misses a free in front of the Kerry goals.

As the game headed towards the forty-five minutes, fifteen minutes had passed since Offaly's last score. Offaly's resilience would be tested at other times during the game, but never as fiercely as this. They had pounded Kerry, yet Kerry were still there. Still untouchable. Offaly had already proven themselves as a team capable of matching Kerry. Now, with the rain slaking down and the game turning against them, they had to find a way to beat them.

A high ball into the front of the Kerry square bounced over John Guinan's head. Even in the muddle of players, Ger O'Keeffe saw a terrifying gap in front of goal. Brendan Lowry was behind John O'Keeffe. If Guinan got the ball and transferred it, Lowry was in. O'Keeffe flung himself towards the ball as Guinan leapt into the air. Guinan's hip caught him flush on his chin. O'Keeffe was laid out, but Offaly had a free 20 metres from goal. This time Connor nailed it, and Offaly were level for the eighth time.

The game was swirling with intensity now. It was becoming clear that, to win five in a row, Kerry could leave nothing behind them on the field. More drama. Páidí launches a line ball at the Offaly defence. Pat Fitzgerald grabs the ball in front of goal but coughs it up. Liam O'Connor sweeps up, but his handpass is pilfered by Tom Spillane. Liam Currams hacks the ball away, but Sean Walsh sends it back towards goal to John Egan. His kick lands on the crossbar. Martin Furlong tries to catch it, but the ball bounces off the black spot into the square. It sits like a grenade waiting to go off. Furlong dives headfirst to smother it. Liston lands on top of him. Free out. Furlong shrugs The Bomber off. He bangs his shoulder with his fist three times, screaming. Not one step back. Not one.

A Sheehy free puts Kerry ahead again and John O'Keeffe wins another ball above Matt Connor. He holds the ball above his head, offers it to the heavens and bounces it off the turf. Kerry pour forward again and Offaly are caught short in defence. With the ball heading towards John Egan, Furlong races out and sweeps the ball away, but Tom Spillane gathers it again and feeds Egan on the edge of the square; Egan leans into Stephen Darby and tries to find a way past. Darby holds his arms out and tries to resist fouling him, but gravity takes over. Egan falls with Darby beneath him. As he gets up, Darby has a clump of Egan's jersey in his hand. Egan leans in to shoot again, and falls for the second time. It's enough. PJ McGrath whistles. Penalty.

Darby throws the ball away, but Offaly's protests dissolve without incident. A bottle comes flying on to the pitch. Liam O'Connor picks it up and flings it back into the Canal End. 'Cop on, Liam,' shouts Mick Fitzgerald. 'Concentrate!'

Kerrymen are looking round for Mikey Sheehy. Offaly are looking at Martin Furlong. Two men. One moment.

17 MIKEY AND MARTIN

The ball sits on the penalty spot, unattended. No one dares touch it. Kerry lead by one point. A Kerry goal now would decide the game. Five-in-a-row could be decided in an instant.

Finally Mikey Sheehy steps forward, and replaces the ball on the ground. He looks at Martin Furlong, then trains his eyes on McGrath. He waits for the nod. His mind is turning over. The memory of his missed penalty in the semi-final against Armagh is gone. The previous Tuesday night in training he had smashed eighteen penalties out of twenty past Charlie Nelligan. He had thought this out. He reckoned Furlong was weaker on his left side. Don't go for power. Place it. Stroke it, don't blast it.

In goals, Furlong is waiting. The game is between them. Everything that went before or that is yet to come could be rendered irrelevant in this moment. Mikey begins his run-up. Six steps between him and immortality.

One step …

Mikey was the first at home to make it as a footballer and nothing ever compared to that. Years later his father would slip on the *Golden Years* video and watch it through when Mikey might call. 'He had it worn out,' says Mikey. 'When I was retired [from football] I often used go over in the evenings during the winter and he'd have it on. He'd have it on two or three days a week. I used say to him: "Unless you put that thing off, I'm going." And he'd put it off and put it on again when I was gone.'

There was a crew of them that headed for the matches. Tom McCarthy and PJ O'Halloran were there. Gerry Savage. Vincent Fuller. The crew followed Mikey everywhere. When he retired they went everywhere to see Kerry.

'There was nothing else only football in their lives. My father would be at every dog fight. Colleges matches, the whole lot. I have a sister, Phil, living in Kilmacanogue and he was up there with my mother seven or eight years ago. Someone said Dublin were playing Kerry in a challenge game to open a pitch or something – this is January or February – he had to get Phil to bring him to the match.'

When Sheehy was a child, they travelled everywhere together to see matches. In 1962 he saw his first All-Ireland final when Kerry beat Roscommon and never missed a game in Croke Park alongside his father after that. They went to Railway Cup matches and Sheehy was enthralled with Connacht's pristine white jerseys.

He started with Kerry seniors in 1973 with a snazzy hair-do streaking down his back and a name as a free-taker. At half-time in the Munster final he spent the break kicking around out on the field in Killarney when Andy Mullin, another sub, came over with news. Eamon O'Donoghue had been taken off. 'You're going in,' he said.

Mick O'Dwyer had cornered the market on free-taking with Kerry for a decade, but coach Johnny Culloty wanted to break the monopoly. O'Dwyer had missed one or two in the first half. Sheehy was sent to take over, but he could deliver the message himself.

Having hit a few points with his first handful of touches, Kerry were awarded a free 30 metres from goal. 'I was kind of half going for the ball, but Dwyer was out. No way was he letting me near it. 'Ah that's grand,' he says. 'I'll take it.' It was like: what part of fuck off do you not understand? He was minding his own corner. And he was dead right.'

Kerry lost that Munster final and another, but in Sheehy they saw the beginning of a future that radiated with promise. His father knew. Everyone did.

Two steps …

People said a lot of things about Martin Furlong. They reckoned he was wild on the field. Reckless. When he came from his goals to challenge for a ball, no one was safe, not even his own teammates. He launched himself to meet it, arms outstretched, bandaged knees sticking out like two battering rams. Sometimes he got hurt. Sometimes it was others. That was the game. That was life.

People didn't always like it. Martin sometimes wondered about that. Did people think about the environment where he learned his football? In the sixties, goalkeeping was a dangerous pastime. When the ball dropped in the square, it was easy for a hefty full-forward to allow the goalkeeper catch the ball before driving him into the net and claiming the goal. In one of his first games as an Offaly minor, Furlong watched a shot sail over the bar, but never noticed the forward charging at him. When he spotted him, it was too late. The forward buried him in the net. Martin punched him. He punched back. By the time the referee got to them, they were tangled up in a fight.

'That's not the way I play football,' he said. 'Now off to the line the two of ye.'

'I swore after to make sure the ball was going over the bar,' said Furlong, 'and after that I'd watch what was coming to me.' He was never sent off again, but he was never nailed like that again either.

Football always drew the Furlongs into battle. He grew up with three brothers in Tullamore: Mickey, John and Tom. Their house became a point of reference for the entire county. On weekend nights after the Second World War and the worst penances of the Emergency had passed, the cinemas and dancehalls of Tullamore were packed out with people. Hundreds of people would cycle to the outskirts of town and park their bicycles at Furlongs' wall. Late at night, the door would reverberate with knocks as people sought a pump to inflate their tyres before heading home.

A garage and engineering works sat across the road, and Furlongs' backyard was often a makeshift store for parts and machinery ready for collection. Accents from all over the country danced through the house when people called to get their purchases, bringing a certain allure about the world beyond Tullamore.

For five decades the Furlongs had a boy on an Offaly team. Mickey came first with the minors in 1946 and the seniors in 1948 before emigrating to New York in 1954. The older people in Tullamore always said John could have been the best of them. He was over six foot tall, built like an old round tower and recalled in the same breath as the venerable old Meath full-back Paddy 'Hands' O'Brien. When he took sick, no one was sure what had happened, but he spent the following three years in hospital. He was diagnosed with meningitis. He lost his hearing, and when he finally left hospital, football was an old memory.

His third brother, Tom, was a prodigy. He made the Offaly minors and missed the All-Ireland senior final in 1961, returned in 1962 and had fitted in a career's worth of football before he was twenty-one. Spectators loved Tom. He was tall and rangy, but blessed with searing pace and a superb kicking ability. He was a genius in goals, but his talent demanded him further outfield.

People saw a precocious talent in Martin, too. In 1963 Offaly minors came looking for him, but soccer already had a hold on him. The GAA's ban on playing sports outside Gaelic games was still in force, and as a child Martin took on the name 'John Smith' when playing soccer. Smith played for Tullamore in the FAI Minor Cup and in the Leinster Cup. They met Athlone in both competitions, a soccer town dotted with stars.

One Friday, Turlough O'Connor lined out for Athlone against Tullamore before playing for an FAI youths' team against West Germany a week later. Turlough played Gaelic football too, and was picked to line out for Westmeath against Offaly. When the Offaly officials got wind, they prepared an objection to O'Connor's presence. But first, they had to cover their own tracks. In the dressing room, Martin was putting on his jersey when the officials told him not to bother. They were objecting to O'Connor, so he couldn't play either. Westmeath won the game. Martin went home that night, and cried his eyes out.

'That hurt. But that's the joys of it. You want to prove you're right. Walking away doesn't prove that. Sometimes fellas quit the game because they fall out with selectors or managers. But you'll never prove your point that way. You're better to stay and fight your corner.'

Tom loved football, but sometimes the people around the game could kill the romance. He was established on the senior team, but threatened not to play in protest at the treatment meted out to his brother. The Offaly board talked him round, but something inside him in relation to playing football for Offaly had been lost. A year later, in September 1964, Tom left for New York and a job with the City Transit Authority.

When Tom left, Martin didn't feel too bad. That was the way of these things. There was nothing in Ireland for Tom but football and fighting with county board men and a lifetime spent scraping out a living. America was new and glamorous, and the Furlongs had never closed their doors to the opportunities presented by the outside world.

A couple of years after arriving in America, Tom called into Jim McDowney's Bar on 44th Street. Eddie McDwyer was an old friend from Daingean, and had asked him to call in. McDowney's had become a regular haunt for a few players from the New York Giants NFL team. Their season was petering out, all for the lack of a good placekicker. Every night they came into McDowney's and grumbled, but there seemed to be no solution. Eddie McDwyer thought he knew someone who might help.

A few mornings later, Tom Furlong arrived at Yankee Stadium at eight o'clock as the ground staff were pulling the tarpaulin off the field. He kicked twenty-eight frees from varying distances up to 50 yards, and converted twenty-four. The Giants liked what they saw, and put him in a 'taxi squad,' a reserve team that trained during the week, but didn't play.

At $200 a week for training, Tom got a taste for the business. He wrote to nine NFL teams offering his services, and got picked up by the Atlanta Falcons. Atlanta was different to New York. They didn't care too much for foreigners, and especially foreigners who reckoned they could play football, but his kicking was too good to be ignored.

His role, solely as a kicker, in the game intrigued him. The maths were challenging. When the ball was snapped back from the line of scrimmage for the kick, Tom had an average of 1.4 seconds to raise the ball eight feet into the air over the first six yards while the opposition attempted to the charge the kick down. There was no margin for error, but Tom was proving a success. As the summer ended and the new NFL season dawned, he had seen off four other kickers and approached the season as the Falcons' first choice.

Then, everything fell apart. During a training session, a team mate fumbled a routine snap. He dropped the ball, Tom kicked fresh air and blew his knee out. His career was over before an autumn leaf had fallen.

Offaly missed Tom at home, but Martin had stepped from his shadow. He was fifteen in 1962 when Tullamore dropped him into goal and won a county title. Two years later, he was making a save in the All-Ireland minor final and withstanding the bull rush from the Cork forward that would endure through Offaly's history to secure the county's first ever All-Ireland title. In 1971 Furlong was there when Offaly won their first senior title. He returned the following year and won another. The celebrations were joyous. Cars were sprayed green, white and gold and mounted on stands. Their All-Ireland winners were heroes. Furlong was a star, but just as his career reached its apex, it suddenly started to fall away.

Three steps ...

By 1982 Mikey Sheehy had already been valued among the most cherished stones in a team that sparkled with gems. Even when racked by injury, he was the only player to play every minute of Kerry's four-in-a-row. And 1982 had already been another good year. He saved Kerry in the Munster final against Cork with a set of points late-on, and ripped Cork to shreds in the replay by scoring 2-4. Of Kerry's four championship matches, Sheehy had been top scorer in three, but as the pressure built all week in Kerry, Sheehy had sensed it more than the others.

On Tuesday night some journalists landed into Killarney to sweep up the last of the quotes and news for the week. That night, training went on, and on, and on. By the end of the session, an early autumn chill had descended and the players felt it. They returned to the dressing room cold and tired. Mikey thought it wrong. On the Thursday night before the final, he watched Mick O'Dwyer hound a hawker selling T-shirts from outside the stadium in Killarney. Then there was the county board official on the Saturday and his talk of homecomings in Sneem and Tralee. He was worried.

When the players went for a walk on the beach in Malahide, Sheehy listened for his instructions. Every year it sounded the same – keep moving, keep swapping with Egan, take the frees, and relax – yet every year Mick O'Dwyer seemed able to infuse it with fresh urgency. He knew the buttons to press. He always knew how to handle Sheehy.

'He'd push me a good bit a lot of years. I might be carrying a bit of poundage and, particularly when we'd be starting out in the championship, he'd say: "Get away out to Banna, you need to shed a bit of weight and watch yourself." Another year he'd say: "Jesus, you're going well now, keep yourself ticking over. Just kick your frees and whatever."

'Injuries? You'd nearly want a doctor's cert with you. Desperate man for injuries. If he knew you were injured though, he'd give you every support, but he'd push you. That's why he was so good. He kept us going when we trained like dogs and no match for three weeks. Fellas were working and driving miles to get there. There was one year and I'd been injured for a while. Probably around April or May. There were seven or eight of us. In one week in Killarney we did four nights and a Saturday morning. It was torture.'

That Saturday night he knew the new jerseys were arriving. It didn't bother him, but he knew it shouldn't have been happening. He roomed with Sean Walsh and had slept soundly as he always did in Malahide, but that morning there was still something in the air. Was it fear? Nerves? His stomach started churning. It stayed around in the bus. It was in the dressing room. It followed him on to the field. Mikey was starting to worry.

In a final he would always try to get a touch of the ball early on. In the 1979 All-Ireland final against Dublin he was marked by Dave Foran. All summer Foran had eaten up good corner-forwards for breakfast. How Sheehy would handle him had been the talk of the few weeks leading up to the final. Inside the first fifteen seconds, Pat Spillane cut through the defence and laid a pass off to Sheehy. He looked for the posts and nailed it. As the play resumed he looked at Foran. 'I wouldn't say he was shattered,' says Sheehy. 'But he was rattled.'

By the end, Sheehy had hit 2-6, and beaten Jimmy Keaveney's record individual score in an All-Ireland final. Dublin had been despatched as a force for a generation and Mikey Sheehy was the standard by which boyhood heroes were measured. Now, he was up against Mick Fitzgerald – Mick, who had spent all summer smashing his own teammates to pieces in training and cutting loose properly during matches. He knew Mick would be tight, vigilant. It had been a good year, but he still needed to find a few breaks.

Four steps ...

Offaly had always kept Furlong straight, but in the four years after Offaly's last All-Ireland title, Furlong had lost his drive. He had nothing left to prove. He drank a bit. He wasn't inclined to train as hard. His life lost its balance and for a year he disappeared into himself. He had his All-Ireland medals and his reputation was secure. Playing on with an Offaly team sinking steadily into obscurity seemed pointless.

When McGee arrived in 1976, one of his first tasks was to cut Furlong from his panel. 'He was right, as far as I was concerned. You don't see it yourself, but I wasn't doing the right things. It was a wake-up call for me. I wasn't putting it in and it probably showed in my game. I was partaking of a little drop of alcohol at the time. Being there as long as I was, I'd gotten comfortable.'

As time went on, Furlong started getting itchy. He needed challenges and big days. He needed football. To find a way back, he first needed to catch a break. In 1977 Tullamore won a county title with Furlong at full-forward. They were drawn against Longford champions Newtowncashel in the first round of the Leinster championship, and lost their goalkeeper before the game. Furlong stepped in and held Newtowncashel out almost on his own. The game went to a replay, and Tullamore won. McGee was in the crowd. The old keeper's eye was tuned in. So was his mind. After the game, McGee asked Furlong back.

'I'll think about it,' Furlong said.

The following day he went for a walk in Tullamore and called into Noel McGee's barber shop. When Offaly won the O'Byrne Cup in 1954, their first ever senior trophy, McGee ascended the steps of the Hogan Stand to accept it. He had hurled with Offaly. His barber shop was a trading post for news and gossip. Furlong was unsure about returning. Offaly were going nowhere, but he had pulled himself back together as a player. Getting back on the Offaly team would be a nice statement to himself, but did he need the hassle?

'When you get to my age,' said McGee, 'you'll wish you never missed a day. If I were you, I'd go back and I'd never leave O'Connor Park again.'

Furlong went back, and stayed till he was nearly forty.

In 1982 he was the team's Achilles: relentlessly brave and ruthless in battle. The week before games passed like a sleepless eternity. He was never at rest. His nerves quivered. In the dressing room he would keep going to the bathroom until he could only generate a dribble. He yawned incessantly, but he talked too. And when he talked, the room was spellbound. He could reduce the men around him to tears before the beginning of a championship game. Some days he could hop up on the table, his eyes flaming with intensity, his dentures removed, leaving chunks of fangs protruding behind his lips. On the field he berated backs and forwards without prejudice. When Liam O'Connor was in front of him, he cajoled and encouraged him. When Mick Fitzgerald was at corner-back, he threw abuse at him. 'If he heard you giving him praise,' says Furlong, 'he'd say: Don't say that to me! Tell me I'm no fucking good!'

If the players had to follow Furlong into hell, they would give themselves a middling chance of making it back to Tullamore.

Kerry had tormented him for years. In the era before the handpassed goal was outlawed, he would watch the Kerry attack string together a necklace of mesmerising passes while advancing towards his square, then wait till the whites of Furlong's eyes were in full view, and dab the ball past him. He was helpless. One day Kerry put five goals past him in a League game in Tullamore in that fashion, but Furlong still came off feeling like he had played well. As he walked off the field, an Offaly supporter slung his arm around his neck. 'Fair play to you, Furlong,' he said. 'You wouldn't stop laughin'.'

By 1982, things had changed. As the week drained down to the final, Furlong couldn't understand people. Had they forgotten Offaly had scored 4-10 in 1980? That it had taken that goal from Jacko to beat them in 1981? People hadn't seen the players on Clonin Hill a couple of weeks earlier after the Galway game, or felt the mood in the dressing room. Furlong knew it. This team was ready to win.

Five steps …

All day Mikey had foraged for a break. He wandered outfield. He switched wings with John Egan. He hung off The Bomber like a bird following an elephant to pick up scraps, but nothing came.

Inside the first minute Egan slipped a pass through to him, but Sheehy's run took him too close to the endline and his shot flashed across goal. Next ball, same thing. He tried to get out in front, but Mick Fitzgerald was always there, snaking a hand to everything. Twenty minutes passed without even a free. The Bomber had a score. Tom Spillane had two. Páidí Ó Sé had sprinted up for a point. Mikey switched to left-half-forward, looking for some room. He looked around. Mick Fitzgerald was still there, right behind him.

Two minutes before half-time, he picked up a ball on the left wing and lofted a pass towards Liston. The ball bobbled. Liam O'Connor gathered it, but under pressure from Liston he hung on to the ball too long. Free in. Twenty-five metres out, Hogan Stand side. Finally. Mikey eased back to the left, ran up and bent the ball towards goal. Martin Furlong jumped, the ball brushed his fingertips but got over. A point. Relief.

Still, as Mikey prepares to take his penalty, the tension is there.

'I didn't have a great record at kicking them, but I didn't mind it. I knew in 1979 [for his penalty against Dublin in the All-Ireland final], I was going to plank it into the top corner because I was playing well. But in '82 when I put the ball down, I had a fear of missing it. I was conscious of the importance of the kick.'

He never believed in designated penalty kickers. Too much about a person's mood could dictate the quality of their kick. Best to leave it to the day of the game. Now, as he looked around, he didn't feel ready to take it. Neither did anyone else.

Furlong shakes his fingers loose. Years of facing penalties have taught him things. Players usually favour their strong side. Right-footed kickers aim at the left side of the goal as they see it. Left-footers at the right. At times during the week Furlong had thought about penalties. He remembered Sheehy taking one against him on an All-Star tour game in Gaelic Park, New York. He favoured his strong side, and Martin had saved it. He looked at Sheehy and screamed at Liam O'Connor and Pat Fitzgerald: 'Watch the rebound!'

He believed it. This ball wasn't going in.

Six steps ...

Mikey's foot is behind the ball. At the last second he has abandoned his theory on Furlong's weak left side, and struck the ball to Furlong's right. He hits it well. It feels good. It rises towards goal and levels off above waist height. But Furlong has seen the trajectory early. He takes two small bouncing strides forward and extends his arms to the right, feels the ball hit the wool of his gloves, and palms the ball away with both hands.

The crowd shrieks. The ball hits the deck. Furlong is prone on the ground. Someone must claim the rebound. As he looks up, Furlong sees

Pat Fitzgerald collect it and drive the ball away. The crowd exhale together and a cheer rattles through the old ground like a hurricane. Everywhere Offaly players have lifted their heads to find the game is still alive while Mikey Sheehy trots out with a weight on his shoulders that will never fully lift.

'I still, to this day, have nightmares about it. You were staring history in the face. I often get slagged about it now. Fellas would be asking why did you kick it?! And now you have all the volunteers, but to this day, when the penalty was awarded, not one fella came and volunteered. The ball was thrown to me. I accepted responsibility.

'I didn't look round, but I'm sure if there was someone else interested, they would've come up. But the boys were great at kicking in training. It's like a fella playing golf with no card in his pocket. It's totally different.'

Kerry were still a point up, but all the bad vibes running through Mikey Sheehy were amplified. The rain was pouring down. Kerry hadn't kicked away as they always did. Kerry players were falling back into defence. Offaly weren't giving up. In the few moments when he held the winning of the game in his hands, when Martin Furlong sprang to his right and pushed the ball away, the ending had been decided in Sheehy's mind.

'I had this vision we were going to lose after that,' says Sheehy. 'I was shattered. I could see it.'

All the while, Martin Furlong was pumping his arms, screaming at his players and drawing on the inspiration of two decades of football to drive Offaly forward. The game was back on, and moving in another direction.

18 THE CALM

As Mikey Sheehy kicked the penalty, Liam Currams was preparing himself for the worst. 'It had started slipping away. Then the penalty came. I says, "Aw Jesus, it's gone." Poor old Stephen [Darby]. He was a fierce nice guy. I felt so sorry for Stephen. That's it, I says. We're done. I was just resigning myself, thinking, "Ah sure, we'll give it hell for what time is left anyway." When he saved it, I couldn't believe it. We still had a chance here.'

The entire team lifted, and for a fleeting few minutes Kerry shuddered. While they regathered themselves, Offaly had set off downfield. Although Páidí Ó Sé cleared the attack, his kick landed to Sean Lowry who returned the ball to Richie Connor. From there, Padraic Dunne looked up and saw Johnny Mooney near goal, in the first patch of space Paudie Lynch had allowed him since half-time. Mooney grabbed the ball, jinked past Lynch, and Offaly were level, 12-12. Twenty minutes to go.

On the line, O'Dwyer is back on his feet, making switches. Sean Walsh heads for centre-forward and Tom Spillane comes out to centrefield. Within minutes, Offaly have coughed up the ball and Sean Walsh is dinking a shot over the bar. Tom Spillane is winning ball at centrefield and the wobble inflicted by the penalty appears to have been steadied. Offaly are still there, lingering on their shoulder, but years of September Sundays have attuned the Kerry players' minds to these afternoons. Offaly's legs are wilting. Time to kick for home.

In eleven minutes Kerry hit four unanswered points. Jacko and Spillane seal up centrefield, Sean Walsh is blowing holes in Offaly's defence and John Egan is still buzzing. Páidí Ó Sé finds the space to push forward and his final attack ends with a point. As the crowd rises to cheer, Páidí turns and races back towards his own goal. A smile is plastered across his face and thoughts of Jacko's goal in 1981 are running through his head. 'We have it now, boy,' he says as he passes Paudie Lynch. Johnny Mooney is standing beside him, still believing, still defiant.

'Ye fucking have not,' he snaps.

With that, Kerry went to the ropes.

Ger O'Keeffe had spotted Mikey Sheehy drifting back towards goal from much earlier in the game. Pat Spillane always utilised his free licence to wander back, but now Ger Power was there too. Sean Walsh was coming back towards centrefield. Jacko was in front of his own goal. Out the field, McGee's words were ringing in Tomás O'Connor's ears: let Jacko go. Hold your own space in the middle. As Jacko cleared more ball from defence, O'Connor started to pick it up.

'We were inside in the backs, telling them to go way up the field,' says O'Keeffe. 'We were under a lot of pressure and there was nobody to kick the ball to.'

They still reckoned they could cope. With so many bodies back, there wasn't space to cause any undue trouble. Down on the sideline, McGee was with his selectors. Gerry Carroll had already swapped with Padraic Dunne and gone to centrefield, but they needed to do more. They needed to get Matt Connor and Brendan Lowry closer to goal. The game was slipping from their grasp, but they still had enough time to pull it back.

John O'Keeffe looked around him. The area around Kerry's goal was beginning to resemble a crowded platform at a train station. There was no way Offaly could breach this. As the seconds ticked down, O'Keeffe allowed himself a moment. For thirteen years he had protected himself against what football could do to him. Nothing was left to chance. No injury was too severe to slow him down. Now he could see it. It was a few minutes away. History.

Five-in-a-row.

'Something went through me that said we're actually going to do it,' says O'Keeffe. 'It was like a confidence with about five minutes to go. We're going to pull this one off. I had a feeling: we're going to do this thing. We're going to get there.

'Then, bang!'

19 THE GOAL

With sixty-three minutes of the game over, John Guinan was running out of steam and looking at the sideline. If Offaly were going to make a switch he knew it would come in the forwards. He also knew he was most vulnerable.

Fr Sean Heaney: Eugene McGee had a stopwatch in his hand. I happened to be standing next to him. Paddy Fenlon was on the other side. We're three points down. Eugene said: 'There's still time if we're good enough.'

Eugene McGee: We'd have to be at our best in the last five minutes regardless of anything. I was absolutely definite about that. If Kerry were ahead with ten minutes to go, the tendency would've been to say, 'That's it.' I had to go to extreme measures to say, 'That's not it.' If they were close enough, we are as good as them, so there's no reason we can't get the last couple of scores. We went four points down with ten minutes to go. On all known criteria, that should've been it.

Sean Grennan: My mother and aunt had decided by then that this game was gone from us. With a young lad like me there they thought they might as well head away now, and avoid the rush.

John O'Keeffe: There wasn't rhyme or reason to the way we were playing. Tactically our shape was totally gone. Mentally it was just a case of hanging on.

It was time for Offaly's final substitution. McGee's first instinct was to look for Martin Fitzpatrick. Fitzpatrick had shown good form all summer, but had never played in a championship game for Offaly before. The other selectors weren't so sure. Seamus Darby hadn't Fitzpatrick's speed, but he had the experience to cope with the demands of the final few minutes. A discussion began on the line. With the game in the balance, the next move would be crucial.

Richie Connor: Eugene McGee wasn't even considering bringing on Darby. Eugene Mulligan, who was PRO, called McGee aside, told him he was mad, that Fitzpatrick was only a young fella. You needed an old head whatever chance you had.

Eugene Mulligan: The game was very tight and the decisions wouldn't have been clear-cut. I just made a comment, something like, 'It's an oul' lad you want.' Martin Fitzpatrick was an exceptionally good footballer but he was only eighteen at the time.

Eugene McGee: The main reason Darby went on was a communication problem. The full-forward line was drifting too far outfield trying to get the ball. We had no chance of getting scores on a wet day if they were 30 or 40 yards out. The first thing Darby was told was to go tell Brendan Lowry and Matt Connor to stay back on the endline, and he was to do the same himself. The rule was, I'd ask the four selectors what they thought on each subject, but the final decision was mine, even if the four said black and I said white. Two said Fitzpatrick, two Darby. On a wet day the older head would be best.

Fr Sean Heaney: John Guinan, who was marking Tommy Doyle, was taken off. Brendan Lowry, who'd be very capable of playing wing-forward, came out and Seamus Darby was put in corner-forward. But Tommy Doyle was put in corner-back where he'd never played before.

John Egan: Tommy Doyle said to me after: 'I looked around and Ger O'Keeffe is standing alongside me. He says, "Your man is gone in there." So Tommy runs back into the corner-back position.

Richie Connor: Seamus Darby was the ideal man to bring on. He'd done it time and time again in training. It wasn't that he was ramming in goals time and again, but he was a skilful player. Very accurate.

Eugene McGee: At that stage he [Darby] was just glad to be back on the team. The Rhode football ethic would take over in this situation. There was no time for acting the bollix.

63 MINS: *Seconds before Darby enters the field, Pat Spillane tumbles over a ball 20 metres from the Kerry goal and ends up on his hands and knees with the ball beneath him. It rolls against his knee and bounces back off his hand. PJ McGrath whistles for a pick-up, and awards a free to Offaly. Kerry look stunned, but none of their players protest. Matt Connor narrows the gap to three points, 0-16 to 0-13.*

Pat Spillane: Little things change games. I always remember the 1977 All-Ireland semi-final, getting my foot to a ball and it going off Brian Mullins's foot over the sideline. Dublin got a sideline ball. Goal. That was the turning point in the game. It was weak refereeing by McGrath.

Ger Power: I think most Kerry people and players would think there were some light-hearted frees given away. But that's the way.

Nelligan's kick-out is broken at centrefield and won by Páidí Ó Sé. He finds Eoin Liston, who returns the ball to the onrushing Ó Sé. As he bears down on goal, Ó Sé taps the ball over the bar and turns with a smile on his face. Kerry lead by four, 0-17 to 0-13.
66 MINS: *Gerry Carroll launches a ball towards Johnny Mooney in front of*

*goal. Mooney initially goes for the ball, but stops himself from jumping at the last second. Paudie Lynch jumps, and bounces off Mooney. Another free to Offaly, **14 yards** out. Lynch shakes his head. Ger O'Keeffe has a word with the referee. Meanwhile, Matt Connor strokes over another free. Kerry 0-17 Offaly 0-14.*

John Egan: We never put pressure on referees. I won't say we were cheated, you'd hate to feel you were. But I felt the referee didn't give us an even break, especially at crucial stages. The game seemed to be running out to a conclusion and maybe the referee thought in his heart he was going to even it up a little bit. But they got two very dubious frees which brought them back into it. I think he didn't believe when he gave the two frees that they'd have an impact. I don't think they were right decisions. I think he was caught himself. It's hard for me to say but I was captain of that team. It's only my opinion, but I have to be honest. I thought we were robbed.

PJ McGrath: I had no doubts about those frees. To me, they were pretty clear.

68 MINS: *Richie Connor grabs a line ball on Kerry's 45 metre line with Kerry defenders funnelling back all round him. He passes to Liam Currams, who has time to pause 30 metres from goal. He stands and looks around. He passes the ball to Sean Lowry. Tom Spillane, Tim Kennelly and Pat Spillane converge on him. Tom Spillane touches Lowry's back with his hand and Lowry falls to the ground 13 metres out. Tom Spillane puts his hands on his head. Everyone assumes Matt Connor will shoot for goal, but instead he taps the ball over the bar. Kerry 0-17 Offaly 0-15. Kerry head back downfield again.*

Sean Lowry: Mikey Sheehy had the ball coming out [of defence]. There was Mikey Sheehy, Pat Spillane and Sean Walsh in a line coming at the Offaly defence. The Bomber was behind me with his hands up, looking for the ball. Mikey Sheehy made a fatal mistake. He tried to kick it to him. I just got in front of The Bomber, got a hand to it, and passed it out to Pat Fitzgerald.

Mikey Sheehy: I felt I did a couple of stupid things. I got the ball and I just kicked it. I didn't have the brains to hold it and look for some fella.

Mick O'Dwyer (from his biography, 1990)**:** We had four men going forward and if I had the choice to delegate responsibility to one man who would take us out of trouble, I would have picked Sheehy.

Sean Lowry: Then The Bomber was coming like a train at Pat Fitzgerald.

Pat Fitzgerald: The Bomber jumped on me. It was a rugby tackle. I never saw him coming. He buried me into the ground with the ball underneath me on my stomach. I was sickened. Winded.

Eoin Liston: Trying to delay time, I threw the ball back under my legs. I was intent on stopping the quick free.

Pat Fitzgerald: I got up, struggling, and Sean Lowry threw the ball back as though to say: kick it. Everyone went up the field, and I'm thinking: What am I going to do with this? I wasn't able to kick it. I looked and Richie was 14 yards away. So I chipped it to him. I wouldn't have been able to kick it in, I was so knackered. I just chipped it to Richie Connor because it was convenient.

Eoin Liston: Next thing I saw my man [Liam O'Connor] shoot to the left. He soloed a few times and lobbed in the high ball.

Liam O'Connor: I could say it was a pinpoint pass, but it was just a question of getting it up and into the forwards. That was when the stamina stood to us, that you were up there and able to take a ball. We weren't going to lose because of fitness.

69 MINS: *Having taken the pass from Richie Connor, Liam O'Connor takes a few strides forward and launches a huge kick towards the Kerry goal. It begins to drop short of the small square, a few yards to the left of the goal, near the point where the corner of the large parallelogram and the 13 metre line meet. Standing there are Tommy Doyle and Seamus Darby.*

Seamus Darby: I got caught behind Tommy Doyle. Tommy is a lot bigger man than I am, and I said to myself: I'm in trouble here. But Tommy just went that little too far out under the ball and I caught it at the last minute.

Johnny Mooney: Darby and me went to the same school. He's only a small man, but he had two great feet in an era when you had to be able to kick with both feet. The moment he had it in his hand, I knew he'd go for it. I wasn't sure when it was up there that he'd be able to catch it, but he did.

Ger O'Keeffe: I was outside Tommy Doyle. I couldn't get to that position. It was all happening behind me. I saw Tommy jumping for the ball, Seamus Darby nudging him and the ball going over Tommy's head, yer man picking it and just throwing a swipe at it. Let God direct it. He had no idea where it was going.

Seamus Darby: I held Tommy with my hip and as I turned I knocked him away. I thought Charlie Nelligan was nearer to me. I thought I just had to put it over his head and under the bar, but I didn't realise Charlie was only a yard off his line. If you asked me to do it again I wouldn't have done it.

Tommy Doyle (from *Kingdom Come,* by Eoghan Corry, 1989)**:** I was thinking like a wing-back, not a corner-back. The man in front of the square is much more dangerous than a man 40 yard**s** out. Paudie Lynch and Charlie Nelligan were roaring at me: 'Come back! Come back!' I was caught out of position at the end. It was coming straight at me. My face was to it, preparing to catch. In the end, I didn't go for it. It skimmed off the top of my fingers. Blast it, I said.

Padraic Dunne: I was around the middle. I was looking with my mouth open. I was right behind him. I thought he shot for a point. He just let fly. Just caught it right.

Seamus Darby: I play golf badly, but the odd time you would hit a perfect shot, you don't even feel it in your hands. It was the same with that goal. I just didn't feel it. I knew it was good. When I saw it hitting the net, I knew it was even better.

Jack O'Shea: I was within inches of catching the ball. I was getting back, but it went over my fingers. I could feel the wind of the ball going by. Another fraction, and I'd have deflected it. He mis-hit the ball. He hit it with his shin. When you hit a ball like that, it dips.

John O'Keeffe: I was maybe seven or eight yards away and possibly could've gone, but Matt was at my side. Lurking. I've had nightmares about that. I've often thought, damn it, there was so much to win. I had absolutely no sense he was going to score a goal. It was the furthest thing from my mind. I actually thought he was going to pass it. I said: there's no way he's going to swing a leg at this. If he does it'll probably go over the bar. I just thought it's not possible. There's too many bodies around here. We have this under control.

Matt Connor: I was closest to the goals if it had come out. But no need. You're going for it, you're running for it and hoping it's going to be kicked into you. It just went the other side of me. A brilliant shot, but he was always good at that. Wouldn't be the first good goal he scored. People might say it was a fluke, lucky or whatever. But he was good at scoring goals. Once he'd get his hands on it you'd always think goal anyway, because he'd be capable of doing it.

John O'Keeffe: I'll never forget the feeling. In one split second I knew our dream was gone. It was dashed.

Fr Sean Heaney: It was a bombshell. It was as totally unexpected to us as anyone else. Unbelievable. It was one of those defining moments in sport. You'll still meet people who know what chair they were sitting in in the sitting room when that went in.

Eugene McGee: The raindrops falling from the net is what I saw. Somebody walked in front of me. I didn't actually see it go into the net.

Weeshie Fogarty: I saw the high ball coming in, Tommy Doyle coming out and going up for the ball, Seamus Darby behind him. He certainly made contact with him, but it was a combination of mistiming by Tommy Doyle and the slightest touch by Seamus Darby. The way he read the flight of the ball, gathered it, the way he turned and the way he finished it. Poetry in motion.

Charlie Nelligan: I felt the breeze going through my fingers. I was a bit out, but not that far. After it hit the net, the wind was blowing back out towards me. I felt the spray from the net just slap me in the face.

Liam Currams: I was over on the left-hand side of the field. I saw the ball going over Charlie Nelligan's head, but I couldn't believe how it got over his head. It dipped down, like a soccer player would put cut on the ball. Then I heard the crowd erupting.

Sean Grennan: When we were coming out we heard a huge cheer. We met a Kerry woman and she asked what was that? We said: 'Kerry must have got a goal. That's that anyway.' We drove out the road back to Balbriggan where my father was. The radio wasn't working right, so until we got there we didn't know Offaly had scored.

Ger Power: You could see Tommy Doyle was pushed from a mile away. The next thing the ball was in the back of the fecking net. But I'd blame nobody for it. Whatever happened, happened.

Mikey Sheehy: I've seen that clip. You couldn't say to this day whether he was pushed or not. If he was, he was.

Ger O'Keeffe: There's no doubt he nudged him. Whether it was a foul or not isn't an issue, but he nudged him. Players do the same today and get away with it. But he had no idea where the ball was going. He just drew a kick at it. God directed it, and it rattled the net.

Tommy Doyle (from *All-Ireland Football Captains*, by Brian Carthy, 1994)**:** Whether I was pushed or not, I'm not prepared to say. All I know is the ball wound up in the back of the net and Offaly won. Good luck to them. The goal was a goal. I was very disappointed. I wished the ground could have opened up and swallowed me. I took it too much to heart.

Matt Connor: I didn't see it at the time. I've seen it a thousand times since, but it was a hard one to call. Some refs would give it. Others wouldn't. I'd say if it happened out in midfield there wouldn't have been a word about it. But it was such a vital thing. If it happened in the first minute, there wouldn't have been a word about it. If it had been given, I don't know. It was touch and go.

Charlie Nelligan: I'll never say whether it was a push or not, or what I thought it was.

John Egan: [The push] made no difference. I'd have done the same thing myself. It was the referee's call. If the referee said it was a free, it was a free. From Tommy Doyle's point of view, it was definitely a push. He would say it was a push. Seamus Darby would say it wasn't. But it's the referee's call.

Johnny Mooney: There was definite contact. Whether it was legitimate, it's hard to tell. He didn't actually push him, but he might have used his elbows on the way up. He definitely made contact. But PJ McGrath allowed it.

Seamus Darby: I held him, and as I took the ball I arsed him out. People say to me, even to this day, 'I saw your hands on his back.' But my hands weren't on the man's back.

Sean Walsh: If it was a push, a traditional corner-back would've been ready for it. Tommy Doyle played very natural football and played like a wing-back would. That's no criticism of him. It just happened. Nobody could make the switch.

Eugene McGee: The reaction of the Kerry people was very significant because they were extremely sporting about it. There was no great whingeing.

Weeshie Fogarty: From a referee's point of view I wouldn't have given a free out. First of all, you couldn't see the push, if there was a push, because you'd be out the field. It was the slightest of slightest nudges. It was the nudge of a highly experienced player. At the end of the day it came down to PJ McGrath and what he saw, and what he didn't see.

PJ McGrath: I had a clear view of it. Offaly people call it the goal of the century. Kerry people probably call it the greatest fluke of the century. I don't care what they call it. My only worry was whether or not it was a goal. And it was. There was no one talking to me [about the alleged push] that evening. The papers picked it up. I spoke to the umpires about it, but none of them saw anything that would warrant any sort of a free. If you look at Darby's hands in the frame, he didn't touch Tommy Doyle at all with his hands. He never pushed him. He pushed out his backside and Doyle backed into him. He never touched him with his hands.

Mikey Sheehy: What a shot it was! Charlie Nelligan was at the top of his game in those years. It took a good shot to beat him.

David Walsh: I was in the Cusack Stand. I was absolutely thrilled. A complete stranger tapped me on the shoulder after the goal and says: 'To think you trained with them!'

Padraic Dunne: I remember at the time being very aware of what to do when the goal was scored. I dropped back straight away. I was very aware not to get wrapped up. It wasn't over. By Jesus, it wasn't.

Eugene McGee: My first reaction was the time that was left, knowing Kerry – and they only needed a point to save it.

Richie Connor: When we got the goal, I went through a few minutes of absolute hell. I could see us throwing this thing away. I found out how much time was left. Three, maybe four minutes. I just wanted players back in their positions. I couldn't believe what was going on. Matt was doing the same thing as me. Calming things down. Lads were jumping around. Seamus would've done his bit. Gerry Carroll was caught in the moment. There was a bit of that going on.

Matt Connor: You're happy but it's not over. Mick Fitzgerald was five yards away from us at the time and he was corner-back. Mikey Sheehy was there. It was just total concentration. He was marking him. No emotion whatsoever. That's the type of fella he was anyway.

Mick Fitzgerald: Everyone else was jumping up and down. Nelligan had the ball and Pat Spillane ran out to the side. Spillane wanted Nelligan to put down the ball quick and kick it out to him. I said to myself: if Nelligan puts that ball down, I'm gone in to kick it away. That's what was going on. That's why I wasn't paying attention to anything else. I was watching the quick kick-out.

Brendan Lowry: Mick walked out as though he was strolling around the town. I was over to Darby, celebrating.

Michael Lowry: Only that you went over to him, he would've jumped out of the park.

Charlie Nelligan: The head was down. I took the kick-out. I might have aimed it at Paudie Lynch but an Offaly man intercepted it.

Johnny Mooney: The very first night I met McGee, he talked about loads of things, but just when he finished up he made one point. He said no matter what happens in a game, carry on. Get on with business. Don't get carried away. Don't get sucked in. There was a bit of celebrating going on, but I was thinking: next kick-out. I went out and won it. The only reason I did that was because I'd been told six or seven years before at the tail-end of the first meeting with McGee. I remember telling him. He just smiled.

71 MINS: *Mooney's pass found Gerry Carroll, whose kick drifted wide. Nelligan's next kick-out found Tim Kennelly who lashed the ball out of defence, only for Carroll to gather the ball at centrefield. He heads for the Hogan Stand, soloing the ball on his left foot. He meets Pat Spillane, and turns to head back infield, where Jack O'Shea is waiting. He turns back towards the Hogan Stand, but O'Shea flicks his hand in and gets the ball away.*

Eugene McGee: I had said to Gerry: 'Look, Gerry, you're not to go on a left-footed solo run. I'd prefer you kicked the ball into the Hogan Stand.' Everybody knew he only had a left foot and could be blocked. He did exactly what I was afraid of. He headed off on a left-footed solo run towards the Hogan Stand. Jack O'Shea came in and steamed him out of it. I could've strung up Carroll. It was madness.

Gerry Carroll: I was trying to kick a low ball into the corner because I'd been boxed in. Afterwards I thought if they'd have scored a point I could make up for it the next day. If they'd scored a goal, I'd have been in America the next day.

71 MINS: *Having regained possession, Jack O'Shea found Tom Spillane racing towards goal. He had options closer to goal, but Spillane attempted to go past Sean Lowry. Instead, Lowry knocked the ball away near the endline, where Martin Furlong had raced out in support.*

Tom Spillane: The ball came down the side [of the field]. Maybe a more mature player might've said: I'll look and see who's around me. But when I got the ball there was only one thing on my mind: beat my man and get into a scoring position. Someone said afterwards: Did I not see The Bomber unmarked? I don't know whether he was marked or not. I was probably hard on myself. I was there. It was me carrying the ball. It didn't happen. End of story. I tried my best.

John O'Keeffe: I think if we'd been a little more composed we could've worked the ball into a scoring position or a free, and he [referee] would've happily given us a free for a draw. But we went mad helter-skelter down the field.

Eugene McGee: I was certain they were going to get the equalising point when Tom Spillane went down. He had opportunities to cross the ball and the referee would certainly have given a free in because he must've known he owed them a favour. Plus, there was a natural tendency to draw matches.

Richie Connor: Then Furlong fucked up. He was out exposed near the corner. I was down beside him that time. He could've been blocked down. The ball could've been taken off him.

John Egan: There was a ball up on the endline. I went down on it and Martin Furlong came out and gave me a push in the back. The referee gave me no free. I didn't feel it at the time, and I won't cry about it now.

As he fell, Egan looked to the referee, but play went on. Furlong slung a pass towards Brendan Lowry, who was standing 25 yards from the endline, but as the ball hung in the air, Mikey Sheehy stepped in and regained possession. With Furlong out of goals, and the Offaly defence in disarray, Kerry had one last chance.

Mikey Sheehy: At that stage there was nothing much to do but I kicked it in high.

Sean Lowry: Any time I played in Croke Park I looked at the clock at the throw-in. I said to myself that day that at 4.35pm it was going to be over. When Furlong got that ball I headed back towards the goal and I glanced up at the clock. It was 4.35pm. I said: if I get this ball I'm giving it to no one, I don't care who it is. Mikey Sheehy kicks this ball across and there was snow on it. It went up into the clouds. I was waiting for someone to hit me in the chest. I was thinking: Will I catch it over my head or into my chest? I had so much time. The Bomber was there, Paudie Lynch, they were all there. But no one came. I couldn't understand it. Then, at the last second, I heard a voice: 'You're on your own, Jack!' So I caught it into my chest. I let on to pass but I had no intention of passing. With that,

PJ McGrath had his hand up. I was going to go to Hill 16 with that ball. I saw the video a few days after the game, and who was standing behind me? Padraic Dunne. After running in from the middle of the field. It was great work for a lad like him.

Fr Sean Heaney: The most satisfying picture in my life is Sean Lowry catching the ball, hearing the whistle and up the hands go. You could never forget that.

Mikey Sheehy: The one thing I'd say about that [Kerry] team, in important games like semi-finals and finals, we used kill teams in the last twenty minutes. That time it was Offaly who did it to us.

PJ McGrath: A fella said to me in 2000 that he was looking at the old matches they were showing on telly. He taped them and he was looking at them. 'I made up my mind finally,' he said. 'You gave the correct decision in 1982'. I said: 'Yes. You had eighteen years to make up your mind. I had one-eighth of a second.'

At the final whistle, there was a moment. A splendidly frozen moment. The ground went quiet, then released a guttural roar of delight. Offaly had won by a point.

The stands burst their banks and the pitch was awash with the delirious Offaly people. The Dublin supporters on the Hill who had cheered their minors to an All-Ireland title came down and hoisted John Guinan on to their shoulders. Martin Furlong met Pádraig Horan in the middle of the pitch. With thousands of supporters pushing in around them they found the space to share a precious moment. Horan had dragged Offaly hurlers through the same bad days Furlong had endured with the footballers. He carried Offaly in his heart like Furlong. He knew what this meant.

Sean Lowry held on to the ball as his wife Nuala got to him and hugged him tightly. All those week nights at home, promising her an All-Ireland medal. He had been right all along. All around them, Offaly footballers bobbed like corks on a sea of people, gradually being washed up on to the steps of the Hogan Stand. Kerrymen graciously performed the rituals of defeat, shaking hands and edging their way towards the dressing rooms. On the sideline, Jimmy Deenihan cradled Mick O'Dwyer's head in his hands. O'Dwyer was broken.

And in the middle of it all, in a potted vision of a life he was yet to live, Seamus Darby was being pulled and dragged by the crowd, his back bruised from slaps.

20 THE LONGEST NIGHT

Eugene McGee stood alone by the dug-out. His clothes were soaked. His light beige jacket was sodden and clinging to him like a cheap suit. As his players celebrated, he stepped back. Maybe it was the journalist in him that made him pull away from the whirl of emotion. Maybe it was the nature of the relationship he had built with the players. This was their moment of fulfilment. In getting them here, McGee had already enjoyed his.

Up at the podium Richie Connor's torrid journey had reached its last stop. When the whistle went he had looked around for someone to leap on. Instead, a Croke Park blazer reached him first, grabbed him and started shouting in his ear about procedure and protocol. As his teammates shipped slaps on their backs and were hoisted on to shoulders, Richie was being forced to straighten up, start thinking about his duties and obligations.

'I would've stayed out in Croke Park for yonks. But yer man whisked me away. He made a beeline for me the minute the match was over. "Come on over here," he says and I was up in the stand on me own. The whole crack is going on down below and I'm getting none of this madness that's going on.'

A million thoughts went through all their heads. Sean Lowry thought of his father and wished he could share this purest feeling of joy with the one man he knew would feel the same. With his last ounces of energy Mick Fitzgerald looked for Stephen Darby and pulled him into his chest.

Darby had beaten Clonin Hill and prospered in a game filled out by big men. His wife had died months after they were married, but football had helped give his life structure and purpose. Bringing an All-Ireland medal home meant something deeper to him than anyone else could imagine. For a moment Fitzgerald let his emotions carry him away.

As he stood on the podium waiting for the players to assemble, Richie Connor improvised a few words in his head. He lifted the cup, and the vast sea of faces in front of the Hogan Stand released a roar that shook the raindrops from the stand. As they descended the steps and set out across the pitch, the Lowry brothers carefully took the cup and shielded it from thousands of hands reaching out to touch its belly. Outside the tunnel, John Guinan met two friends from home, trying furiously to pierce the cordon and get into the dressing room. 'Tell ye what, lads,' said Guinan, 'one of ye take this arm and you take the other.' They lifted him up. As Guinan played injured, the crowd opened in front of him. They dropped him down in the middle of the dressing room and started to take it all in.

Players were in the shower area around the Sam Maguire cup singing 'The Rose of Tralee'. Johnny Mooney spotted a priest squeezing his way through the throng. Fr Moriarty had officiated at his wedding in San Francisco a few weeks before and promised Mooney he'd be picking up an All-Ireland medal in a few weeks' time. Evelyn Currams, mother of Liam, appeared in the dressing room wearing a chain with her son's All-Ireland hurling medal attached and kissed McGee. 'Next year,' she said, 'I'll have two.'

Seamus Darby slugged on a bottle of milk. In the middle of chaos, Eugene McGee gave an interview to RTÉ's Mick Dunne. As reporters squeezed into the dressing room, McGee asked about the game. 'Was it good?' he wondered, so absorbed had he been in the details.

Martin Furlong sat on the bench and took a long draw from a cigarette and considered their achievement. 'We beat one of the best teams of all time,' he said. 'We mustn't be too bad ourselves, so.'

When Richie Connor returned to the dressing room, he opened his gearbag to find everything had been robbed. A new tracksuit, socks, wristbands and other gear had all been pilfered. All he had left was enough to dress himself with.

'I don't know what eejit took them. We got very little stuff at the time. It was something you'd use in winter training. Often I thought I'd love to see somebody wearing the tracksuit with my name.'

All the while, Matt Connor took the congratulations with a quiet, dazed smile. 'The dressing room was very good, but fellas are so drained. You just want to get on to the next part. [You tell yourself] the next part will be great. What you'd love is to get the lads in a small place on your own and just have a chat. That'd be my ideal. Even for a couple of hours, just to get away from it. But that never happened.'

As the reporters filed out and the players tightened the knots on their ties, McGee emptied the dressing room, leaving only the players and his selectors. Those who travelled to Ballycommon for training and pulled themselves up Clonin Hill only to see themselves dropped off the panel in mid-summer were there. Even after their demotion, many of them had pledged their assistance if required for practice games in training. Anything. This was their day too.

In the middle of the room, sitting on a battered old table, was the cup. The silence was impeccable. It was the quietest moment they had known since losing in 1981. There was no one hounding them, no thoughts about Kerry rattling around their heads. Every debt had been settled. Every task had been accomplished. This was their greatest moment. Suddenly, there was nothing left to do.

Seconds passed and the silence remained unblemished. Like Matt Connor, Pat Fitzgerald suddenly felt this strange sense of emptiness. Was this it? Was this what they had given six years of their lives for? The cause that had held them all together was gone. When the dressing-room door opened again, all the players would step into another life. They had foiled history. Kerry's ordained place was now theirs. On the other side of the dressing-room door, the whole world was waiting for them. Everything they once knew was gone.

Then, from somewhere in the room, a great roar exploded the silence. The moment had been broken, and everyone smiled and cheered. The party could begin.

*   *   * ·

Outside on the pitch, downtrodden Kerrymen strolled towards their dressing room. As Eoin Liston neared the tunnel, an Offaly man landed nearby, having clambered over the wire at the Canal End. Liston brushed him aside, and patted Jack O'Shea on the back. Charlie Nelligan walked to the dressing room, dazed and devastated. As he went across the pitch, a Kerry supporter came up behind him and punched him in the jaw. Charlie didn't feel a thing.

'I didn't see who it was, but I was told after that whoever it was got a bigger dusting himself. It was about three weeks later a man came into the shop and said: "Jesus, what happened was desperate." And I said: "What happened?" The minute he told me, I remembered. At the time it never registered at all.'

He remembers other moments. Seconds after the punch, Donie Houlihan, an old friend from Tralee, slung his arm around Nelligan's shoulders. Tears were welling in his eyes. 'He was bawling his eyes out. He said to me: "Never mind. Ye gave us fabulous years of football. We'll never forget ye." That meant more to me than the clatter I got before.'

Nelligan entered a dressing room smothered by silence. Boots clattered on the concrete floor. The only sounds came from the pitch outside, the dressing room next door and the spatter of water on the showers on the tiled floor.

John O'Keeffe came in and sat down. His hip ached. He had cradled history in his hands. Now, it was gone. After years of focusing on the next ball, the next game, the next training session, he had allowed his mind to drift to the podium. He looked down at the ground, as the tears dropped. 'The dressing room then was the worst I ever knew,' he says. 'Lads were saying, more or less, that's the end of it.'

The press quietly filed in and began the doleful business of gathering the thoughts of a shattered team. O'Dwyer pulled himself together as best he could. 'They played very well,' he said. 'We didn't get far enough away from them at any stage. Retirement? This isn't time to talk about things like that, but naturally the thought is in a few minds. We'll have to wait for that.'

That evening, Mick O'Dwyer sneaked out of the dressing room, into the back of Eric Murphy's car, and lay down across the back seat. As Murphy drove through town, O'Dwyer didn't utter a word. When they reached the Gresham hotel, O'Dwyer relocated to his room, and stayed there.

'Reporters were coming in, trying their best,' says Charlie Nelligan. 'But what do you say? It was unique. We had it and the next thing it was gone. The fabulous five-in-a-row. Next thing you had four-in-a-row.

'It would've been nice to have won it all right but I don't know was it meant to be. We had everything. We'd won everything. We'd all the joys that had gone before. The winning of the four-in-a-row. If you could bottle all the losses of the teams we'd beaten, it would equate with the loss we had in 1982. We had the four years' losses all in one year. It was desperate.' The following morning Nelligan disappeared to Castleisland where he didn't speak for three days. Jerseys were left dripping on the benches for whoever wanted them.

But as Mikey Sheehy stood in the Croke Park shower, replaying the day over in his head, he remembered something. The girl from Armagh. She might be outside looking for autographs, he thought, but she won't want this jersey now. As he headed for the team bus, he heard a familiar voice call his name. It was the girl. Kerry had been beaten, but as for Mikey's jersey, it still had value for her.

Outside in the corridor beneath the stand, Richie Connor was stepping out of the Raidio na Gaeltachta broadcast van having given an interview, when he saw John Egan, fully clothed, heading for the exit.

'We stole it on you, Johnny,' he said.

After everything: the name pulled from a hat, the embarrassing evening in Ennis, the hundreds of miles between Kildorrery and Killarney, after all the silly questions from pressmen and officials, enduring the referee and listening to the guff about five-in-a-row, here was where it ended, in a dull tunnel, shrouded in darkness. It could have been his day. Egan smiled and walked away.

Ger O'Keeffe's chin was cut and bloodied after his collision with John Guinan's hip, and having showered and changed, he set off for the Mater Hospital to get the wound stitched, on foot and alone. The others headed for the Cat and Cage pub, their refuge on the best nights and the worst. As O'Keeffe waited in the accident and emergency unit, a man sat down beside him.

'Were you in a fight?' he asked.

'Yerrah, I was in a bit of a fight, all right,' replied O'Keeffe.

'Were you at the match?'

'I was.'

'What did you think of it?'

'Sure, I suppose it was unfortunate Kerry lost.'

O'Keeffe's companion smiled. 'Ah, I was delighted. It's great to see a new team winning.'

O'Keeffe started to bristle. 'By the way,' he said, 'I'm one of the Kerry fellas who lost.'

'He suddenly changed his tune and was disappointed in what he'd said,' says O'Keeffe. 'Then he talked to me about it and actually made me feel good. He actually sat me in the car later and brought me back up to the Cat and Cage.'

John O'Keeffe sought out his wife, Liz, for support. Tom Spillane walked to the pub alone, spattered by passing cars and taunted by the beeping horns of those who recognised him. The Spillanes had gathered in one corner with the Templenoe crew. Other players mingled around the bar, supping pints and trying to forget. In one corner a group of players had gathered round Tommy Doyle. He took defeat hard. He could still feel Darby behind him, a phantom hand leaning against his back. If he had been behind the man, he could have stopped him. In his mind, his mistake had lost Kerry everything.

'Tommy took it very personally,' says John O'Keeffe. 'That was all wrong really. I won't forget it. Tommy took it very badly. We won as a team, and we lost as a team, but he took the whole thing on himself, which was wrong. I remember trying to get him to come round. It wasn't nice.'

When Ger O'Keeffe arrived from the Mater, he headed straight for Doyle's group. 'When I arrived up, Tommy Doyle was crying. The motto for the night when fellas had a few drinks was: *Five-in-a-row, five-in-a-row, by Christ we were close to five-in-a-row.*'

*　　*　　*

The Offaly players filed out from the Hogan Stand through a human corridor of backslapping and whooping. From there, the team bus headed straight for RTÉ for the post-match television show, a pre-recorded show with the winning team to be screened that night. Already players were restless. As the hours drew on in the television studio, the players were getting hungrier and thirstier.

'We were starving,' says Richie Connor. 'Fellas wouldn't have ate much that morning and all you want is a couple of pints and a bite to eat with your friends. We were put on a bus out to Montrose. Michael Lyster was doing his thing in twenty-minute slots. We were in the studio for about two hours. No drink, nothing.

'There was a meal in the Montrose next door afterwards and by then it was time to go out to the Ambassador [hotel, Kill, County Dublin]. Fellas might've had two pints drank. Not that all you wanted was to fill yourself with beer. But you're after winning this thing. You just wanted to chat to your friends. We had no control. Kerry wouldn't have gone to Montrose. RTÉ were delighted we won.'

The Ambassador in Kill, on the route home, had become a magnet for every stray Offaly car and supporter since the end of the game. By the time the players arrived, the hotel was bursting at the seams. The crowds streamed out into the car park. Water dripped down from the ceilings caused by the condensation steaming up from the thousands that had packed themselves into the function room. By the time the players arrived at the hotel, it was near eleven at night.

'Nothing could have prepared me for the scene there,' says Connor. 'Everybody was pissed. They were after running out of Guinness and Smithwicks in the hotel. Fellas were buying crates of large bottles. It was mad. There was broken glass on the floor. We thought we were going to walk in and everybody would be the same as ourselves. We weren't thinking. While we were caught up in Montrose, fellas were giving it a lash.'

The players were swamped. The greater the compliments that were delivered the harder came the backslaps. The post-match analysis was also suffering under the conditions.

Connor found himself cornered for the night.

'Well done, Tom! That was a great ball you kicked into Darby!'

'I'm Richie and it was Liam that kicked in the ball.'

'Next thing,' says Richie, 'fellas are being hoisted over our heads by drunken slobs. There was beer spilt and there's glass on the floor. It was crazy. It was a cattle mart. A fucking disaster.'

Sometime around one in the morning, Johnny Mooney headed for his room, but found the door already open when he arrived. 'There were about twenty people in there. I didn't even know them. It was like Woodstock. The whole night was like the Fleadh Ceoil in Ennis or something. We'd nowhere to stay, so we stayed up all night.'

*   *   *

At some stage during Kerry's banquet in the Gresham hotel, someone asked Páidí Ó Sé where he was headed afterwards. 'Oblivion, perhaps,' he replied. 'And if I don't get there, perhaps limbo.'

The room was draped in sorrow. As the bell rang for the banquet to begin, Kerry county chairman, Frank King, was still looking for

O'Dwyer. He went to his room and knocked on the door, and found him inside, lying on his bed staring at the ceiling. The mask had slipped. O'Dwyer was shattered. He had invested everything in his team. He had protected them all year, and had carried the pressure himself. Now the roof had come crashing in. Throughout his time as county chairman, King had supported O'Dwyer. Now, O'Dwyer needed him again.

'Mick,' he said, 'I want you to carry on as the trainer of the team.'

They went downstairs together, and for a few hours the guests gathered around the players and insulated them from disappointment. As the night drew on, the guests started getting loose and the cordon around the players started to unravel. Some guests went looking for Mikey Sheehy. When they found him, they had words.

'[They were saying] You bottled it,' says Sheehy. 'You cost us five-in-a-row. That sort of thing. It comes with the territory. They're not supporters. You knew the genuine guy who'd come over and throw the arm around you. He might be saying something else privately, but at least he came over and said something to you anyway.'

With the hotel bulging with people, the security gates outside the Gresham had been locked. Out on O'Connell Street some Kerry players who had left earlier had returned but found their way barred by bouncers. One player made a burst forward but was kicked back on to the street. There he sat, looking at the stars, with nowhere to go.

All across town there were parties and wakes. Declan Lynch wandered back to the Ormond hotel and headed for the bar. Galleon's dreams had been shattered too, but Lynch didn't care so much about that. They all had jobs waiting for them at home. They weren't broke. Winning five-in-a-row was bigger than any earthly concerns.

The Kerryman beside him was more agitated. The telephone in the bar rang for him once. Fifteen minutes later it rang again. And again. He explained it was his wife. His fondness for porter worried her, and the trauma of the day could send him hurtling off the rails. But there was more. Out in his car, he had thousands of T-shirts. Five-in-a-row shirts. What good were they now? He drank his pint.

'But I'll tell you the truth, Declan, there's always a way out. I'm after getting a right good deal on ten thousand plastic macs. If the Lord is any way fair at all, it'll pour rain for the week at the Listowel Races.'

They drank their pints, forgot their sorrows and waited for morning to come.

* * *

The party went on the following morning in Mulligan's pub, where Con Houlihan held court. When he spotted the Kerry contingent, Houlihan sent over a bottle of champagne. Up at the bar, Pat Spillane settled in beside Houlihan and saw a chance to fluff up his feathers.

'Con,' he asked, 'who were the best team you saw in1982?'

Con paused, and thought. 'Italy,' he replied.

The champagne disappeared quickly and Eoin Liston was into his set list, including his own altered version of 'Five in a Row'. People laughed, and as lunchtime came they headed back to the Gresham for the annual post-All-Ireland lunch with Offaly.

Liston was the personality Kerry wished the world to remember as theirs, gracious and good humoured. As Sean Lowry ordered a drink at the bar, Liston walked up behind him, pulling himself up to his maximum height. 'Lowry,' he said, remembering the sweet hook that had caught him on the jaw the previous day, 'I owe you one.'

Lowry looked him up and down. 'Bomber, I don't care if you owed me ten belts right now,' he said, and the tension dissolved in laughter.

As Johnny Mooney stood at the bar, he felt someone tap him on the back. He turned to hear a familiar voice that took him back to alarm-clock calls and early Sunday mornings in San Francisco. Micheál O'Hehir. For a minute, Mooney's throat went dry.

There were more songs from The Bomber and from a contingent of Dublin minors who were celebrating their own All-Ireland. John Egan sat beside PJ McGrath and chatted. Before long it was time to catch trains and head home.

That night Killarney and Tralee both teemed with people and sadness. The players stood on the trailer in Killarney in front of the Park Place hotel, looking shattered. O'Dwyer was broken. 'I know we let ye down,' he said, but the rest of his speech was carried off in a hail of cheers. The crowd chanted: '1983. 1983.' As he put the microphone down, O'Dwyer pulled his handkerchief from his pocket, and wiped his eye.

'Fate dealt us a lethal blow,' said John Egan, still smiling, still keeping his feelings in check. Páidí sang 'An Poc Ar Buille'. The Bomber led the crowd in 'The Rose of Tralee'. The rest of the week dissolved into nothing. Ger O'Keeffe got wind that Jimmy Keaveney and a few old Dubs were down and disappeared with them to Ballybunion. The rain spilled down all week on Listowel and the hawker's plastic macs sold like hotcakes.

On Wednesday night, the team followed Egan back to Sneem. A mighty bonfire illuminated South Square in the village, but the posters that had been prepared acclaiming Egan's return with the Sam Maguire were put away. Hundreds turned out, unsure what to say or do.

'It was like attending your own wake,' says Pat Spillane, 'only the corpses were having a drink with you. It was horrible. It's not that we didn't know about losing, but when you're standing there saying we'll be back next year …'

Local people queued up to pay John Egan a tribute. PJ Burns, the club chairman, recalled how Egan had raised more than IR£1000 when the club fundraised for their new pitch. People spoke of the debt Sneem owed to the Egans that could never be repaid. Frank King told Egan's friends and neighbours the team regretted nothing as much as failing to see Egan return home with the cup. 'We all know he deserved that honour.'

When Egan spoke, he simply said the right things. 'I can't believe just how genuine and sincere everybody is in welcoming us home. It's unbelievable.'

Sneem had shown Egan what he meant to them, but he didn't have what he wanted to give back. He was heartbroken. They all were.

PART IV

THE DECLINE

21 DISINTEGRATION

Declan Lynch woke up on Monday morning with talk of plastic macs swirling around his head and porter churning up his guts. He felt rough, but a day off rolled out ahead of him. He left Dublin and stopped in a pub in Portlaoise to decide his next destination.

Cork or Killarney.

In Cork, sympathy might be hard for a Kerryman to find, but Killarney? Losing homecomings didn't promise much either, especially this one. Then he started thinking outside the box. How far was Tullamore?

That night, Tullamore was thronged. As the train carrying the Offaly team pulled in, a mighty bonfire burned in the car park with a banner in front proclaiming, '*Veni, Vidi, Vici.*' The team bus slowly edged through the main street. Nuns, perched on the roof of their convent, waved tricolours. Waitresses emerged from the Bridge House hotel with trays laden down by glasses and bottles of champagne for the players. When the players reached the GAA centre and stood on the stage, they looked out across a sea of faces and remembered 1981. This time there were no tears, just smiles.

John Guinan saw his father hoist his youngest brother on to his shoulders for a better view, just as he had with John when Offaly came home with the cup a decade before. Tomás O'Connor gazed off into the distance and spotted his father at the back of the crowd, away from the mayhem. Their eyes fixed on each other for a moment, and Tomás saw him nod. Praise enough.

When Eugene McGee spoke, he took himself back to 1976. He recalled the old days travelling to Askeaton to play Limerick and Lahinch on a freezing winter's afternoon.

'Those that weren't there don't know what they missed,' he said. 'Lahinch in December takes some beating.'

The week that followed was manic. On Tuesday morning, John Guinan woke up feeling bleary and struggled into the kitchen for his breakfast. The house was empty except for his mother. Everyone was at work. The All-Ireland had been won. Time that normal life resumed.

He took a walk into Clonygowan, the local village, for the newspaper. Having paid one of the two village pubs the courtesy of calling in the previous night, he decided to drop into the other. 'It was about noon,' he says. 'What was along the top of the bar? A whole load of lunchboxes and my father and my two brothers in the middle of them. Padraic Dunne's father was there and a few more. Everybody thought they'd gone to work!'

That night, Richie Connor brought the cup back to Walsh Island. On Wednesday they hit Ferbane, where green, white and gold Fianna Fáil election posters had been doctored to read: 'Welcome to Lowry Country'. Back in Offaly, Edenderry came after Ferbane. That night, Richie Connor called Sean Lowry aside. 'I've something to show you,' he said. He reached into his jacket and pulled out a crumpled envelope. The address read: 'Richie Connor, Offaly captain, Offaly'. The handwriting looked feeble. Lowry took out the letter. It was from an old woman in Fermanagh, thanking Richie and Offaly for the joy they had brought her on Sunday. She was the old woman down the country lane. She was everyone.

By then the team were moving through the county like a travelling circus. One night they hit Gracefield, where a player met a local car dealer and swapped his old Fiesta for a brand new car. On Thursday, Johnny Mooney, Matt Connor and a crew headed for Listowel races, fell in with a few of the Kerry boys and were fêted all weekend. Free passes for the races were produced, while their money was no good anywhere they tried to spend it. This was their week. They showered in people's houses and bought clothes as they needed them.

Weeks of celebrating turned into months and they quickly became enslaved by their obligations With requests for the Sam Maguire cup rolling in, Mick Fitzgerald was given custody of the trophy and provided with a diary to keep a schedule of appearances. The players tried to share the workload, but public demand didn't allow that. People wanted to see Darby – Matt – Richie – The Lowrys – Furlong. Players were out for nights on end. Their days were clogged with appointments at schools. There was no escape.

'I did thirty-two schools that winter,' says Sean Lowry. 'And there was no point in going at three in the evening, they wanted you there in the morning so they could give the kids a half-day and no homework.

'I went to Leitrim with it. Longford. I went to the strangest places. The biggest problem was people had jobs. I was working with the ESB but I had a very good supervisor. I was going to him at eight in the morning with the Sam Maguire in the boot outside, saying: "I've promised to go to three schools this morning. I'll be back at lunchtime." It was the only way it could be done. I'd have the cup booked for three days.'

The cup went everywhere in the evening, and everywhere there was drink. One weekend, Offaly played a league game against Down in Newry and were afforded a civic reception by Newry and Mourne District Council the night before. A long table was covered with bottles of beer. A local official approached one player: 'There's tea being served over there,' he said. 'We can get tea at home,' the player replied. The following day, Down ate Offaly alive.

One evening, deep into the winter of 1982, Liam Currams headed down from Longford to a function in Tullamore. As the night drew on, Currams didn't leave till half-four in the morning and braced himself for a treacherous drive home. As he neared home, Currams approached the brow of a hill when the car swerved out of control. It lurched to the left and went flying through a ditch, landing in a field. Currams shook himself. He felt okay. Then, he fell asleep.

As dawn broke, he was woken by a thudding sound. He opened his eyes to find a calf rubbing its face against the window. He turned the key in the ignition. The car was turning over and the wheels were moving, but the car stayed in the same spot. When he got out to check, he found the car balanced on a tree stump, suspended in mid-air. This life was becoming too much. The wheels were still spinning, but Offaly were starting to slow down.

That winter, Richie Connor got a phone call from Jack O'Shea to see if he could borrow the cup. All those years and he had never got a picture taken with it. It had suddenly struck Jacko he might never see it again.

* * *

Winter passed slowly in Waterville. As the tourists emptied out, the cold weather set in and the Atlantic began to churn with temper. Mick O'Dwyer was left alone with his thoughts.

He brooded for months. Some nights he watched the video, pausing the tape at vital moments, forensically deconstructing every frame with sadistic precision. One wild winter's evening his old friend Owen McCrohan called to one of O'Dwyer's hotels in Waterville to see him. When O'Dwyer descended the stairs, McCrohan met a broken man. The twinkle was gone. The spark of enthusiasm for football was extinguished. When the talk turned to the final, O'Dwyer could reel off moments where the game had turned from Kerry. As they chatted, the wind rattled the window frames and howled through the empty hotel. In this ghostly place, O'Dwyer pondered his future. Rumours rumbled around Kerry that he would leave, and as Christmas approached he was beginning to agree with them. 'I'll never start from the bottom again,' he said.

Eoin Liston had been in Waterville since 1979, where O'Dwyer had taken him on as a personal winter project and turned him into a serious player. They were tight. When the local council asked O'Dwyer to organise keep fit classes during the winter, he brought Liston along to work through his aerobics. They ran circuits around Waterville together, with only O'Dwyer's guttural breathing breaking the night silence.

They played rounds of golf on the links course. They played handball and badminton. When the squash court in Cahirsiveen was free they travelled in for a game. O'Dwyer was always the referee, and Liston rarely questioned his decisions. They played cards on a Saturday night, always stopping to watch 'Dallas' at O'Dwyer's insistence. 'Maybe he saw himself as some kind of JR,' Liston teased.

O'Dwyer always pushed Liston hard, but Liston loved him for it. Now, O'Dwyer needed people like Liston around him. There were days when he and Liston would be striding down the fairway at the links course when O'Dwyer would return to an incident in the game, recalling the minutiae of the moment with chilling clarity. The clamour had been too much. The jerseys, the hype. Páidí's *piseoga*. Mikey Sheehy's loose kick-out of defence. The nudge on Tommy Doyle. The crazy frees called by the referee. Spillane's injury. It was harrowing.

Liston had sensed O'Dwyer's hunger for five-in-a-row all summer. Throughout his life, O'Dwyer had raged against the conventions of Kerry football. He had proved himself a footballer of rare worth despite almost being discarded as a Kerry minor. He had taken a willowy senior team in 1975, when Kerry was sinking to its lowest ebb, and won an All-Ireland. He had torn up the old manual of catch-and-kick, re-invented Kerry's style and increased the levels of training and devotion required to succeed. He had survived the abuse and derision thrown at him. Five-in-a-row would have shown them all. Five-in-a-row would have carried him and his team to a peak where they could have seen for miles, safe in the knowledge that no team in the history of football would ever possess the talent or the perseverance to join them. Now, he was left with nothing. The 31½ counties were sharpening their claws again.

'The biggest psychological problem Kerry ever came across was the five-in-a-row,' says Ger O'Keeffe. 'Psychologically, we were in trouble going into that game. We had been built up into something superhuman. We allowed ourselves to become embroiled in a lot of fantasy. We would've walked ourselves into a false sense of security. Mentally, most of the players forgot to play, or couldn't play, because psychologically they were battered.'

Meanwhile, Eugene McGee was gleefully thinking about history. Tom Donoghue had run the team up Clonin Hill during the spring of 1983 and noticed no change in their fitness or their mood. John Guinan was starting to show real pedigree. All the Connors were in good fettle. Surfing on the wave of the previous year, Johnny Mooney had decided to stay at home and bought a pub in Geashill. Offaly strolled through the league and were toasted wherever they went. As All-Ireland champions they could pick their challenge matches from the dozens of offers. One evening they travelled to Castleisland to play Kerry. With a few minutes left, Offaly sprang Seamus Darby. As the game wound down, he burst through with only Charlie Nelligan left to beat. On his home pitch, after everything that had gone before, Charlie couldn't allow himself get beaten. He sprinted out and smothered the shot. The crowd cheered, and Darby smiled. 'I remember saying: "Why the f*** didn't you kick that one and I'd have saved the other one?" said Nelligan. "You could have this one!"'

Offaly collected six All Stars that winter – Martin Furlong, Mick Fitzgerald, Liam O'Connor, Sean Lowry, Liam Currams, Padraic Dunne, and Matt Connor – and they prepared for the trip to America. This was living. Freedom.

On their way from Los Angeles to San Francisco, John Guinan, Liam O'Connor, Padraic Dunne, Richie Connor and Galway's Seamus McHugh escaped the main party, rented a car and headed for the desert. They ventured into Indian country. Death Valley. Vegas. For three days they drove from town to town, cramming themselves into double rooms at the local motels. They partied hard, yet made San Francisco in time for their battery of functions and matches. On the flight home, Padraic Dunne celebrated his twenty-first birthday. Guinan was twenty. They had All-Ireland medals in their pockets and sore backs from the slaps of two weeks' adulation on the west coast.

They felt invincible. But problems were brewing.

Gerry Carroll and Eugene McGee were bugging each other again. Winning an All-Ireland hadn't softened the edges on their relationship, and the night before Offaly played their first Leinster championship game against Kildare, they got snagged again.

That night, McGee called Carroll. He was dropping him from the team for disciplinary reasons. He wasn't putting in the effort at training, said McGee. On the other end of the line, Carroll was seething with rage. 'It was the closest I came to quitting,' he says. 'People talked me out of it. I'd had enough then. That's when I lost a lot of respect for our manager, and things started to turn sour.'

That night, Carroll drank a few pints and forgot about football. The following day McGee put him on at half-time. Offaly smashed Kildare in the end, but by then further cracks had started to appear. Late in the game, Sean Lowry ran out to contest a ball, caught his foot in a hole and tore ligaments in his ankle. Liam Currams was struggling too. During a club game one evening in April, he leapt to catch a ball and came down heavily on his ankle, snapping the ligaments. They started him in the Leinster final on Barney Rock, but two months without training or a game knocked the sharpness out of him.

Mick Fitzgerald was nursing a pulled hamstring. Half of Offaly's defence should have been ruled out. Seamus Darby had regained the weight he had lost on Clonin Hill in 1982, and a winter of turkey-and-ham dinners and porter hadn't been shed by many of the rest. A few weeks before the Leinster final, Offaly travelled to Enniscrone to play Sligo and ripped them to shreds. Donegal would win an Ulster title that summer, but Offaly had taken them apart too. At the functions afterwards, the players remember McGee laying out his theories on how to achieve All-Ireland victory. Six years of trial and error were now being condensed into one easy-to-swallow pill.

The week before the Leinster final, McGee and Leo Grogan had travelled to Cork for the Munster final. O'Dwyer had pulled himself and Kerry back together for 1983, but, like Offaly, cracks were showing. John

Egan and Jack O'Shea had won another county title with South Kerry, and this time Jacko was captain, but the team was creaking as they headed to face Cork.

Jimmy Deenihan and John O'Keeffe had pulled hamstrings. Sean Walsh was gone from centrefield. Ger O'Keeffe and Paudie Lynch had approached this year as their last. Cork had given them frights in 1982, but nothing that had Kerry quaking in their boots.

That morning, the rain came again. Haunted by more *piseoga*, Páidí Ó Sé spotted McGee negotiating the deep pools of water in his wellington boots as he entered Páirc Uí Chaoimh. 'McGee is here,' he said. 'We're not going to win again.'

With two minutes left, his omens looked like being shattered for good. Kerry were two points up and the sun was out. Their rehabilitation looked complete. Time was almost up when Cork's Denis Allen sprinted for a ball in centrefield with Páidí on his tail. Allen gathered the ball, felt contact on his back and went sprawling to the ground. The ball was sent in long, where Tadhg Murphy was waiting. He had time to let off a shot. The ball slithered beyond Charlie Nelligan and rolled helplessly to the net. Cork were a point ahead. Nine years of relentless defeat and humiliation evaporated.

Kerry were beaten. Another last-minute goal. Losing to Offaly had hurt them badly, but to Cork? 'That was worse than '82,' says Sean Walsh. 'Cork is Cork. No Kerryman likes to lose to them. They were the one crowd I found it hard to lose to.'

Defeat to Cork brought some kind of closure for others. The previous winter had passed like an age for Mikey Sheehy. For nights he had lain awake in bed, thinking about Furlong and the penalty. When he slept, the sudden jolt of missing the shot often woke him again. People could see it in him.

And while O'Dwyer wrestled his own demons, he also took Sheehy's on. Forget about it, he told him, it's done. By 1983, Sheehy was worn out. A short summer gave him a chance to draw breath.

'I won't say there was a sense of relief, but the level of

disappointment was very little in comparison to the previous year. The jokes were going round then that Kerry are never beaten till the last minute. Tadhgie Murphy and Cork did us a major favour because it gave fellas time to rest and recharge, and see would they go again.'

Either way, losing to Cork still inflicted an incurable kind of pain. On the way home from Páirc Uí Chaoimh, McGee made some deductions: Cork in the All-Ireland semi-final; Galway on the other side, and a Donegal team Offaly had recently massacred. Even with players carrying weight and injuries starting to mount, the summer was theirs for the taking. When the team reconvened in Edenderry the night before the Leinster final with Dublin, McGee was in boisterous mood. Offaly weren't chasing anyone now. Everyone was chasing them.

'His attitude changed to: we were to go out and beat Dublin in the first five minutes and game over,' says Richie Connor, 'instead of telling us we were the luckiest shower of fuckers ever to win an All-Ireland – Dublin are going to come out and hit you with everything. Be ready for them.'

'We had it won before we went out,' says Pat Fitzgerald. 'I saw a couple of Dublin players, Mick Holden and a few others, walking into Croke Park. I pitied them. They were on a hiding to nothing. We were going to give them such a beating. The one message I remember from the night before was: a good team wins one All-Ireland. A great team wins two, and we had the capability to be a great team. This was before the Leinster final.'

The game was a disaster. Dublin hit two early goals and while Offaly never let them further away than four points, they never looked like reeling them in either. Darby was taken off, Matt Connor missed a penalty. By the end, even Mick Fitzgerald, the standard bearer for proper attitude and relentless concentration, had snapped.

'The crowd was in on the sideline,' says Fitzgerald. 'On one occasion Martin Furlong was looking for the ball to kick it out and here was a Dublin supporter at the back of the goalmouth going on a solo run. Paddy Collins [referee] had given a few iffy decisions which I thought were a bit harsh, so it was building. Martin Furlong took a short kick-out to my brother. Pat went down on it. Ciarán Duff came in with his knee on top of him. I calculated: the game's over; we're not going to win this. If Collins isn't going to do something about that, I will.

'I took off and leapt with my feet into Duff and scraped my brother's back as I was doing it. The crowd came on the field. I got a belt of a flagpole off a supporter. Collins says to me, "For your own safety, I'm sending you off." And that was it.'

In the end, Dublin won by two points. McGee was shattered. Kevin Heffernan had trumped him. Offaly were shattered.

'It was largely my own personal fault because I never thought we were going to lose it,' says McGee. 'We were going into the Leinster final after annihilating everybody in Leinster, beating Dublin the year before and Kerry were gone. We had this All-Ireland won. That's the way we were. Immaturity. And an element of pomposity, obviously. That was one of my worst days because I took a lot of the blame on myself.

'I wouldn't have overestimated the value of the team, but I'd have overestimated how good we were for that day. Kerry were gone and there didn't seem to be anybody else who could beat us. That was a big mistake on my part.'

That September, Dublin clobbered Galway in a vile All-Ireland final. Five players were sent off and the joyous rush of the previous year had been forgotten. 'I remember walking out of the Cusack Stand,' says Tom Spillane, 'and some fella saying to me, "Jesus, ye better get back." He didn't have to say it twice. We knew in our own minds.'

Kerry were gone and suddenly the world missed them. The Wednesday before the All-Ireland final, O'Dwyer had called the players together in Tralee. He ran them around the pitch. He watched their body language. Bringing them out this week poked at their psyche, helped see if there was another year in them. He knew his defence needed restructuring, but the rest of the team still beamed with health. He still had the Spillanes and Bomber. Jacko and Sean Walsh. Mikey. Power and Ogie. Ó Sé and Charlie. Tommy Doyle had begun to conquer the demons that had assailed him since the 1982 final and almost tormented him into early retirement. That was enough. If he could keep them keen, there was nothing to be afraid of. Offaly in 1982 and then Cork had soaked up all their fear. Nothing else could possibly go wrong. He ran them around the field, and started planning a new team for 1984. Kerry would start again.

Offaly were drifting towards the end. In 1984 they began the Leinster championship against Longford looking weary and dishevelled. All the urgency that had once marked their training sessions was gone. Players were worn out. The precision that defined their preparations had been replaced by carelessness. When they arrived in Longford for the game, someone realised they had forgotten to bring the jerseys. By the end of the match, only Matt Connor's accuracy salvaged a draw.

The replay at Croke Park was even more haphazard. Martin Furlong had picked up an injury late in the week, leaving Offaly reliant on reserve keeper Dinny Wynne. By half-time, Offaly were in trouble. McGee decided on drastic action. Laz Molloy had played some Under-21 football for Offaly as goalkeeper, and had been spotted entering the ground. An announcement was made on the public address system asking Molloy to make his way to the Offaly dressing room. Molloy was downstairs beneath the stand, eating sandwiches and soup with his brother. His boots were in his car, which was parked a short distance away on Mountjoy Square. His brother collected the boots and Molloy took his place in goal, looking out on a team decimated by injuries and drained of life. Offaly beat Longford 3-15 to 3-10, but, with the team now nursing seven injured players, they didn't get the break they needed to regroup. The following week, they met Dublin.

Seamus Darby had struggled with injury all summer and the week before the Dublin game he settled himself for a day on the bench. That Saturday he attended a funeral, and let his guard down. He had a pint, then another. An afternoon's drinking stretched into the night. The following morning he awoke with a blinding hangover, and news that he was starting.

He lasted till half-time, but by then Offaly were gone. Injuries had reduced the team to rubble. They tried to rough Dublin up, but got beaten to a pulp. In the end, they lost by eight points. The reporters filed into the Offaly dressing room after the game and gathered round their colleague. McGee delivered a eulogy.

'This Offaly team has done a fabulous job,' said McGee. 'But clearly it has come to the end of its tether. It's the price it had to pay for five years of hard slogging.'

After almost fifteen years of fighting Dublin, trailing Kevin Heffernan along the sideline and irritating Dublin like a thorn in their paw, McGee had sensed Dublin would be the team to finish them off. 'The will to win,' he said, 'is no longer there.'

After the Dublin game, Gerry Carroll headed to Boston with Richie Connor for the summer and enjoyed the pace of life there. At twenty-five he had grown tired of Offaly and McGee. Just as his father had known when to let Offaly go, so did his son.

McGee's appetite was waning too. This business of winning two All-Irelands and securing greatness didn't entirely make sense to him. Winning one had been his driving force. That was done. He made a phone call to Matt Connor and asked him how he felt about another year's training. Connor couldn't give McGee a straight answer. It helped settle McGee's mind.

It was over.

22 MATT

Offaly GAA star Matt Connor is paralysed from the waist down after a Christmas Day accident. The 25 year-old Tullamore Garda received critical spinal injuries in a car crash as he drove to join his parents and family. He was the most injured over a two-day fatality-free Christmas holiday.

The Connor family, Mr and Mrs Jim Connor and Matt's five brothers and two sisters, are awaiting the opinion of top surgeons on whether Matt will walk again or not. The Offaly scoring ace – the leading scorer nationally for the past two years – won three Bank of Ireland All-Star awards. He was a member, along with his brother Richie, of the Offaly team that put paid to Kerry's five-in-a-row dream in 1982.

Garda Connor was driving home from Tullamore to his home in Walsh Island when his Ford Escort car careered out of control at Kellellery, Geashill, about thirteen miles from Tullamore.

The Escort struck a tree, throwing Garda Connor from the car and critically injuring his back. He lay on the roadside for almost half an hour before another motorist saw him.

Garda Connor was taken by ambulance to Tullamore General Hospital but was later transferred to Dr Steevens's Hospital, Dublin where he underwent surgery.

Irish Independent, 27 December 1984

Matt Connor: *Half an hour? I could've been there all day and not realised it. My mind was strangled in shock. There was no blood. No feeling. Just silence.*

So weird. I tried to twitch my legs. Nothing. Maybe it might wear off. I couldn't feel the cold. Christmas morning and no cold.

It must've been a puncture. I felt the tyre blow out. Next thing, the car was gone flying at the corner. It was only a small lump of a tree. Nothing to it. They reckoned it wasn't the fall that did the damage but the car door. I think my back hit the door handle. I wasn't going hard. No speed involved. Now I'm lying there, trying to move my legs and wondering, is this temporary or what?

It was an old tradition in the Garda station on Christmas Day. I just called in, had the crack, met a few lads, then headed home for the day. Someone came across me and called for help. The ambulance arrived and took me to Tullamore General. I remember the staff talking about me. When I got there they examined me immediately. They checked for feeling in my legs, but I already knew there was something wrong. They transferred me to Dublin. They talked to me without telling me anything. They didn't need to. I knew.

Richie Connor: We got a phone call that Matt was in an accident, that he was all right but he was badly broken up. I drove straight over to the hospital. I was expecting blood and broken bones but there wasn't a drop of blood. The surgeon said they were transferring him to Dublin because there was a danger that some damage had been done to his spine. But we were still holding out hope.

I was in Dr Steevens's Hospital that evening, just opposite Heuston Station. It was where they operated on me. The following morning I was told I'd be recuperating there for a fortnight. The injuries needed to settle down. For a while it didn't really register. There was so much happening. People were calling in. Family were around. All the time the doctors kept holding out hope. I was holding out hope. Maybe the swelling will go down and my toes will start to move. Two weeks would tell everything. People still calling. Two weeks to decide the rest of my life. Waiting for news. Hard to take it all in.

Padraic Dunne: I never thought at the time he was going to end up in a wheelchair. I remember going in to see him and he was upside down in the bed. I was talking to him, laughing and joking. And I came out thinking to myself, 'Matt'll be all right now', but he knew at that stage.

Sean Lowry: I remember calling up to see his parents a couple of weeks after the accident. Richie's father was one of my biggest fans. Richie was always telling me he was a fan of the old-type player. They were heartbroken. They were getting older and it was tough. Matt Connor will never grow old. He's like James Dean on a football field. No one ever saw him in his thirties. He will always be remembered as the athlete he was.

Michael Lowry: A whole lot of us went up. He was in great form that time. He was so quiet before that. It was like he accepted it quick and just got on with it. There was four or five of us there that night and he never stopped talking. He never gave us time to chat.

Mick Fitzgerald: I remember the previous League game we'd played – I think it was Mayo in Tullamore – I'd had a go at all and sundry at half-time when I thought they weren't trying, including Matt. That was the last thing I said to Matt on the field of play. 'For fuck's sake, cop on, show a bit of something.' That was difficult.

The two weeks passed and I ended up in a rehabilitation centre in Dun Laoghaire. Feck all can be done. This is it. I'll be here for six months and in a wheelchair for the rest of my life. Time to harden. Time to adjust.

These are the worst moments. People have stopped calling. Life is starting again. You can go mad and lose the head, but that's not going to do any good. I don't think I did. I hope I didn't. The rehabilitation work took three months, but I stayed six.

They did some occupational therapy with me, lots of physio. They put me through some counselling. Total rubbish. I look around the hospital and meet so many people in the same position as me, and some who are much worse off. A good talk with them helped me more than hours with a psychiatrist. They know what's ahead. They're living it. A lot of people are coming back to the centre for check-ups, people who have been in wheelchairs for four and five years. They seem happy enough. They're able to get along with life. That's the best part of the rehab. People.

Brendan Lowry: I'll never forget the joyrider sitting in the bed beside him. He wasn't able to move. The joyrider had a bit of wire around his finger with the wire extended out and another hole at the other end where the nurse used put a fag in it. His family had disowned him. He was slagging Matt because Matt only wrote off an Escort while he was in a BMW. I'd say Matt got some kind of inner strength when he looked round and saw the people around him; he was the best of the ten or eleven in the ward.

Richie Connor: Dun Laoghaire was a kind of tonic for us because he was one of the best cases in there. There was a lad from Mayo who fell off some bales of hay and was paralysed from the neck down. We had been warned, Murt and myself, that Matt might be inclined to say things he didn't mean, that he might lose it at times. But he never said a bad word. I wrote an article for a programme at a benefit game where I said that when Matt played for Walsh Island and Offaly, he played in front of handfuls of people and before seventy thousand in Croke Park, yet he seemed to be the same guy in both situations. Sport probably helped him come to terms with things.

Liam O'Connor: The only day I saw him sort of down was the day when I went in and I knew he'd been told. But it only lasted three or four minutes and he was back. He never made you feel uncomfortable, did Matt. When you were with him, you could talk football. In fact, he wanted you to talk football. He never made you feel: Jesus, I have to be careful, I can't mention this. To me, the way he handled his accident far exceeded his exploits out on the field. It was really, really brilliant. He must have had his hard times, but he never let you see them.

I made it back to Walsh Island in June, sitting in my wheelchair with a new life ahead of me. Football was gone and I missed it, but that wasn't the biggest part of it. It was the simplest things in life were now hardest for me. Just sitting there wanting to take the dogs for a walk, that was hard. As the years went on I missed playing football even more, but that wears off too. I was twenty-five when I finished playing, but I put so much into it. I'd spent hours kicking frees every day in Walsh Island, bringing the bag of balls to training in Tullamore before a session with Offaly and practising even more. I'd done my bit. I would've liked to have done more, but it didn't work out that way. Feck all I could do about it.

The joy in football was always in the simplest things, not in the claps on the back and the medals but in excelling yourself as a footballer. It was in kicking a sweet free or shooting a goal. Setting up a score or out-running a defender. For years I used to spend time on my own, working out ways to shimmy past a defender. Maybe throw my hip to the right and swing around to the left, try and leave the defender behind.

It was the nights inside in training trying to beat Martin Furlong.

You were always proving yourself. Whenever McGee brought a new player on the panel, he always seemed to single me out for a hard time. I never liked it. I always thought he picked on me. Maybe he was trying to make a point about no one being bigger than the team. I never thought I was bigger than anyone, but I wasn't going to answer back anyway.

You dreamed of winning All-Irelands, but it was only afterwards I realised that wasn't really what I was dreaming about. Winning the All-Ireland never quite felt like I thought it would. The final whistle goes, you cheer and whoop and shake hands, but then there's a fella in a blazer dragging the captain away to make sure he gets to the podium. RTÉ are organising to get you into studio later on. Nothing stops. People have jobs. Life goes on.

Mick O'Dwyer (from his biography, 1989): After [1982] I was inconsolable for months and months, but it was only fitting that Matt Connor should win an All-Ireland medal. He was a brilliant footballer and if he had been playing for Kerry we might have won ten-in-a-row.

Tomás O'Connor: It had a serious impact on me. I haven't seen Matt a lot since that. I don't think I ever really handled it that well. I didn't go see him that much in hospital. Maybe it was a fault of mine. I regret it a bit.

I didn't ignore football. Even if I wanted to, I couldn't. The first match I went to was Walsh Island's first game in the county championship against Edenderry. When I came in, people clapped and cheered. People were very good, but at the time it was all a bit much for me. I didn't want the attention as a footballer, and I didn't want it now. I'd have preferred to be away from it all, but you have to go through that.

At times the wheelchair got me down, but you have to endure those times too. That's what helps you recover. Eventually you have to accept there's absolutely nothing you can do about it. If there was even a sliver of a chance I could have recovered, maybe I'd feel different. But from the moment they loaded me into that ambulance, I knew.

I missed exercise. I tried getting involved in wheelchair basketball, but you had to go to Clontarf to play, which meant a day's travelling to play a bad game of basketball. Maybe if I hadn't played football I would've kept it on, but it was too much for too little.

I started doing a little coaching. In 1986 I took over the Offaly minor footballers. It energised me again. I took it so seriously. When I played football, I practised my kicking every single day. After I took on the minors I didn't miss an underage game in Offaly for ten years. I went to club matches. I was at colleges games. Any new talent that was coming through, I knew of them.

In 1989 we got to an All-Ireland final. We worked with hundreds of players and over the years a few came through that started getting Offaly back on track at senior level. Years later, John O'Keeffe got me involved with the Irish International Rules team that played Australia in 2002 and 2003. I worked as a selector when Gerry Fahy was in charge of the Offaly seniors in 2004.

Was getting involved in coaching a form of therapy? I wouldn't think that way. I liked it. I had an interest in it. Getting around and travelling to training sessions and matches was hard, but the satisfaction in getting teams to perform and watching players develop into something special was something else.

Football and sport go on. You gear up to achieve something. Then you move on. Whether you're standing up or sitting in a wheelchair makes no difference. For twenty-three years I've tried to live a happy life. That much I've done.

Fr Sean Heaney: I always think of the way the Greeks commemorate their heroes in ancient times. If you see any of the statues of their greats, even the gods, they're always depicted at their peak, the moment of their greatest deed. They're immortalised in that. I always think of Matt scoring one of his goals. That is Matt.

23 THE THREE-MINUTE MEN

Back in Boston, as 1985 began, the same dreams haunted Gerry Carroll over and again. As he drifted off to sleep, a showreel of Matt Connor's greatest moments ran through his head. He could see Matt catching and kicking. Matt sliding out of tackles and jinking away. He saw Matt walking. He couldn't sleep nights. The only way for Carroll to carry on was to leave the game behind for a while.

He lost interest in every sport. He stopped playing football. When he started again he was rooted in America with no desire to return home. At twenty-five years of age, his time with Offaly was over.

'I had no problem leaving. It was a good time for me to leave. It was when I had lost interest in playing for McGee. I probably played some of the best football of my career in Boston and New York. The final here in 1984 went to a replay. One team brought on two subs: John Kearns [Dublin] and Ambrose Rodgers [Down]. It was All-Star stuff. I played with John Egan. That was class. Every ball I got, it was: Here, John.'

The memories from 1982 still warm him. The day after the 1982 final, Carroll called into a bookies' in Edenderry. Having laid IR£20 on Offaly at 5/1, he was there to collect. Later that week, he left the celebrations behind to take part in the latest round of the Superstars TV show with Seamus Darby, doing squats and dribbling a football through traffic cones for a day. Later that winter, he agreed to take part in a charity race around a dog track along with some other Offaly players. He remembers running a 1050-yard race around a greyhound track for charity that winter with some other Offaly players, including Pat Fitzgerald, the King of Clonin Hill. To stand any chance, the rest of the boys needed to find a way to hold Fitzgerald back. The race amounted to two laps. Gently, they convinced him to take it easy for the first lap.

'I was a pretty decent sprinter in my day,' says Carroll, 'but if it got too long I wasn't very good. I went to Belfield the week before to see what time I'd run 1000 yards in. I didn't even finish it. I talked to my boss at the time who played for Shamrock Rovers. He said: "You fucking eejit, when you run a race like that, save something for a sprint at the end. At least you'll finish the race".'

With Fitzgerald already agreed to a gentle first lap, Carroll had reduced the chances for humiliation. That night, everything went to plan. As they rounded the track and began the second lap, Fitzgerald stepped on the gas. Carroll was still running. With 100 yards to go, he was still there. With 50 yards to go, he was on Fitzgerald's shoulder. At the tape, he had passed him out. *Chariots of Fire* music in his head, and bragging rights for all eternity.

In time, his grief over Matt's accident left him, and he began to remember better times. When he married in 1996, Matt travelled from Offaly for the wedding. And when Matt suddenly turned up in New York a couple of years later to get married, Carroll and Martin Furlong were the only Offaly players there. The frustration about how his time with Offaly had ended dissolved, too.

'I wouldn't say I ever fell out with McGee. I don't know if people think I did. I wasn't the easiest player to deal with. I guess I was young and reckless at times. When you're young you think it's so good – you don't think about it ending. I had my disagreements with him. But I've had them with a lot of people.'

He remembers picking up an Irish newspaper in New York one Sunday containing an article about Offaly's decline. In the middle of the piece, Brendan Lowry was asked what he missed most from the old team. 'I miss Gerry Carroll landing the ball into my chest from forty yards,' he replied. The line touched Carroll. He turned the page. Those days were done.

Back home, the team was drifting apart. Sean Lowry had moved to Crossmolina in 1985 and was persuaded to play one more year with Mayo. They started him in the Connacht final, and he picked up a medal before retiring that autumn.

Tomás O'Connor's life was getting busy. He had a young family to rear and a career to deal with. Matt's injury haunted him. He retired in 1987 with a mind to return in a year or two, but he never did.

'It just didn't seem right any more. Offaly had gone down with Matt there in 1983 and 1984, so we can't say the decline came because of Matt's crash, but what hope we had of coming back was largely dependent on Matt. Once he was gone a few people started to drift away. It just seemed too much hassle to get back into it. It died away a bit. Things just didn't seem as important.' His brother Liam's life became troubled and complicated. By the mid-eighties he had finished with football. His marriage had broken down.

Others hit problems too. With Offaly in decline, Johnny Mooney struggled to knock any fun from the games any more. In 1987 he headed back to America for a couple of years, then rejoined the Offaly panel in 1990. He lasted a few months. 'It was terrible,' says Mooney. 'We were at nothing. There was only a handful turning up for training. It was unbelievable. What was worse was, it was accepted. It was considered the norm.

'With respect to anyone who came in to train Offaly, the bar had come down an awful lot. It was accepted that Offaly were in the wilderness.'

Mooney couldn't settle. In 1989 he sold the pub he had bought in Geashill on the wave of optimism triggered by 1982, and hopscotched between England and Offaly for the bones of a decade. He trained teams in England and worked different jobs. Eventually he came home to Rhode, alone. His marriage had ended and his family had grown up. Recently he started building a house. A home.

'Starting for the second time,' he smiles.

Other players were cursed with misfortune. Having torn ankle ligaments in April 1983 and started the Leinster final without a training session or a game behind him, Liam Currams blew his knee out in 1984 during a game with the ESB. By September 1985 he had recovered to make the Offaly hurling panel that won the All-Ireland, but at twenty-five years of age, playing football had become too much for him.

'I had gotten awful tired. I was mentally tired from playing matches. The fun had gone out of it. I wasn't able to compete. My ability as a footballer was running and athleticism. I thought I was a pretty handy hurler and I liked it. But when I couldn't run properly, the edge went off my game. Then my confidence went.

'Maybe I had too much done too soon. I was burned out. When I injured my knee, I didn't want to play in that match. I was physically tired. My last football game for Offaly was against Waterford in Dungarvan. I went on a solo run, but I couldn't solo the ball. We were all muscle bound from the training in Rhode. I remember McGee giving out shit to the lads. I was so mentally tired. I wasn't at the races.'

Around the same time John Guinan's knees gave out, while the Fitzgeralds drifted quietly out of the scene. By 1985, Martin Furlong was thirty-nine years of age. When he finally let go at the end of the year, the timing felt right. A year later he was suffering. He needed his fix.

In 1988, his brother Tom rang home from New York with an invitation. He had a bar in upstate New York that needed a manager. Furlong was forty-two. His kids were growing up. His football career was behind him. They had a day to decide. He and his wife stayed up all night talking. They sat by the fire, looking into the glowing embers. 'Martin,' his wife said, 'we could be here in twenty years' time doing the same thing. We'll do the worrying after. Let's go.' They never came back. America had claimed the last of the Furlong boys.

By then, America was teeming with the young Irish. The football teams were packed with stars that had emigrated, seeking a living. At the weekends more players flew over to play matches for badly needed envelopes filled with dollars. Padraic Dunne worked on building sites with Larry Tompkins in Dublin during the eighties when Kildare were struggling, but Tompkins was already a star. In 1985 Dunne headed for New York to play football for two weeks, and he and his wife stayed five years. Tompkins was on the same flight.

They shared a house for a while: part home, part boot camp. Tompkins's devotion to fitness was maniacal, and Dunne was forced to endure alongside him. 'You don't stay with Larry Tompkins unless you want to stay fit,' says Dunne.

They were just two stars in a vast constellation. One year, Dunne returned home with the local GAA club in New York for a summer tour. They played Laois, Mayo, Donegal and Cork, and stayed unbeaten. Only a draw with Donegal blemished their record.

'All the footballers were over there,' he says, 'I drove around looking for work here. There was none. I know now if a good young lad in Offaly, or anywhere, was leaving for America someone would say to him, why aren't you staying around? I was working on a building site. I was starting to learn a trade in blocklaying. Not one person ever came to me. I've only thought of that in the last few years. At the time I didn't think of it.'

Dunne kept returning to play with Offaly during the summers till the early nineties, but the thrill was gone.

*   *   *

A bank holiday Monday morning, and the gentle aroma of frying sausages wafted through the Greyhound Bar in Toomevara. The night before had been a good one. Seamus Darby had sung a few songs. The place had crackled with people and business was good. The morning brought a tinge of a headache, but he could live with that. This was his life now. Simple. Happy. Content.

Seamus Darby always loved pubs. It was the people, the warmth in their company, the yarns, the banter. When he spent the night before matches in Paddy McCormack's pub, it was for the company, not the drink. He knew pubs and he knew people. Pubs gave him a living and good friends.

Con Linehan had emigrated to London from near Scartaglin in Kerry years before Darby. Football was Con's link to home. Darby's pub in the Elephant and Castle was his local. Con and Darby were close.

'Are you fit?' Darby would ask him.

'I'm training all the time.'

He referred to Darby as 'The Three-minute Man.' Darby always chuckled. 'Ye were lucky I wasn't on all the time.'

Con died young from asbestosis, a chronic inflammatory condition that results from prolonged exposure to asbestos at work. When they brought him home to Scartaglin, Darby said a few words at his funeral. Con's death hit his old friend hard. They were close in age. The Three-Minute Man was Con's greatest line, and promised to be Darby's epitaph.

All of the players will carry 1982 with them for the rest of their lives, but none was as profoundly affected by the game as Darby. Three minutes suddenly defined how the world saw him. People from all over the country visited his pub. Reporters still call to record his story. When the anniversaries of the 1982 final popped up, the same old pictures and yarns were rolled out and he politely retraced the goal again. People still wanted to be near him, to hear his stories.

The goal was never a curse on him, but it changed his life for good. As the cup travelled around Offaly during the winter of 1982, Darby was its most regular companion. Weeks were built around his social engagements. He couldn't move for backslaps and free pints. He loved company and good humour. He was living the dream.

'I didn't have a routine. That's probably where I got this reputation of being a drunkard, or a fella who followed his beer. I would've been out every night of the week. No matter where I went, people would mean well and buy you a drink. I don't regret any of it. In the seventies I was only a boy; Tony McTague and Willie Bryan, Paddy McCormack – they were the people that people wanted to know and meet.

'I didn't really enjoy the seventies. I was married at twenty years of age the Saturday after the 1971 All-Ireland final, which was too young for me, and my wife. The world then just opened up. I thought I'd seen it all, but I hadn't.

'I would've missed a lot in terms of being here and there. There was an awful lot of people in Offaly who wouldn't even know I played in 1972. I always said if it ever happens me again, I'll fucking enjoy it. Suddenly I went from there to being half top-dog, the person people wanted to see.'

The months since the end of 1982 had been a riot. Winning the All-Ireland had brought fame and recognition beyond anything he imagined. For years his life had been Edenderry and the hardware shop. Veronica and the kids. Another world was starting to tug at his arm, and life was getting complicated.

By the beginning of 1983, late nights were backing into early mornings and Darby was growing tired of the grind. His hardest work had gone into proving his point in 1982. There was nothing left for him to do.

'It [1982] left a hangover for me. I'd have found training hard enough to get back to. I probably shouldn't have bothered, and left it at that. I trained hard and all that, but I would still have been out and about. It was well into 1983 and I was still going to dinner dances. I'd have been out maybe five nights a week. It's a lot if you're having a jar yourself. It'd be different if you weren't drinking.

'I kind of felt this was it. I'd done it all at that stage. I wasn't really that bothered. I felt I'd proved to myself what I had to prove. I felt good about it, and I probably should have packed it in.'

His fame brought him recognition, but times were hard. His hardware shop had been a prosperous business, but Edenderry was beginning to fall apart. Factories all round the midlands were shutting down. Inside a few years almost a thousand people in Edenderry were made redundant. Money was scarce. Darby's hectic schedule was starting to burn up his energy.

'It wouldn't have helped; you wouldn't have been on the ball every morning, but it wouldn't have been the reason the business fell asunder. I wasn't the only one in Edenderry. Bigger people than me went down.'

Life was hitting him hard. The 1982 final was seven years gone, but it still hadn't left his system. He drank a bit. His marriage had broken down. There were women. Business was suffering and the debts were rising. He took on a pub in Borrisokane but it did none of the business he was promised. He was in deep trouble. At thirty-nine years of age, Darby was forced to leave for England.

'It wouldn't have been something I ever planned to do, but I didn't have any choice. At that stage I owed a lot of money. Businesses had fallen down around my ears. Times were bad in Ireland. The banks wouldn't give you a light. I couldn't get a job. I applied for an awful lot of repping jobs. I had been on the road for years. The odd person would reply to you with a big circle around your age. There was nothing left. I had to go.'

One weekend he saw an advert in a newspaper looking for a bar manager in London. He rang the telephone number. The voice on the other end was Irish. They chatted for a while. The conversation turned to football. He asked where Darby was from.

'Offaly.'

'You're not the footballer, are you?'

'That's right,' replied Darby.

The atmosphere softened immediately. There wasn't, in fact, a managerial post available, 'and I wouldn't insult you with a barman's job,' the man said.

'I'll take it,' said Darby.

He moved to London and started work in the Fiddler's Elbow in Chalk Farm. Soon after, he got a managerial job in Kentish Town. Things started to take off. He lived in a one-bedroom flat and took a job on the railways to supplement his income. He worked as a look-out, watching for oncoming trains while labourers worked on the lines. 'It was a monotonous job, but you had to be on the ball,' he says. 'One mistake and you could kill ten lads.'

His new life started taking shape. He had met a new girl at home, and she followed him to London. He took on a pub in the Elephant and Castle, and business took off. GAA clubs visiting London became a crucial source of trade, and his stories kept them coming back. Sometimes the burden was hard to carry. The nature of his fame sometimes troubled him.

'I can walk into a bar and sit down, and people will come to the table and call you by your name. That's something I always found hard to deal with. I'd enjoy company and chatting and the crack. That'd be my scene. But going to a strange place where someone already knows you can be strange.'

There were other stories too. After hearing about the goal, people wanted to hear the story of the aftermath. His life in England. The drinking. The irony of being the central protagonist in an epic moment of history, then fading into the background like an old prize fighter, where the greatest fascination lies not in the ring but in the darkened corners of the life that follows.

'I've had nights when I didn't want to be out. I've had nights like that where I've said: Fuck's sake, I don't need this shit. But you can always stay home as well. I would've been one of the lads who would've been at a lot of dinner dances and presentations. With that would come a few jars. I probably did more than a lot of lads, but I wouldn't have any regrets about that.

'Drink is not a problem with me. Like anyone who takes a drink, I can get in with the wrong company. In the right company, I can sit down, have a few jars and there'll be no more about it.'

A few years back, he decided to come home. He bought the Greyhound Bar and developed a solid little business. He helps Richie Connor sell some houses on the side, and lives comfortably with his old stories. The walls are dotted with newspaper articles and pictures. There is one of George Best with Darby from 1983 at a charity soccer game in Newry. There are pictures of the goal, and framed articles telling the story of 1982. There is one of a reunion with the 1972 team. Darby sits down front, his legs crossed, with a beaming smile. Still a boy among men.

'The only game they think I played in was '82. People often say to me: "I heard you'd prefer you'd never scored it." That's not true either. There's an awful lot better players than me and they won't be remembered at all. I was lucky enough to get the goal and I'll probably be remembered for that as long as I live. It's always been a good memory. Never a regret.'

24 DECLINE AND REVIVAL

In September 2005, Charlie Nelligan and Mikey Sheehy were chatting outside Nelligan's bakery in Tralee when they spotted Darragh Ó Sé coming down the street. A few days had passed since Tyrone had beaten Kerry in the All-Ireland final. Ó Sé was still raw, still hurting. He wondered what two men with fifteen All-Ireland senior medals between them could tell him of defeat.

'Jesus, lads,' he said. 'This feeling is sick. How long does it take to get out of this thing?'

Sheehy smiled. 'We were beaten by Offaly in '82, and we still haven't got out of it!'

A few weeks after he met Ó Sé, Sheehy was sitting in a pub in Tralee, watching a Premiership game. There was a good crowd in when a telephone call came through to the bar for him. He picked up the receiver. The voice on the other line snarled: 'You fucker, you bottled it in '82!'

Sheehy thought someone was joking with him, but no one ever came to him claiming the punchline. 'You get over it,' he says, 'and you don't. A lot of other people obviously don't get over it either. People would bring it up. You know when they bring it up what they're thinking, but they're not saying it.'

From his bakeries in Castleisland and Tralee, Nelligan sees it all the time. People come in looking to talk football, and he's happy to oblige, but the conversations always flow the same way. 'They'll say: Jesus ye were a fabulous team,' he says. 'Then they'd say: How many [All-Ireland medals] do you have? Is it seven or eight?' And they always finish up:

Wasn't it an awful pity about the five-in-a-row? I'd see it coming, and when I do I always say it first. And they always say: Jesus, I was just about to say that.'

In Kerry, too, 1982 changed lives. As Jimmy Deenihan's recuperation continued through the summer, people came to him with different projects. During the world tour, Deenihan had spoken strongly in Australia about the merits of Gaelic football and the links it could forge with Australian Rules. In Croke Park, crudely formed notions about some kind of compromise game were being floated and Deenihan was added to a committee to examine the idea. Eventually he and referee John Moloney were sent away to hammer out a set of rules. Down in Tarbert Vocational School he stuck up two extra posts and used his pupils as guinea pigs during PE class. He would meet Moloney in Limerick to exchange notes. Eventually a set of rules emerged that are still in use.

Other, more profound, changes were happening too. In 1982, the country was plunged into political turmoil. Two elections came and went, and with the economy leaking jobs, money and people, no political reputation was safe.

Adversity also bred opportunity. Fine Gael were struggling to preserve their support base in north Kerry and sought a rallying force. The Deenihans had always carried the party colours. Jimmy's father had nurtured a devotion to Michael Collins, and his support for the party had never been in doubt. They had relations who been Fine Gael TDs. The bloodlines suggested Jimmy might run. When they came looking for him Deenihan bargained for time, and headed for John B Keane.

He always looked to John B. When an evening's socialising brought him to Finuge, John B would always seek out Deenihan's father. Deenihan was eleven when he won his first football medal in Listowel primary school. John B was at the match with his sons, Billy and Conor. He called Deenihan over to show off his medal. 'From then on,' says Deenihan, 'I was his buddy.'

John B travelled to Deenihan's games and put Deenihan's name on the guest list for all his opening nights. Deenihan, John B and Billy travelled to Thomond Park together in 1978 to see Munster defeat the All Blacks. Deenihan drank his first glass of stout in John B's bar. The town was steeped in literary talent and wisdom, and Deenihan was drawn to them. Writer Bryan McMahon became a friend, so did actor Eamon Kelly.

To Kerry's greatest writers and poets, their footballers were divine creators on a par with the greatest artists the world had seen. When Ger Power came to work in the Listowel social welfare exchange, they were inextricably drawn to him. 'John B wrote some article called "The Boss",' says Power, 'so the boys used all call me The Boss because they were all unemployed. It was gas fun.'

When John B was once asked what he'd like to be remembered for, his answer was simple: 'As the individual who scored the winning point against Duagh in the 1951 North Kerry intermediate final.' They lived their footballing fantasies through Deenihan, but now that chapter seemed over. O'Dwyer had been on, but Deenihan sensed he didn't truly need him. O'Dwyer had played into his late thirties, but Deenihan always sensed he was suspicious of any player over thirty. For years he had heard O'Dwyer goading them: 'Ye're getting old, lads.' He trained for 1983 but a bad hamstring injury slowed him down. John B reckoned Fine Gael needed him. In the fifteen previous elections, the party had managed to get just two TDs elected. On a Thursday, Deenihan was approached to run for Fine Gael. The following Saturday, he had been endorsed as a candidate in Kerry North.

The following few weeks tested him. In the end, he was pipped by 140 votes, but people had warmed to him. New Taoiseach Garret FitzGerald nominated him for the Senate, and Deenihan had been catapulted into a new life.

'If I had a week to think about it and gone to a few political meetings,' says Deenihan, 'I doubt I'd have run. It's a very, very tough game. I was still a PE teacher in Tarbert. I'd have been training every hour of the day. Then I was a senator and under pressure. To some degree I was public property, but I was still a very private individual. I just couldn't do both things. I was just thirty years of age, and that was it.'

Politics reluctantly took over his life and it took time to let football go. The days of matching Johnno's weights in Dinny Mahony's gym were gone. He still had Finuge and the fanatical quest for a North Kerry championship to sustain him, but he missed Killarney and the warmth of the summer.

'Breaking my leg was a turning point in my life. Psychologically, it was. I suffered from that trauma for a while afterwards. I used to dream about it. Football was our lives for so long. It was my life since I was seven years of age, right up to 1982. That's all I did. The only reason I did physical education was because I wanted to be fit for football. Everything I did was geared for football. Next thing, you break your leg, and it was all over.

'I was fairly traumatised. Not being part of the five-in-a-row team when you were part of it for so long, just being there on the periphery took a lot of re-adjustment. I wanted to be part of it.'

Before the next general election in 1987, Tim Kennelly canvassed for him. When he was elected in 1987, Deenihan's supporters struggled to hold him on their shoulders until Kennelly butted in and took him on his own. He looked up.

'Deenihan, I've carried you all my life.'

'Sure, isn't that what horses are for,' he replied.

When Deenihan went, the old Kerry defence started to fall away. Ger O'Keeffe relocated to Kenya after 1983, contracted malaria and never fully returned to football again. As Paudie Lynch left the field after defeat to Cork in 1983 Munster final, he pulled his old sidekick Páidí Ó Sé by the jersey: 'The next time you see me on a field, Sé, will be with the Jimmy Magee All Stars.'

Kennelly went in 1984 and behind him John O'Keeffe had already yielded to his creaking body. Having returned for 1983, a ruptured hamstring ended his Munster final, and a glittering career petered out in the rain. His hip continued to ache every day. Soon after the final, he finally made the trip to the orthopaedic surgeon he had been dodging for years. The doctor told him what he had always feared, but what he had also known.

'He told me to hang up the boots straight away. He said you'll jeopardise your career as a PE teacher. So I took his advice. Eventually I had to have it replaced. The surgeon said to hold on, and I didn't get it done till the late nineties. I suffered too much pain with it. But I've never regretted it. I'd love to go through it again. They really were the good years. Great years.'

For years Pat Spillane repeated the same mantra, but recently he has started to question his beliefs. By the beginning of 1984, Spillane's knee had healed. He collected three more All-Ireland medals between 1984 and 1986, playing the best football of his life, but the journey to greatness left him crippled.

It hurts the most in school. His greatest fear is the ball that rolls toward him during PE followed by two hurtling teenagers. His battered knees won't allow him move out of the way in time, so he braces himself for the hit.

It's also the mornings when he's walking across the school yard as a shower of rain begins to fall and he knows he won't be able to scurry for shelter. Over the years his other knee suffered from overuse. He can't go for walks anymore. Jogging is long gone. Even kicking a ball, the simplest expression of the game he joyously mastered, is now impossible.

'At fifty years of age, when you can't do the normal things, it suddenly dawns on you. You're an invalid. You're not an able-bodied man any more. Since the last problem with my knee, the "I'd do it all again" attitude comes with a "maybe" now. You'd do it all over again, but you wouldn't be as gung-ho about it.'

When players think back to the dressing room after 1982, some of their most vivid memories contain John Egan. Of them all, they reckoned he had the most to lose, yet, in his darkest hour, Egan was fighting the gloom. He moved through the dressing room that day, smiling, trying to drag them all back from the depths. 'Sure, lads, it's only a game,' he kept saying. It's only a game.

They had grown used to Egan's demeanour before games. He was always cool, unnervingly calm. They remembered him like that before the 1982 final, and never remembered him the same way again.

'It only hit me later on,' says Egan. 'I felt sorry for the club who really expected it. It was disappointing, but I've had lots of disappointments. I was anointed that I didn't leave the side down. I led from the front. Anybody who thought I might have been a bad captain – I certainly wasn't.'

As winter drew in that year, his life got mercilessly harder. That autumn, his twin brother Jerry was at a party hosted by the Caseys of Sneem, famed as international wrestlers, and the set of brothers who almost rowed for Britain at the 1936 Berlin Olympics. Some time during the night, Jerry left the party to head to the shop for supplies. The following morning they found him in Casey's pool. In the next three years Egan would also lose his father and his brother-in-law. When people thought of Egan, they imagined the depth of despair losing the final must have created, but 1982 was only part of it.

'What happened in the next three years was tragic. It's only that sport is such a transparent thing. There's so many people involved and it's a massively emotional thing to be involved in, especially when you're carrying the can. We were the men who had to do it.'

He had always thought about football's place in his life. Now it was changing. He remembered the reporters in the lead-up to the All-Ireland final. Some asked him about the number of All-Ireland medals he had won. When he had first joined the panel? What club he played for? After thirteen years playing with Kerry at different levels, he was still a stranger to them. They knew nothing of his life, nothing of the sacrifices, and they didn't care. That hurt.

'What is really disappointing is that you get no thanks for it. There's no sentiment, only people waiting to take the legs from under you. It's an awful cruel place to be.'

Egan's form in 1982 was recognised with an All Star, but football was getting hard to focus on. He drank harder. He was slowing down and other players were catching him up. One evening in 1984, he travelled to Mayo for a challenge game and was pulled aside by a selector before the game. He hadn't been playing well, the selector told him. If he had serious notions about this year, he should take the frees this evening, so he could notch a few points beside his name.

'I nearly took the jersey off and threw it at him. It's those things that hit you. I should've retired after '82. It was effectively the end of my career. It was disappointing to go out in that respect, because when you lose at that stage, everything is negative, irrespective of being gallant losers. When you're a winner, it's easy to talk about being a gallant loser. But it hurts when you're a loser.'

He battled all summer for his place, won his sixth All-Ireland medal and retired that winter. Kerry moved on without him. For years people described Egan as the most underrated component of the Kerry forward line, but time has changed that. His place among the greats is enshrined.

'I was lucky to be where I was and achieve what I did. If I owned the world I could never meet the people I did when I was young. Travelling to all those cities. Being heroes. Being appreciated. We were treated like kings. But we had to work hard at it. We had to be the best.'

Some players carried 1982 in their hearts. Others recycled it into motivation and used it as the fuel to drive future teams to greatness. With John O'Keeffe gone, Mick O'Dwyer again compelled Sean Walsh to move. This time, it was to full-back. He never settled fully in the neighbourhood, but having Páidí Ó Sé beside him at corner-back made it feel more homely.

Mick Spillane returned to the team and Tom slotted in at centre-back. Pat Spillane had taught his right leg to do everything his left leg couldn't do and was on the cusp of the best football of his career. Jacko was revived. So was Bomber. Charlie Nelligan was only twenty-seven and eager to get on. Ambrose O'Donovan came from Gneeveguila, a little village tight on the border with Cork as captain, joined Jacko at centrefield, and helped stir the fire again.

'He was way different to us,' says Sean Walsh. 'He'd never won an All-Ireland medal and suddenly he was captain. But he had the strength of character to be a good captain. He had a different approach altogether. He wouldn't be over-analytical. It all came straight from the heart.

'Of all the times our teams were revved up, it was during Ambrose's time. I remember before the Munster final he hopped up on the table that day and said it was a privilege for him to captain all these guys who had won medals, "But my only worry," he says, "was to wake up the following day listening to fellas from Kiskeam and Ballydesmond." He was going into border stuff about Cork and Kerry. He brought us back to basics. It was pure passion. He wanted to win an All-Ireland and he had that fire in his belly. That was a whole new scene again.'

They tore Cork to shreds in 1984 and won another All-Ireland that September against Dublin. It was a new team, refreshed by O'Donovan's leadership and the young blood now circulating through the team, but the drive was rooted in hurt, the roots sown by Darby.

What grew from those roots will live through football history for good. After 1984, Kerry stitched three consecutive All-Ireland titles together. Five players: Pat Spillane, Ger Power, Ogie Moran, Páidí Ó Sé and Mikey Sheehy each finished their careers with eight All-Ireland medals. The core of O'Dwyer's team had finally proven themselves the greatest of them all. Their last All-Ireland title in 1986 was collected by Tommy Doyle. The phantom hand had disappeared. All the tears had been wiped away.

'Walking up the steps [of the Hogan Stand] in '84,' says Charlie Nelligan, 'it was like winning our first again. I remember looking at Bomber and Ogie going up and the tears in their eyes. It was great. We'd suffered in '82 and '83 but that was forgotten about. The mourning period was over then.'

***

In December 2005, thousands travelled to mourn Tim Kennelly in Listowel. The Dubs were there. Old Cork men. Football people from across the country who had grown up backing The Horse in every game.

A delegation of Kerry players had slipped into a local pub for a drink when Richie Connor came through the door, his broad frame blocking the sunlight out. Behind him was Seamus Darby. As he edged towards the bar, a local accent shouted at him: 'Get out of Darby's way, lads. If you don't let him to the bar, he'll push.'

The crowd erupted in laughter. Someone asked Darby about the title of his autobiography. 'Not Pushed,' he replied.

Circumstances have rarely brought the Offaly and Kerry players together like history does. Charlie Nelligan occasionally hosted Darby in his coffee shop in Tralee and they laughed about 1982 and the challenge game in Castleisland. On one visit home, Gerry Carroll and his wife were hosted in Dingle by the Ó Sés.

Years have softened old differences among them. Gerry Carroll has enjoyed pints with Eugene McGee in New York. In time, McGee married Marian O'Connor, a sister of Liam and Tomás. Players who once couldn't fathom McGee's personality now include him among their friends. They never underestimated his contribution to their footballing careers. Now they can fully enjoy his company, too.

Sometimes the Kerry players wonder about 1982, and what their lives might be like had they won the five-in-a-row. Some players reckon it would have finished their careers early. The weight of carrying such history could have capsized some of them, or inflated their egos so much they would have floated away from their real selves and become unrecognisable as the amiable, gregarious group who had charmed the world.

Even the holidays would get drab. For Mick O'Dwyer, the years spent coming to terms with 1982 had given him perspective. Five-in-a-row would have been too much for them all to handle.

'It was best for the Kerry players who were drinking too much that they did not break any more records,' he said in his 1990 autobiography. 'In the end, I suppose everything evens itself out.'

'I don't know how I would've reacted but I know I would've been very difficult to live with,' says Ger O'Keeffe. 'In my job I'd have felt untouchable. I think it was better, in hindsight, to lose than win. There was somebody above saying: These guys will go apeshite.'

After 1982, fame and football extracted the same toll from Kerry as it had Offaly and other teams. Marriages and people broke down. Men wrestled with drink and other addictions. The misfortunes that befell them made them vulnerable and human. The commitments they made to each other as young men and the football they played made them immortal.

In time, Offaly's unbending will and sheer refusal to submit would transcend the generations. Their spirit would accompany Cork to All-Ireland titles in 1989 and 1990, embolden a string of Ulster teams in the nineties and be revived again by Tyrone and Armagh in the last decade. Kerry's blessed generation will be remembered as the last great dominant force. No team will ever rule and shape football as they did. On one September Sunday, it seemed like both teams were playing for their legacy.

In the end, history found room for them all.

POSTSCRIPT

THE KERRY TEAM

Charlie Nelligan

Made his last appearance with Kerry in Croke Park in the 1991 All-Ireland semi-final against Down. and returned to manage the Kerry minors alongside Mikey Sheehy in the late nineties. Also an accomplished musician, runs a successful bakery businesses in Tralee, Killarney and Castleisland.

Ger O'Keeffe

Was set to play on into 1983 but was forced into retirement having contracted malaria on a trip to Kenya. Worked as a selector with Kerry manager Jack O'Connor from 2004 to 2006, as Kerry won two All-Ireland titles in three years. Works as an engineer.

John O'Keeffe

Injury forced him to end a magnificent career in 1983, but O'Keeffe made a brief comeback to win one last county medal with Austin Stacks in 1986. Coached Clare and Limerick in the nineties, and worked as Kerry physical coach with Páidí Ó Sé and worked with Kerry hurlers alongside Ger Power. Also coached the Irish International Rules team with Matt Connor as selector in 2003 and 2004. Endured a hip replacement operation after years of damage. A teacher in Tralee CBS.

Paudie Lynch

Retired after the 1983 Munster final against Cork but remained active with Beaufort club. A solicitor in Killarney.

Páidí Ó Sé

Played on with Kerry until 1989 when O'Dwyer dropped him for the Munster final, prompting a rift that took years to heal. Ended his career among the record eight All-Ireland medal winners and took over Kerry Under-21s in 1994 before being appointed senior manager in 1996. Guided Kerry to two All-Ireland titles, six Munster titles and a League title before stepping down in 2003. Took over Westmeath in 2004 and watched them win their first Leinster title in his inaugural year. Took charge of Clare in late 2006, but resigned in July 2007. Runs a venerated pub in Ventry.

Tim Kennelly

Continued playing for Kerry into 1984 where he won a ninth Munster medal to compliment his five All-Ireland titles. Also acted as Kerry selector that year, but retired in mid-summer. Acted as selector again in 1990, and watched his sons, Noel and Tadhg, play for Kerry – Tadhg has forged a career with the Sydney Swans in the AFL. Kennelly remained a prominent character in Listowel, running a bar in the town up to his sudden death in December 2005, aged fifty-one.

Tommy Doyle

Having considered retirement after 1982, he captained Kerry to a third successive All-Ireland title in 1986 having had both ankles encased in plaster ten days before the final. Still a part of the team when Mick O'Dwyer stepped down in 1989. Suffered severe ankle problems after retirement. Now employed as a company rep.

Jack O'Shea

Retired after defeat in the 1992 Munster football final against Clare and began a brief managerial career with Mayo the following year, winning a Connacht title. Finished his playing career with seven All-Ireland medals and ten Munster medals, while also winning six consecutive All Stars between 1980 and 1985. Named on the GAA's Team of the Century in 1984. Became a respected newspaper columnist and runs a successful plumbing business in Dublin.

Sean Walsh

Won three more All-Ireland medals at full-back between 1984 and 1986, before retiring in 1988. Worked with the Kerry minors and teams at his club Kerins O'Rahilly's in Tralee. Suffered problems with his hip in later life, and underwent replacement surgery. Runs an estate agency in Tralee.

Ger Power

Played on past his teammates as far as 1990 and ended a dazzling career without a scratch and eight All-Ireland medals. Part of John O'Keeffe's international rules management team and currently working with O'Keeffe and the Kerry hurlers. Works in the employment exchange in Tralee.

Tom Spillane

Reverted to centre-back to win All-Ireland medals between 1984 and 1986, and eventually finished his Kerry career at full-back with four All-Ireland medals and three All Stars. Still involved with Templenoe underage teams and runs an auctioneering business in Killarney.

Denis 'Ogie' Moran

Another who ended his career with eight All-Ireland medals. Took over as Kerry manager in 1992 and coached various teams at underage level at Kerins O'Rahilly's. Works with Shannon Development in Tralee.

Mikey Sheehy

Retired in 1988 with a record haul of eight All-Ireland medals, a place on the GAA's Team of the Millennium and among the greatest players of all time, and with a list of injuries that left him with aches and pains for the rest of his life. Coached a succession of Kerry minor teams with Charlie Nelligan in the late nineties. Runs a financial consultancy firm in Tralee.

Eoin Liston

Won seven All-Ireland medals and made a brief comeback with Kerry in 1993, under his old friend Ogie Moran, having retired in 1990. Spent seven years managing Kerins O'Rahilly's club, finally guiding them to their first Kerry senior county title for forty-five years in 2002. A selector on the Irish international rules management team in 2006. Works for Irish Nationwide in Tralee.

John Egan

Retired after the 1984 All-Ireland final with five All-Ireland medals and settled in Bishopstown, Cork city. Acknowledged as one of Kerry's greatest ever forwards. Works as a Garda in Bishopstown.

Pat Spillane

Played his final game with Kerry in the 1991 All-Ireland semi-final with Down having enjoyed a career that earned him a record eight All-Ireland medals, nine All Star awards and a place on the GAA's Teams of the Century and Millennium. Became one of the most controversial media pundits in Irish sport on RTE's 'The Sunday Game', estranging many of his former teammates with his comments there and in his divisive autobiography. Now presenter of 'The Sunday Game', proprietor of the family pub in Templenoe and still teaching in St Goban's College, Bantry.

Jimmy Deenihan

Was appointed to the Senate having retired from football in 1982, and was elected to the Dáil as TD in Kerry North in 1987. Was appointed Minister for State at the Department of Agriculture and Food in 1997, and worked as Fine Gael spokesperson on Arts, Sports and Tourism before the last election. Continued to play with Finuge until the late eighties and subsequently coached the team. Also did some specialist defensive coaching for Mick O'Dwyer with Laois during 2006.

THE OFFALY TEAM

Martin Furlong

Ended a magnificent inter-county career in 1985 aged thirty-nine. Emigrated in May 1988 to help his brother Tom run a pub in upstate New York before taking a job with a construction company in 1994. Still lives in upstate New York.

Michael Lowry

Continued to play with Offaly until 1991 and ended his career in the Leinster championship against Meath. Still living in Ferbane and involved with the local club.

Liam O'Connor

Retired after a lively inter-county career in 1985. Continued to play football with Bray Emmets until he was 50. Lives in Dublin and employed in security.

Mick Fitzgerald

Moved to Cork in 1985 and drifted away from the Offaly scene soon afterwards. Currently living in Tipperary and working for South Tipperary County Council in Clonmel.

Pat Fitzgerald

Held on to the right-half-back spot till 1985 when he disappeared from the panel. Managed Kildare and later Offaly in the mid-nineties. Lives in Newbridge and works for Bord na Móna.

Sean Lowry

Moved to Crossmolina in 1985 and popped up on the Mayo team that won the Connacht title that summer before retiring following their All-Ireland semi-final defeat to Dublin. Moved back to Shannonbridge in Offaly in recent years, where he works with ESB.

Liam Currams

Having played in All-Ireland football and hurling finals in 1981, winning a hurling medal, and collecting the football equivalent in 1982, successive knee injuries devastated Currams's career. Finally had a knee operation to repair his cruciate ligament in September 1984 and managed to make the Offaly hurling panel the following August 1985, collecting an All-Ireland medal that year. Never returned to the football panel again and underwent further knee surgery in 1986. More knee problems followed in 1990 and his time with Offaly was over. Moved to Donegal in 1999 where he played his last football game with Four Masters. Works for the ESB.

Tomás O'Connor

Played for Offaly till 1987 but transferred from Walsh Island to Round Towers in Clondalkin where he continued to play and coach. Moved to Clane and coached Rathcoffey in Kildare, bringing them from intermediate to senior level. His son, Tomás, is a current member of the Kildare senior panel. Works as a psychiatric nurse.

Padraic Dunne

Emigrated to America in the mid-eighties but continued to travel home to play championship football with Offaly till 1991. Came home soon after and now runs a pub and delicatessen in Portarlington and trains underage teams in Gracefield.

John Guinan

Lasted with Offaly till 1990 when knee injuries forced him to retire, but played club football and the occasional game of rugby till 1999. Coached Ballinagar at junior level for a spell. Works as an electrician in Portarlington.

Richie Connor

Continued playing with Offaly till 1989 before calling time on a fourteen-year career. Immediately took over as Laois senior football coach, guiding them to a thumping win over Offaly in the 1990 Leinster championship. Still involved in coaching with Walsh Island.

Gerry Carroll

Emigrated to Boston in summer 1984 aged twenty-five, and never played for Offaly again, but enjoyed a successful football career in Boston and New York, before finally retiring from football in 1993. Runs a pub in Manhattan.

Brendan Lowry

Played on during a difficult decade for Offaly before retiring in 1993, his reputation among the county's finest forwards assured. Managed Westmeath in the late nineties. Worked with Eircom and retired in 2003.

Matt Connor

Retired following his accident in 1984 with a brilliant record of 82 goals 660 points from 161 games with Offaly, five county medals with Walsh Island, two All Stars and a B&I Award from 1980. Worked with the Offaly minors from 1989 and with the Irish International rules team in 2003. Served as Offaly selector in 2004. Works as a Garda in Tullamore.

Johnny Mooney

Returned to America in 1987 and worked in New York before coming home and briefly rejoining the Offaly panel in 1990, an experience that left him deeply disillusioned. Sold his pub in Geashill in 1989 and emigrated to England for four years. Trained Warwickshire to an All-Ireland junior football final in 1990. Now returned to Rhode and works for a mobile phone company

Stephen Darby

Continued to be an influential figure in Rhode after his footballing career ended, guiding an array of players through to play for Offaly. Managed Rhode to a Leinster club final in 2006 and teaches in the local school.

Seamus Darby

Having ended his Offaly career in 1984, Darby continued to play for Rhode and Borrisokane having moved to Tipperary in 1989. Emigrated to London in late 1991 and ran a pub where his notoriety as the man who denied Kerry five-in-a-row flourished. Returned home to Toomevara where he runs the Greyhound Bar. Still has his jersey from the final.

THE MANAGERS

Mick O'Dwyer

A glorious association with Kerry stretching over four decades ended in 1989 following a third consecutive defeat to Cork in the Munster final, and addressed the dressing-room one final time with tears streaming down his face. Took over in Kildare in late 1990 where he enjoyed two stints as manager, leading them to an All-Ireland final in 1998. Took over Laois in 2003 and brought them to their first Leinster title in forty-seven years. Having turned seventy in 2006 and left Laois, turned up as Wicklow manager that November. The story continues.

Eugene McGee

Briefly managed Cavan in the late eighties and got involved with his local club Colmcille, having left Offaly. Managed the Irish Compromise Rules team in 1990 and remains a respected national newspaper columnist, having also served a variety of roles with the *Longford Leader*, including editor and managing director. Still a well regarded media pundit on Gaelic football, and widely acknowledged as one of the most revolutionary coaches the game has ever seen.

***

John Dowling

Left Offaly county board in 1988 after twenty-three years as county secretary to become GAA President. Served till 1991 and laid the foundations for the reconstruction of Croke Park. Later honoured as President of Offaly County Board. Died in 2002, aged seventy.

Weeshie Fogarty

Became a respected broadcaster with Radio Kerry. A voracious collector and recorder of Kerry sporting folklore. Recently published a book on his former mentor and legendary Kerry coach Dr Eamonn O'Sullivan, and continues to present his 'Terrace Talk' radio programme.

Sean Grennan

Grew into a gifted dual player, playing in both All-Ireland minor finals for Offaly in 1989. Later specialised in football, winning a Leinster senior medal, Offaly's first since 1982, in 1997 and a league title in 1998. Was part of a committee charged with finding Offaly's new football manager in 2006. Runs a farm machinery business in Edenderry.

Fr Sean Heaney

Finally ended his time as Offaly county chairman in 1984 having tried to extricate himself from the job four years previously. Worked in parishes across the country was given the title 'Monsignor'. Currently parish priest in Tullamore.

Sean Kelly

Climbed the administrative ladder in Kerry, serving as county chairman before a stint as chairman of the Munster Council. Served as GAA President from 2003 to 2006, seeing through the opening up of Croke Park to soccer and rugby before taking up his current post as Executive Chairman of the Irish Institute of Sport.

Declan Lynch/Galleon

Having been voted Gobshites of the Year by the *Sunday World* in late 1982, Galleon returned to their day jobs but the band went on. Later refitted different lyrics around the 'Five in a Row' tune and re-released the song in 1983 as a humorous tribute to Michael Fagan, who broke into the Queen's bedroom in Buckingham Palace. Re-grouped in recent years and play gigs in Germany and around the country. Still receives countless enquiries about the availability of 'Five in a Row'.

Tom O'Donoghue

Having concluded his stint as physical trainer with the Offaly footballers in 1983, Donoghue coached a variety of clubs in Westmeath and Laois. Briefly worked as physical trainer with Longford footballers in 1994 and was brought in by the Offaly hurlers in early 2000. Currently principal of Kilcormac Vocational School.

Gerald Whyte

Remains an active administrator and member of the Causeway club. Currently vice-chairman of Kerry County Board.

ACKNOWLEDGEMENTS AND SOURCES

While the source material for this book also comprised newspaper clippings, books and radio interviews, the principal sources were the participants from the 1982 All-Ireland final, all of whom were exceptionally generous with their time and their recollections.

Special thanks to Charlie Nelligan, Ger O'Keeffe, John O'Keeffe, Páidí Ó Sé, Jack O'Shea, Sean Walsh, Ger Power, Tom Spillane, Denis 'Ogie' Moran, Mikey Sheehy, Eoin Liston, John Egan, Pat Spillane and his scrapbooks, Jimmy Deenihan, Gerald Whyte, Sean Kelly, Owen McCrohan, Weeshie Fogarty, Eric Murphy, PJ McGrath, Martin Furlong, Mick Fitzgerald, Liam O'Connor, Michael Lowry, Pat Fitzgerald, Sean Lowry, Liam Currams, Tomás O'Connor, Padraic Dunne, John Guinan, Richie Connor, Gerry Carroll, Johnny Mooney, Matt Connor, Brendan Lowry, Stephen Darby, Seamus Darby, Eugene McGee, Tom Donoghue, Mgr Sean Heaney, Eugene Mulligan, David Walsh, Sean Grennan and Declan Lynch.

Thanks also to Carthage Buckley, Mick Mangan, Colleen Nelligan, Pat Nolan, Tom Humphries, Der O'Connor, Martin McHugh, Joan Herbert, Martin Rigney, Willie and Andy McCarter, Tomás Ó Sé, Junior Murphy, Declan Carroll, Alan Kerins, Brud Sullivan, Paddy Reidy, Mick Dineen, Mick Higgins, Pat Teahan, Kevin Corrigan, PJ Cunningham, Dr Paul Rouse, the staff at the National Library and at the Gilbert Library, Pearse Street, and Gracefield GAA club.

For the use of their pictures I am indebted to Sportsfile, the Offaly Archaeological and Historical Society, John Kearney, Joe O'Sullivan

Photography, Tullamore, and Don MacMonagle in Killarney.

For references and sources I specifically utilised the archives of the *Irish Independent*, *The Irish Times*, the *Examiner*, the *Sunday Independent*, the *Sunday Tribune*, the *Evening Press*, the *Sunday Press*, *Sunday Times*, *Tullamore Tribune*, *Westmeath-Offaly Independent* and the *Kerryman*. I also sourced material in *Kingdom Come* by Eoghan Corry, *Dublin v Kerry* by Tom Humphries, *Football Captains, the All-Ireland Winners* by Brian Carthy, *Football's Top 20* by Colm Keane, *Mick O'Dwyer, Manager of the Millennium* by Owen McCrohan, *Páidí*, the autobiography, as told to Sean Potts, *For Love of Town and Village* by Jack Mahon, *Fighting Back: The Rocky Bleier Story* by Rocky Bleier, an extensive article with Tom Furlong by Dave Hannigan which appeared in the *Irish Echo*, September 2002, and in radio interviews conducted by Weeshie Fogarty with Seamus Darby in 2002 and by Eamon Dunphy with Mick O'Dwyer, April 2007.

Thanks to The O'Brien Press for the faith to undertake this project and the encouragement to ensure it got done, to Emma for a wonderful design job and Íde Ní Laoghaire for exhibiting great patience in getting the final manuscript ready for public consumption.

Thanks also to an array of friends and colleagues who kept me sane during a long, trying year. To all at the *Sunday Times*, particularly to Denis Walsh, whose prompting, encouragement and example was a constant source of inspiration. Thanks also to Paul Rowan, Peter O'Reilly, Donn McClean, and to my former sports editor Alan English, who kept keeping the idea for this book alive whenever I threatened to kill it. Also a special word of gratitude to Dave Hannigan for his assistance towards the end of the project and his regular emails of encouragement.

Index